US Investment in Latin America and the Caribbean

US Investment in Latin America and the Caribbean

Trends and Issues

Ramesh F. Ramsaran

ST MARTIN'S PRESS
New York

 For information, write:
St. Martin's Press, Inc., 175 Fifth Avenue,
New York, NY 10010
Printed in Great Britain
First published in the United States of America in 1985

ISBN 0-312-83317-2

Library of Congress Cataloging in Publication Data
Ramsaran, Ramesh.
U.S. Investment in Latin America and the Caribbean.
Includes index

1. Investments, American—Latin America.
2. Investments, American—Caribbean Area. I. Title.
HG5160.5.A3R36 1985 332.6'7373'08 84-18364
ISBN 0-312-83317-2

Contents

Acknowledgments

My interest in capital movement was first aroused during my tenure as a research assistant with Alister McIntyre (now Deputy Secretary-General of UNCTAD) and Beverly Watson who were spearheading the Foreign Investment Studies Program (under University of the West Indies auspices) in the late 1960s/early 1970s. To these two people I owe a great intellectual debt. This interest was sustained by my subsequent involvement in the Monetary Studies Program which has been a significant forum for the discussion of monetary and financial problems facing regional states by academics and policy makers. In writing this book I have had access to a number of libraries in the region. I am particularly indebted to the staff of the Documents' Centre and the Library at the Institute of International Relations at UWI, St Augustine. The assistance of my friends and colleagues at this institution often goes beyond the call of duty. The staff at the libraries of the London School of Economics, the University of Hull, Florida International University, Colombia University and the World Bank/IMF Group were extremely helpful. I also owe a debt of thanks to Herb Addo for encouragement, and for providing me with some of his provocative theoretical insights. Finally I must thank Mrs. Norma Ferreira and her staff for the secretarial assistance provided me, and in particular, Jackie Roberts, who was subjected to the ordeal of typing the first version of this manuscript.

Needless to say the shortcomings of the work remain my responsibility.

Preface

The US Caribbean Basin Initiative (CBI) announced by President Reagan in early 1982 places great store in the role of the private sector and the role of foreign private capital in economic development. In a sense, it defines a particular kind of strategy which countries willing to participate in the programme may have to adopt. Given the historical experience of the Latin American/Caribbean region and the nationalism which has grown out of it, and given the way economic development is being increasingly conceptualised, this situation has given rise to a certain amount of concern in some quarters. The region has long been the recipient of private foreign capital, but the impact has been of a limited nature. In some instances, it has contributed to growth without making any significant contribution to broad structural transformation. The fact that development now tends to embrace goals like greater local ownership and greater national control over economic decision-making exerts a crucial influence over the policies relating to private foreign capital.

Private capital flows take several forms. The most important form in recent years (as far as developing countries are concerned) is that of direct investment which is now synonymous with the transnational corporation. Direct investment, as we shall see, connotes ownership and control and may involve a transfer of capital, technology, management and sometimes marketing connections. The fact that these benefits often tend to be exaggerated has given rise to a certain amount of skepticism which has led to calls for a code of conduct for transnationals. In this study our aim is a limited one. Since the US is the most important source of direct investment in Latin America and the Caribbean, we examine the historical growth of American investment in the area, and discuss some of the main problems and issues which have come to be associated with the role of private foreign capital in the development process. It might be useful to point out here that, since most countries in the region do not publish data on the source of foreign investment flows or the ownership of capital assets, the discussion is often carried out in general terms. Even the US official data that are available often tend to be of an aggregate nature which do not permit detailed analysis.

As far as the structure of the study is concerned, it is not possible at this juncture in time to discuss meaningfully the role of private foreign capital, either in historical perspective or in the context of current controversies, without taking into account existing social and economic conditions or the perception of capital movements as obtained in the theoretical literature which often has a critical influence on policy formulation. Also, the experience with other types of resource flows needs to be examined if the issues pertaining to direct investment are to be seen in proper perspective.

In Chapter 1 we look at the treatment of capital movements in economic theory and the attempts to quantify the relationship between capital movements and economic growth. Chapter 2 reviews the development experience in the post-war period. In Chapter 3 we examine the broader resource flow question in the context of the balance of payments. These may be called the background chapters. Chapter 4 provides data on the growth and pattern of US direct investment in the region, going back to the turn of the century. In Chapter 5 we undertake a discussion on some of the main issues arising from US direct investment activities. In Chapter 6 we look at the policy framework and experience of selected countries, or group of countries, with respect to private foreign capital. Clearly in a work of this scope it is not possible to focus our attention on every single country in the region. The case studies chosen tend to highlight different approaches in the policy framework. Chapter 7 outlines the broader context in which US investment flows take place and provides a discussion on the Caribbean Basin Initiative. In Chapter 8 we conclude with some final observations.

Notes

1. The money figures are all in US dollars except where otherwise stated.
2. Symbols used:
   - = nil or negligible
   n.a. = not available
   FDI = Foreign Direct Investment
3. 'Billion' refers to a thousand million throughout.
4. As far as the statistics are concerned, the most recent figures available at the time of writing have been used.

Dedication

To those Striving for a Better Tomorrow

1

Introduction

Raising the rate of capital formation remains one of the most critical development issues facing poor countries. In the early post-war years it was widely believed, both among academics and policy-makers alike, that the problem could largely be solved by the inflow of external resources in the form of private foreign capital and bi-lateral and multilateral assistance. The academics became pre-occupied with the formation of simplistic but elegant models (largely keynesian in nature), which they used to determine the amount of foreign resources that would be required to attain particular growth rates under various assumptions. The policy makers on the other hand set about creating the legal and politico-economic framework to attract and protect private foreign capital to which privileged treatment was extended on many fronts. The provision of industrial sites, freedom from taxation for a stipulated number of years, guarantees for the repatriation of profits, constitutional provisions giving assurances of fair and prompt compensation in the event of nationalisation, double taxation agreements, accelerated depreciation allowances, guaranteed local markets, etc. soon became standard incentive packages aimed at transforming agricultural or mono-product societies into diversified industrial economies. There was a built-in contradiction in this strategy in that some of the incentives offered encouraged capital intensive production techniques in situations characterised by large amounts of un-employed and under-employed labour. This shortcoming, however, like several others that were to emerge, was not to be recognised until much later.

In Latin America, and later in the Caribbean, industrialisation came to be seen as a way of overcoming structural weaknesses in the economy and of improving their terms of trade position in the international economy.[1] The international division of labour in which developing countries were relegated as essentially primary producers was severely criticised and the basically nineteenth century theory used to justify its perpetuation soundly attacked.[2] The assumptions of the theory, it was felt, were not in accordance with reality, and became even less relevant with post-war developments in the international economy. In both the classical and neo-classical theories of international trade, productive resources are assumed to be fixed both in terms of quality and quantity, but in the real world the factors of production are constantly changing in both respects. The international movement of people and capital are also at variance with the explicit immobility assumption of traditional trade theory. The emergence and growth of transnational corporations are ample demonstration that open national boundaries, even in the context of rabid nationalism, cannot be assumed away in a world where the evidence points to increasing internationalisation of capital. The concept of perfect competition so basic to economic theory is an ideal that is to be found neither in factor nor product markets. 'The assumption of fixed world-wide consumer tastes and preferences dictating production patterns to market-responsive atomistic producers is another fiction of economic theory. Not only are capital and production technologies disseminated throughout the world by means of the multinational corporations often aided and abetted by their home governments, but consumption technologies (i.e. consumer preferences and tastes) are often created and re-inforced by the advertising compaigns of the powerful financial giants who dominate local markets. By creating demands for imported goods, market-dominating international enterprises can manufacture the conditions for their own further aggrandisement.'[3] Free markets are also affected by trade unions and other interest groups who are able to exert significant influence on national decision-making relating to areas such as industrial protection, employment, wages, etc. One of the most contentious issues in trade theory relates to the division of benefits. At the national level it is implicitly assumed that the benefits accrue to the nationals of the country – an assumption that fails to recognise the movement of factors of production in practice. Just as unrealistic is the assumption that technology is freely available or that the fruits of technical progress are shared equally by all countries through higher incomes or lower prices for the goods they buy. The large gap in living standards between the industrial countries and developing countries would seem to indicate that this is far from being the case in practice. A number of observers have argued that the fruits of increased productivity resulting from technological improvements have largely been expropriated by the developed nations in the form of higher wages and higher prices for their exports.[4] In this connection, industrialisation has come to be seen not as an end in itself, but as the principal means at the disposal of developing countries for obtaining a share of the benefits of technical progress and of progressively raising the standard of living of the masses.[5]

A further criticism[6] made of traditional trade theory is its lack of attention to certain 'power' relationships in the economy. It is argued that government preferences for say industry over agriculture, government ownership over private ownership, national ownership over foreign, import substitution over export expansion, etc. determine a pattern of behaviour quite different from that predicted by international trade theory. Also, since 'the government does not usually use market criteria for its production and pricing decisions, the observed level of production and consumption in an economy will depend not only on private tastes, technologies, and factor endownments, as theory suggests, but also on the preferences and decision rules used by the government.'[7] To take account of these factors there is a need to incorporate certain power equations explicitly into traditional theory. In other words 'pure' economic theory must incorporate an increasing element of political economy.

Private capital movement takes different forms. Some (e.g. portfolio) may be explained simply in terms of differentials in the rate of interest or the rate of return on investment. Others, like private direct investment, are more complex in nature and require analysis that often transcends simple relative rates of return. In an effort to obtain more satisfactory explanations of capital movements than classical and neoclassical theory can provide, attention in recent years has shifted to the theory of the firm which is the main agent for private direct investment. Some of the early writers on imperialism like Hobson and Lenin saw expansion abroad as a response either to deficient demand or surplus capital resulting from falling rates of profits at home.[8] The tendency in recent years has been to move away from the text-book perfect competitive model (in which no firm has an advantage over any other) to frameworks based on 'imperfections,' oligopolistic interdependence, and the possession of monopolistic advantages.[9] Hymer, for example, associates foreign investment with oligopolistic firms competing for market shares under imperfect conditions.[10] Caves[11] argues that 'foreign direct investment occurs mainly in industries characterised by certain market structures in both the "lending" (or home) and "borrowing" (or host) countries. In the parlance of industrial organisation, oligopoly with product differentiation normally prevails where corporations make "horizontal" investments to produce abroad the same lines of goods as they produce in the home market. Oligopoly, not necessarily differentiated, in the home market is typical in industries which undertake "vertical" direct investments to produce abroad a raw material or other input to their production process at home.' Vernon[12] explains foreign investment in terms of a multi-stage product cycle theory which puts 'less emphasis upon comparative cost doctrine and more upon the timing of innovation, the effects of scale economies, and the roles of ignorance and uncertainty in influencing trade patterns.' As the input requirements of a product change as it becomes standardised, the cost advantage may shift from one country to another. 'The essence of oligopolistic theories is that firms operating across national boundaries and over long distances, suffer an intrinsic disadvantage—caused by difficulties of communication, linguistic and cultural differences, lack of knowledge of local market conditions, and so on – which, for transnational investment to prove profitable, must be sufficiently offset by some sort of special advantage over potential local competitors.'[13]

Recognising the many flaws in traditional international trade theory, and in view of the increasing skepticism of international trade as an engine of growth, development theorists have tended to turn their attention to the reorganisation of resources at the domestic level. Over the years poor countries have been inundated with models and strategies seeking to explain how poverty can be overcome and self-sustaining growth achieved with particular policies. Rosenstein-Rodan,[14] for example, some years ago argued that in order to create a sufficiently broad market that could support large scale production there was need for simultaneous expansion in a wide range of industries (a 'big push') either by government or the private sector or both working together. Hirschman[15] saw little merit in this approach and instead advocated the creation of 'forward' and 'backward' linkages in a sequential pattern, with external economies providing inducements to the creation of a series of industries which may not have otherwise been undertaken. For Lewis,[16] a developing country could easily be described as having essentially two sectors: a capitalist sector and a subsistence (agricultural) sector. The existence of surplus labour in the latter meant that the former could easily draw on the latter (with a wage slightly above subsistence) without affecting total output. The reinvestment of profits by the capitalist class (which is crucial in the model) is the driving force behind economic expansion and the creation of greater productive employment.

The experience of the post-war period has shown that real life situations are not as easy to control or influence as neat text-book models with their simplistic assumptions often lead us to believe. These models often assume an abundance of the very factors that are in scarce supply and in a sense define the development problem. The need to attract factors from abroad means that certain guarantees and incentives often have to be proferred, and this may mean abandoning control over certain aspects of behaviour (e.g. the reinvestment of profits). Latin American industrialisation has relied heavily on foreign factors of production, particularly capital, technology, managerial skills from the metropolitan countries. These have tended to come in package forms rather than in an individual capacity. Out of this relationship has emerged new forms of dependency. Under the old form (which to some extent is still intact) the Latin American/Caribbean countries exported food and raw materials to the centre, earnings from which were used to pay for the manufactured goods supplied. Under the new form, import-substitution, far from decreasing dependence, has led to increased vulnerability. The share of consumer goods has fallen in many cases, but the proportion of intermediate and capital goods has increased correspondingly. The internal orientation of the industrialisation process has meant that net export earnings have been minimal, and dependence on traditional exports remains crucial. The implication of this development style is that imports cannot be reduced easily when export earnings fall without affecting the level of domestic economic activity. In this context, the crucial role of foreign finance becomes readily apparent as a means of forestalling economic (and political) instability. This dependence on foreign resources itself, however, also creates problems of its own. In recent years foreign borrowing has been undertaken not only to finance trade deficits, but to service past loans and investment. The extent of the borrowing and the terms and conditions associated with foreign loans have led to a situation where in many cases there have been significant increases in the level of foreign debt outstanding. Failure to secure funds in private markets on the scale and terms desired often means increasing reliance on institutions such as the IMF and the World Bank whose assistance tends to be highly conditional. The greater this reliance, the greater the possibility of loss in terms of control over desired development paths and policy instruments which are often refashioned to suit the ideological perspectives of the lenders.

The import-substitution strategy pursued by Latin American/ Caribbean countries in the post-war period has resulted in the emergence of a dependent-type capitalism which Prebisch has referred to as peripheral capitalism.[17] In this phase of the region's development, penetration has been effected in more complex and subtle forms for which many Latin American economists have found traditional modes of analysis highly inadequate. As we saw earlier, the assumption of neoclassical theory are such that this framework is not a particularly useful one for analysing the experience of developing countries in the international economy. One of these assumptions of which some observers have been particularly critical is the identification of the concepts of 'economy' and 'country' implying that countries are conceived as self-contained economic units which exchange products in the international market place.[18] Sunkel has pointed out that quite 'apart from the very partial aspect of international economic relations implicit in this approach, it fails to grasp one of the essential characteristics of the international economy, namely that it is basically made up of international firms which operate simultaneously in various national markets, thus constituting an international economic system which penetrates and overlaps with national economic systems.'[19] He further makes the point that, while the Marxist theory of imperialism has been able to grasp the implication of this in its concept of international monopoly capitalism, it has tended to ignore a very important element, i.e. 'the "spread" and "backwash" effects of the international extensions of some national economic systems into other national economic systems, and the influence of these processes on the structural configuration of the under-developed economy.'[20]

In some of his recent writings, Raul Prebisch has elaborated extensively on this latter point.[21] He argues that, in its struggle to develop, the periphery tends to follow in the tracks of what is done and thought in the centres. In contrast to the innovative capitalism of the centres, however, peripheral capitalism is essentially imitative. 'We adopt the same technology, we imitate the centres' consumption patterns and life styles. We copy their institutions; and their cultural manifestations; ideas and ideologies are constantly gaining ground in our countries.'[22] This type of development has certain built-in contradictions which are not easy to resolve. 'The penetration of technology from the centres requires more and more capital, which is not available, while it tends to absorb less and less a labour force which is relatively abundant per se, and is, moreover, growing at an exceptional rate.'[23] The imported technology has both economic and social implications for the domestic economy. On the one hand it leads to higher productivity and thus increases the potential for capital accumulation. A large part of the surplus generated, however, either finds its way back to the centre countries or is frittered away by the consumption habits of the upper strata to whom an increasing proportion of the income generated accrues in the process. What is implied here is that the rise in productivity leads to changes in the structure of society, 'in the course of which the upper income strata increase their power by concentrating most of the means of production in their own hands, with the result that they have the institutional capacity for primary appropriation of the fruits of technological progress. The middle income strata also strengthen their position as they expand with the development of industry and other related activities, but the lower strata remain largely excluded.'[24] The distribution of income, of course, manifests itself in the pattern of demand, and hence exerts its influence on the structure of production. The stronger this influence, the greater would be the bias in favour of luxury and semiluxury goods and against wage goods.

The foregoing analysis is essentially an extension of the ECLA thesis formulated during the 1980s, which blamed Latin America's problems on the region's position in the international economy and the uncritical adoption of liberal-capitalist economic policies. The dependency school which has emerged in recent years was in reaction to both the results of the import-substitution strategy during the 1950s and the 1960s and what it saw as serious analytical inadequacies in both the Marx-Lenin theory of imperialism and the ECLA framework. With respect to the latter, dependency theorists (among whom it should be pointed out are to be found differences in approach and perspectives) generally take the position that the ECLA thesis was correct in linking under-development with the international economic system, but did not go far enough. 'It fails, for example, to examine the conscious policies and specific needs of the nations of the center; it mistakenly attributes Latin America's backwardness largely to traditional or feudal oligarchies; it inappropriately assumes that development would be promoted by a progressive, nationalist bourgeoisie, an assumption thus far negated by historical experience; and its stress on import substitution has led to greater dependence on the international system and to economic stagnation.'[25] As indicated earlier, dependency theorists tend to differ among themselves in terms of conceptual approaches, focus and analytical frameworks. There are certain essential aspects of the model, however, which can be taken as broadly representative of the general position. One of the central points in this respect is the link between under-development in the periphery with development in the centre within one global system. 'Instead of hypothesizing under-development as an original state it asserts that the now developed countries were never under-developed and that contemporary under-development was created.'[26] The very forces responsible for expansion in the centre are the very ones creating under-development in the periphery. The latter has been conditioned by the needs of the expanding centre and lacks any autonomous capacity to generate its own growth and development. Though the metropolis may have shifted since the colonial times, and the structure of trade changed, the nature of dependency has not changed a great deal. Some argue it has deepened 'through greater foreign corporate, governmental and foundation penetration of banking, manufacturing, retailing, communications, advertising and education.'[27] 'The political result of economic dependency also has not changed. Just as the landed elites and merchants who exported Latin America's wealth pursued their interests in maintaining dependent economic patterns, modern industrial managers and military elites favour foreign interests. They also fear the demands of the masses within their own nations, preferring military dictatorship to nationalistic reform or revolution.'[28] The argument that the fruits of growth will 'trickle down' to the masses has been considerably overestimated.

The link between internal relationships and external factors forms one of the most important elements in the dependency theory. Underdevelopment tends not to be seen simply in terms of external constraints. 'Dependency in any given society is a complex set of associations in which the external dimensions are determinative in varying degrees and indeed internal variables may very well re-inforce the pattern of external linkages.'[29] The argument that developing countries can develop along the lines of the industrial nations ignores the history of the former and the class formations and structural characteristics which it bred in these societies. As we shall see in following sections even observers whom one may not wish to classify as dependency theorists take the position that internal behaviour can be influenced (and not always in the desired direction) by foreign factors which with local interests can perpetuate a state of dependence and under-development.

Capital inflows and economic development

High rates of capital formation have long been recognised as a major factor in the process of economic development. Investment can be financed from domestic sources as well as from foreign sources. If capital formation were dependent solely on domestic resources then the level of investment would rest critically on the level of savings in the local economy. Implicit here is the prior-savings approach which basically argues that the problem of low savings must be resolved before investment can increase. In the early post-war years many economists argued that developing countries were caught in a trap or 'vicious circle', i.e. savings were low because income was low, and income was low because there were not enough savings to finance the desired level of investment. In order to break out of this trap foreign capital was required. What was not generally suspected was that the savings level and potential of these countries were far greater than was thought to be the case. The problem was that, because of the colonial institutional arrangements, a significant part of their savings were being exported for use elsewhere, sometimes in the same countries that were providing loans and grants. Also, the tendency to use the concept 'gross national savings' as an indication of the level of savings generated by an economy is misleading since it excludes the re-investment earnings of non-resident owned enterprises, which have come out of local output. The broader concept 'gross domestic savings' includes both national savings and re-investment income (which is also treated as part of new investment) of foreign enterprises.

Assessing the capital needs of developing countries has been a favourite pastime of many economists, working individually or in collaboration with international development agencies.[30] Estimated needs tend to depend on the kind of assumptions that are made with respect to such variables like the required rate of growth, domestic savings, the capital output ratio, etc. A starting point for many of the models used is the well-known Harrod-Domar growth equation which grew out of the keynesian income/employment short-run theory, and sought to provide an answer to the longer term question of the rate of growth necessary to maintain full-employment over time. Given 's' as the ratio of savings to income and 'k' as the incremental capital-output ratio (ICOR) the rate of growth 'g' can be written as

$$g = \frac{s}{K}$$

Alternatively,[31] this equation can be written as

$$g = sk^* \text{ where 'k*' is}$$

the incremental output-capital ratio or the reciprocal of the capital-output ratio. If domestic savings are supplemented by an inflow of foreign aid 'a' (expressed as a percentage of national income), the growth rate 'g' can be written as

$$g = \frac{s + a}{k} \quad \text{or } g = (s + a)k$$

We can put this in words as follows: if a country is saving and investing 15% of its national income, and its incremental capital output ratio is 3, then its growth rate will be 5%. If foreign savings received is equal to 3% of national income, then the economy can grow at a rate of 6%. The above equations can be used (and often are used) to calculate the total amount of savings (including foreign aid) necessary to achieve a planned or target rate of growth. Thus if g* represented the target rate of growth then the rate of savings necessary to achieve this rate can be written as

$$c - g^*k \text{ where 'k' is}$$

the incremental capital-output ratio (as before) and 'c' the rate of accumulation or

$$c = \frac{g^*}{k^*} \text{ where 'k*' is}$$

the incremental output-capital ratio (i.e. the productivity of capital as before). The difference between 'c' and 's' is the savings gap and gives some indication of the amount of foreign aid necessary to achieve the planned rate of growth. Many proponents of foreign assistance argue[32] that in time a country may be able to generate its own savings requirements from domestic sources and thus become less dependent on foreign capital. In this connection an important assumption often made is that the marginal propensity to save is greater than the average propensity, so that as income increases the savings ratio will also rise.

There is some debate in the literature on the extent to which domestic savings can be substituted for foreign resources. This arises from the fact that developing countries tend to depend to a critical extent on outside sources for capital goods and many types of essential inputs, which they are unable to produce in the early stages of development. So even if domestic savings are high, foreign exchange may still be needed if earnings from exports are not adequate to pay for the level of imports necessitated by the desired rate of growth. In this context economists tend to speak of two gaps: a *savings gap* (the difference between savings and investment) and a *foreign-exchange gap* (the difference between foreign exchange earnings and expenditure). Ex-ante the two gaps need not be equal. In a formal or ex-post sense, however, they tend to be identical by definition, as can be seen below.[33]

Income= Consumption + Imports + Savings
Output= Consumption + Exports + Investment

Since, Income = Output
then Investment − Savings = Imports − Exports.

One of the major criticisms levelled against models using the gaps approach to foreign aid is that they tend to rely on fixed 'technical' relationships (e.g. the ICOR) and stable savings and import propensities.[34] In order to overcome this shortcoming some studies on foreign aid have sought to combine the gaps approach with what is often called the capital-absorptive capacity approach 'which regards capital requirements as being determined by the ability of an economy to employ both domestic and foreign capital productively in the sense that aid yields some minimum rate of return.'[35] In the absence of adequate and acceptable definitions for concepts relating to 'absorptive capacity' and 'rate of return', this latter approach itself is also not free from controversy. Disagreements over the approaches and methods used in assessing capital requirements for developing countries represent one set of issues. Another set arises from the position taken by some economists who challenge the assumptions that the rate of development will increase if the ratio of investment to national income rises and that the investment ratio will rise if capital imports increase. 'It is now generally agreed, I believe, that increased investment is neither necessary nor sufficient to achieve a high rate of growth in an under-developed country. In some circumstances expenditure on investment goods may have a negative return and expenditure on certain items usually classified as consumption may have a high positive return. It is less widely accepted that capital imports often tend to increase aggregate consumption more than investment. The reason this last point has not been accepted is that the possibility of capital imports supplementing consumption has been excluded from the typical aid model.'[36]

In the process of economic transformation many economic (and social variables) undergo change. The direction of change is not always in the desired direction. In the quantitative models, as indicated earlier, the tendency has been to deal with this problem by assuming stability in certain important coefficients. As far as the inclusion of variables is concerned, economists differ widely among themselves in terms of the critical variables that instigate change in an under-developed situation. The role of foreign capital has been subjected to examination in a number of econometric exercises a summary of which is provided in the Appendix to this chapter.

Appendix
Foreign capital and domestic savings and growth: some econometric results

1. *Griffin and Enos (1970)*[37]

(a) Using United Nations data for fifteen African and Asian countries over the period 1962–64, these two authors found 'no close association' between foreign aid received and the rate of growth of GNP. The results are given in Equation (1), in which Y is equal

to the average rate of growth of GNP and $\frac{A}{Y}$ is equal to the ratio of foreign aid to GNP. Not only is the correlation low, but the high standard error

$$\text{Eq. (1) } Y = 4.8 + \underset{(0.26)}{0.18}\,\frac{A}{Y}$$

$$R^2 = 0.33$$

casts serious doubts on the significance of the aid coefficient.

(b) Using data for the period 1957–64 relating to twelve Latin American countries they found an inverse relationship between the average rate of growth of GNP (Y) and the ratio of foreign aid to GNP $\left(\frac{A}{Y}\right)$ The results are shown in Eq. (2). The fit is clearly not good.

$$\text{Eq. (2) } Y = 42.97 - \underset{(\text{n.a.})}{6.78}\left(\frac{A}{Y}\right)$$

$$R^2 = 0.13$$

(c) Recognising the unreliability of the data used in the above exercise, they decided to look at the experience of one country, viz. Turkey over the period 1951–65. In Equation (3) the percentage change in GNP per capita (Q_{t+1}) is correlated with the amount of foreign aid received. (A_t). The relationship between the two variables is again

$$\text{Eq. (3) } Q_{t+1} = 12.5 - \underset{(0.011)}{0.047}\,A_t$$

$$R^2 = 0.62$$

negative. With an R^2 of 0.62 and with the regression coefficient significant at 0.005 level, the fit is much better. The lag between the independent and the dependent variables here is one year, but the authors make the observation that 'different lags and different forms of variables provoke no significant change in the sign of the relationship.'

2. *K. Griffin (1970)*[38]
   (a) Using the United Nations data for the period 1962–64, Griffin did a cross-section study of 32 under-developed countries in which he examined the relationship between the savings ratio and foreign savings. In Equation (4) $\frac{S}{Y}$ represents gross domestic savings as a % of GDP and $\frac{A}{Y}$ foreign savings as a % of GDP. Savings are calculated

$$\text{Eq. (4)}\quad \frac{S}{Y} = 11.2 - \underset{(0.11)}{0.73}\,\frac{A}{Y}$$

$$R^2 = 0.54$$

   as a residual and the net inflow of foreign capital is assumed to be equal to the deficit on current account. Here again, a negative relationship is suggested between capital inflows and domestic savings.
   (b) Within the sample of 32 countries, 13 were from Asia and the Middle East. The regression equation for these countries, Eq. (5) shows similar results.

$$\text{Eq. (5)}\quad \frac{S}{Y} = 16.1 - \underset{(0.52)}{0.82}\,\frac{A}{Y}$$

   (c) In a study of Colombia using 1950–63 data, Griffin smoothed out the bi-annual coffee cycle by using a two-year moving average, and then regressed domestic saving on foreign capital. The result shown in Eq. (6) is similar to Equations (4) and (5)

$$\text{Eq. (6)}\quad \frac{S}{Y} = 21.5 - \underset{(0.29)}{0.84}\,\frac{A}{Y}$$

$$R^2 = 0.43$$

3. *W. Leff (1968)*[39]
   Nathaniel Leff is another scholar who has expressed skepticism over the favourable effects of foreign capital on domestic savings and investment. In a study of Brazil covering the period between 1940 and 1960 he found a negative relationship between foreign investment inflows and domestic savings. In Equation (7), DS_t represents annual domestic savings,

$$\text{Eq. (7)}\ DS_t = \underset{(4.72)}{1.78} + \underset{(0.02)}{0.1545}\,(Y_{t-1}) - \underset{(0.33)}{0.1560}\,NFCI_t$$

   Y_{t-1} national income in the previous year, and $NFCI_t$, the current volume of net capital inflow. While the equation may be affected by the unusual years of the Second World War, Leff found that the domestic savings ratio tended to fall over the period 1939–60. The fact that this occurred while the economy was experiencing a growth rate of about 6% on average would seem to challenge the assumption often made that rising levels of income in developing countries may be enough to raise savings rates.

4. *T.E. Weisskopf, (1972)*[40]

In an effort to assess the average extent to which net foreign capital inflow substitutes for ex-ante domestic savings, Weisskopf pooled the time series data for seventeen countries into a single set of observations. The data related roughly to the period between the mid-1950s and the mid-1960s. With dummy variables to distinguish each of the countries, a pooled regression was undertaken to estimate the overall ex-ante savings function. Equation (8) was the result. The value of the intercept 'a' varied from

Eq. (8) $S = a + 0.183\,Y - 0.227\,F + 0.176\,E$
$(t = 65.9), (t = 5.3), (t = 4.6)$

Where S = Gross Domestic Savings
F = Net Capital Inflow
Y = Gross Domestic Product
E = Total Exports

country to country according to the estimated coefficient of the corresponding dummy variable. The coefficient of capital inflow (F) which is negative and highly significant indicates that about 23% of net foreign capital inflow substitutes for domestic savings.

5. *M.A. Rahman (1968)*[41]

Rahman uses 1962 data for 31 less developed countries to test the hypothesis that foreign inflows might be negatively related to domestic savings. He obtained the following estimated relationship:

Eq. (9) $\frac{S}{Y} = 0.14 - 0.25\,\frac{F}{Y}\ (t = 2.5)$

where S = Domestic Savings
F = Capital Inflow
Y = Gross National Product.

6. Not all writers share the view that foreign capital inflows are negatively related to domestic savings. Grinols and Bhagwati[42] take the position that it is difficult to judge whether foreign aid has been beneficial or not to recipient countries 'without adding several other relevant dimensions of a social welfare function.' Papanek[43] feels that a more fruitful approach than trying to measure the impact of foreign inflows on savings by regressing one on the other is to assume that they are independent variables in explaining growth. He also thinks a better insight can be obtained by disaggregating inflows into their principal components. The equations in Table 1.1 (which are based on a sample of 85 observations—34 in the 1950s

and 51 in the 1960s) summarise his results. In equations (10) to (13) aid has a coefficient nearly twice that of any other variables. In Equation (14) it is higher than that of private foreign investment, and in equation (15) it is more than twice that of the coefficient of the latter.

7. *Ramesh Ramsaran*[44]

Using time series data the author ran a series of linear regressions for three Commonwealth Caribbean countries (viz, Jamaica, Trinidad and Tobago and Guyana), with the aim of establishing a relationship between foreign capital inflows and domestic savings and growth. The results were as follows:

(a) *Jamaica* Observations: 1968–80

X_1 = Gross Domestic Savings as a % of GNP
X_2 = Total Autonomous Capital Inflows as a % of GNP
X_3 = Transfers as a % of GNP
X_4 = Annual % Change in GNP
X_5 = Net Direct Investment as a % of GNP
X_6 = Other Private Capital as a % of GNP
Figures in parenthesis are standard errors

$$\text{Eq. (17)}\ X_1 = \underset{(2.41)}{17.23} + \underset{(0.31)}{0.96X_2} - \underset{(1.38)}{1.45X_3}$$

$$R^2 = 50.15\%$$
$$D.W. = 1.28$$

In this equation foreign capital inflows has a positive relationship with the savings ratio, while transfers have a negative one. These two variables explain about half of the movements in the savings ratio.

$$\text{Eq. (18)}\ X_4 = \underset{(6.24)}{1.31} - \underset{(0.53)}{0.62X_2} + \underset{(0.38)}{1.01X_1}$$

$$R^2 = 43.07$$
$$D.W. = 1.45$$

In this equation the foreign capital variable is negatively related to the growth variable. Together with the savings ratio they explain only about 43% of the changes in growth.

$$\text{Eq. (19)}\ X_4 = \underset{(5.16)}{3.62} - \underset{(0.57)}{2.01\,X_5} + \underset{(0.52)}{0.58\,X_6} + \underset{(0.31)}{1.17\,X_1} - \underset{(1.51)}{2.43\,X_3}$$

$$R^2 = 76.19\%$$
$$D.W. = 2.10$$

In this equation net direct investment, other private capital inflows, the savings ratio and transfers explain more than 75% of growth. The coefficients of both net direct investment and transfers are, however, negative.

Table 1.1 *The Papanek Equations*

Equation		Intercept	Savings	Aid	Foreign Private Investment	Other Foreign Inflows	Corrected R^2	F Statistic
10) Growth	=	1.5	+ 0.20	+ 0.39	+ 0.17	+ 0.19	0.37	13.5
		(2.5)	(6.0)	(5.8)	(2.5)	(2.1)		
11) Growth	=	4.4	+ 0.07	. . .	. . .	. . .	0.02	3.9
		(8.7)	(1.7)					
12) Growth	=	4.9	. . .	+ 0.20			0.08	9.6
		(20.0)		(3.1)				
13) Growth	=	2.0	+ 0.18	+ 0.39	. . .	. . .	0.28	17.9
		(3.3)	(5.0)	(5.5)				
14) Growth	=	1.5	+ 0.21	+ 0.46	+ 0.35	+ 0.13	0.46	8.7
Asia		(7.7)	(4.2)	(4.4)	(1.7)	(0.8)		
(N = 31)								
15) Growth	=	1.1	+ 0.23	+ 0.47	+ 0.21	+ 0.12	0.44	8.8
Asia		(1.2)	(4.5)	(4.8)	(1.3)	(0.9)		
and the Mediterranean								
(N = 38)								
16) Growth	=	2.5	+ 0.11	+ 0.29	+ 0.19	− 0.06	0.11	2.4
Americas		(2.7)	(2.0)	(1.7)	(1.4)	(−0.3)		

Notes:
Growth = annual rate of increase in GDP; saving = gross domestic savings; aid = net transfers received by governments, plus official long-term borrowing; foreign private investment = private long term borrowing plus net private direct investment; other foreign inflows = net private transfers, net short term borrowing, other capital (net), and errors and omissions in the balance of payments; all independent variables expressed as percentage of GDP; regression (15) includes the same countries as regression (14), plus Cyprus, Tunisia, the UAR, Greece and Morocco; N = number of countries included in sample; figures in parentheses = t − ratios; R^2 corrected for degrees of freedom.

Trinidad and Tobago Observations: 1956–80

Y_1 = Gross Domestic Savings as a % of GNP
Y_2 = Autonomous Capital Movements as a % of GNP
Y_3 = Previous Year GNP
Y_4 = New Direct Investment
Y_5 = Other Private Inflows
Y_6 = Gross Domestic Savings
Y_7 = Annual % Change in GNP
Y_8 = Public Sector Inflows

Eq. (20) $Y_1 = 0.23 - 0.64\,Y_2 + 0.34\,Y_3$
(0.25) (0.29) (0.77)

$R^2 = 53.18\%$
D.W. = 1.45

This equation shows a negative relationship between total foreign capital inflows and the savings ratio.

Eq. (21) $Y_7 = 8.56 + 0.79\,Y_4 - 0.23\,Y_5 + 0.27\,Y_8 + 0.76\,Y_6$
(0.16) (0.30) (0.16) (0.33)

$R^2 = 45.76\%$
D.W. = 1.61

In this equation net direct investment is positively related to growth, but the former combined with other foreign inflows of both the private and public sectors and gross domestic savings could only explain 46% of the movements in the dependent variable, viz., growth.

Guyana

Observations: 1961–1980

Z_1 = Annual Percentage Change in GNP
Z_2 = Current Account Balance
Z_3 = Net Autonomous Capital Inflow
Z_4 = Gross Domestic Savings

Eq. (22) $Z_1 = 466.18 - 2.58\,Z_2$
(44.60) (0.56)

$R^2 = 53.75\%$
D.W. = 1.39

Where the current account balance is used as a proxy for capital inflows as in this equation, the relationship with the growth variable is a negative one.

Eq. (23) $Z_1 = 584.11 + 7.20\,Z_3$
(27.08) (2.27)

$R^2 = 35.95$
D.W. = 0.45

When net autonomous capital inflows are used as the independent variable the sign becomes positive, but the R^2 falls from 54% to 36%.

$$\text{Eq. (24)}\ Z_1 = \underset{(76.61)}{212.67} + \underset{(2.06)}{0.67}\, Z_3 + \underset{(0.65)}{3.23}\, Z_4$$

$$R^2 = 73.98$$
$$D.W. = 1.00$$

In this equation net capital inflows and gross domestic savings explain about 74% of the changes in growth, but the two variables appear to be seriously correlated. In addition the coefficient of the net capital inflows variable is not significant.

Summary

While most of the studies cited above tend to indicate a negative relationship between capital inflows and domestic savings, the poor quality of the data pertaining to savings and capital inflows would suggest some caution in interpretation of the results. In several cases the capital inflow concept appears to be too highly aggregative. It is possible that, with a greater degree of disaggregation both in the dependent and independent variables, more useful relationships could be obtained. For instance, the impact of aid might be felt more by government savings than by total savings. On the other hand, a high correlation between the inflow of foreign savings and growth does not necessarily imply any connection with welfare of the masses of the population. Papanek uses GDP as his dependent variable, but a significant part of the GDP may be accruing to foreigners as owners of factors of production. Also, while growth might be taking place, only a small proportion of the population might be sharing in its fruits. The imitative consumption habits of developing countries, as we saw earlier, tend to result in a high propensity to consume, which in turn reinforces dependence on foreign sources for funds to finance development. Higher income, as we indicated, may not necessarily lead to higher savings, so that what Papenek might be addressing himself to is not 'growth' but 'dependent growth' – i.e. growth dependent on continuous foreign inflows. The logic of having savings as the dependent variable stems from the assumption in the whole aid idea that in time the savings ratio would rise, enabling growth to be sustained on the basis of local resources. Of course, this assumption could be wrong, and the purpose of aid might be more sinister as Griffin has suggested.

Notes

1 The Economic Commission for Latin America (ECLA) set up in 1949, and its first Secretary General, Raul Prebisch, played a lead part in providing the theoretical framework for the acceleration of the Latin American industrialisation process in the post-war period.
2 For a most brilliant critique, see Raul Prebisch, 'The Economic Development of Latin America and its Principal Problems', *Economic Bulletin for Latin America*, Feb., 1962
3 Michael P. Todaro, *Economics for a Developing World* (London: Longman Group Limited, 1977), p. 310.
4 See, for example, Prebisch, op. cit. See also Hans Singer 'The Distribution of Gains between Investing and Borrowing Countries', *American Economic Review, Papers and Proceedings*, Vol. 11, No. 2, May 1950.
5 Prebisch, op. cit.
6 See S.H. Hymer, and S.A. Resnick, 'International Trade and Uneven Development', in J.N. Bhagwati *et al.*, *Trade, Balance of Payments and Growth* (Amsterdam: North-Holland Publishing Co., 1971).
7 Ibid.
8 For a critical summary of early imperialist theories, See D.A. Offiong, *Imperialism and Dependency, Obstacles to African Development* (Washington, DC: Howard University Press, 1982), Chap. 3.
9 See S. Lall and P. Streeten, *Foreign Investment, Transnationals and Developing Countries* (London: Macmillan Publishers Ltd., 1977), p. 18.
10 S.H. Hymer, *The International Operations of National Firms: A Study of Direct Investment*, (M.I.T. doctoral dissertation, Cambridge, Mass., 1960). See also his article, 'United States Investment Abroad', in Peter Drysdale (ed.), *Direct Foreign Investment in Asia and the Pacific* (Toronto: University of Toronto Press, 1972).
11 R.E. Caves, 'International Corporations: The Industrial Economics of Foreign Investment', *Economica*, Vol. 38, 1971.
12 Raymond Vernon, 'International Investment and International Trade in the Product Cycle', *Quarterly Journal of Economics*, Vol. 80, No. 2, May 1966.
13 Lall and Streeten, op. cit., p. 18.
14 See P.N. Rosenstein-Rodan, 'Problems of Industrialization of Eastern and South-Eastern Europe', *Economic Journal*, June–Sept., 1943. See also his 'Notes on the Theory of the "Big Push" ', in H.S. Ellis (ed.), *Economic Development in Latin America* (New York: St. Martin's Press, 1961).
15 A. Hirschman, *The Strategy of Economic Development* (New Haven: Yale University Press, 1958.)
16 W.A. Lewis, 'Economic Development with Unlimited Supplies of Labour', *The Manchester School*, May 1954.
17 See Paul Prebisch, 'A Critique of Peripheral Capitalism', CEPAL, *Review*, first half of 1976.
18 For example, see Osvaldo Sunkel, 'The Pattern of Latin American Dependence', in V.L. Urquidi and R. Thorp (eds.) *Latin America in the International Economy* (London: Macmillan Publishers Ltd., 1973).
19 Ibid.
20 Ibid.

21 For example, see his 'A Critique of Peripheral Capitalism', op. cit.
22 Ibid.
23 Ibid.
24 Ibid.
25 R.H. Chilcote and J.C. Edelstein, (eds.), *Latin America: The Struggle With Dependency and Beyond* (New York: John Wiley and Sons, 1974), p. 41.
26 Ibid., p. 27.
27 Ibid.
28 Ibid.
29 See J.S. Valenzuela and A. Valenzuela, 'Modernization and Dependency: Alternative Perspectives in the Study of Latin American Development', in Heraldo Munoz, *From Dependency to Development* (Boulder: Westview Press, 1981).
30 See, for example, H.B. Chenery and A.M. Strout, 'Foreign Assistance and Economic Development', *American Economic Review*, Sept. 1966.
31 See K. Griffin, 'Foreign Capital, Domestic Savings and Economic Development', in *Bulletin of the Oxford University Institute of Economics and Statistics*, May, 1970.
32 See, for example, H.B. Chenery and A.M. Strout, 'Foreign Assistance and Economic Development', *American Economic Review*, Sept. 1966.
33 It shoul be noted that in accounting terms the amount of foreign borrowing required to supplement domestic savings is the same, whether the need is just for more resources for capital formation or for imports as well. See A.P. Thirlwell, *Growth and Development, with Special Reference to Developing Countries* (London: Macmillan Publishers Ltd., 1978), p. 292.
34 See K. Griffin, 'Foreign Capital, Domestic Savings and Economic Development', op. cit.
35 R.F. Mikesell, *The Economics of Foreign Aid* (Chicago: Aldine Publishing Company, 1968), p. 76.
36 K. Griffin, op. cit.
37 K.B. Griffin and J.L. Enos 'Foreign Assistance: Objectives and Consequences', *Economic Development and Cultural Change*, April, 1970.
38 K. Griffin, 'Foreign Capital, Domestic Savings and Economic Development', op. cit.
39 N.H. Leff, 'Marginal Savings Rates in the Development Process: The Brazilian Experience', *Economic Journal*, Sept. 1968.
40 T.E. Weisskopf, 'The Impact of Foreign Capital Inflow on Domestic Savings in Under-developed Countries', *Journal of International Economics* (1971).
41 M.A. Rahman, 'Foreign Capital and Domestic Savings: A Test of Haavelmo's Hypothesis with Cross-Country Data', *The Review of Economics and Statistics*, Vol. 50, 1968.
42 E. Grinols and J. Bhagwati, 'Foreign Capital, Savings and Dependence', *The Review of Economics and Statistics*, Vol. 58, 1976.
43 G.F. Papanek, 'Aid, Foreign Private Investment and Growth in Less Developed Countries', *Journal of Political Economy* Jan/Feb., 1973.
44 I am indebted to Mr Vincent Maraj for assistance with some of the computations.

2

Post-War Development Experience

The Latin American/Caribbean region is in socio-geographical terms largely the poor part of the Western Hemisphere, or broadly the Western Hemisphere minus Canada and the United States. It is one of the several 'developing' (some prefer the terms 'underdeveloped' or 'less-developed') areas of the world. Depending on the analytical context, it is sometimes referred in more colourful terms as the 'Western Periphery' or the 'Western Third World' or the 'Western South'. Many American politicians prefer to see it simply as the 'American Backyard'. The region comprises a heterogeneous group of countries that differ in size, population per capita income, resource endownment and levels of development. The five languages currently spoken (viz, Spanish, Portuguese, Dutch, French and English) reflect the fact that these countries were at one time (some are still) part of the competing European-based Empires. There are, of course, other manifestations and legacies of the colonial experience, particularly in the area of economic organisation and external economic relations, which persist long after formal ties have been severed. By the end of the 1820s all the Spanish and Portuguese colonies (excepting Cuba)[1] had won their political independence. The decolonisation of the British Empire in the Caribbean started in 1962 when Jamaica attained its constitutional independence. The process is still continuing, and its formal conclusion seems to depend on the decisions of the few remaining colonies themselves whose size and resources raise serious doubts about their ability to survive as independent states. The only Dutch colony to seek and attain independence so far is Suriname (formerly Dutch Guiana) in 1975. The French presence is maintained in French Guyana, Martinique and Guadeloupe which are 'Overseas Departments'[2] of France. Haiti declared its independence from France in 1804.

The colonies of all the Empires were developed (exploited) to serve primarily the interests of the metropolitan powers. They provided food and raw materials to the 'centre' from which they purchased manufactured goods. Products of the resource-based industries were exported largely in raw form for processing abroad. Domestic manufacturing activities were discouraged since they were seen to compete with industries in the 'centre'. Investments in the colonies by individuals or corporations based in the metropole were like investments in the home country, since they were subjected to the same laws, the same guarantees and the same exchange control regulations. The monetary systems of the colonies were closely integrated into those of the 'centre' countries, and this facilitated the movement of capital not only into the colonies, but out of it as well. Thus, while the colonies were seen as short on investment capital, whatever little domestic savings took place were remitted in various forms to the centre countries. Development of the local economies was not a central concern of the latter who were primarily interested in their resource potential and the strategic importance they held in global security. Concessions to private foreign investments paid little consideration to the long term interests of the particular colony concerned.[3] Once political independence was achieved many countries found it necessary to re-examine the terms on which foreign capital was operating in such key sectors like the utilities and the resource based industries which were important to national development.

In the following sections we look at recent social and economic trends in the Latin American/Caribbean region in order to provide a background to subsequent chapters.

The population of the Latin American/Caribbean region increased from an estimated 160 million in 1960 to around 370 million in 1980 at an average rate of 2.8%. As a proportion of the world total, the ratio increased from 6.5% to 8.3% over the period. A glance at Table 2.1 shows that the population growth in recent years differs widely from country to country, but generally has been over 2% per annum. For most countries in the region real income has grown at a faster rate than population, resulting in a positive rate of change in per capita real income. Between 1935 and 1961, the GDP for Latin America as a whole increased at a cumulative annual rate of 4.6%. During the 1960s the growth rate was around 5.2%. At 1970 prices GDP grew at an average rate of about 6% between 1970 and 1980, while real per capita GDP increased at a rate around 3.5%. Table 2.2 shows that both nominal and real income (and even population) growth rates can fluctuate widely from period to period. A glance back at Table 2.1 will show that there has also been great differences in the growth experienced by individual countries. During the 1970s for example, while real per capita GNP for certain countries grew at a rate exceeding 5%, in a few cases the growth rate was actually negative.

Table 2.1 *Basic data on selected Latin American/Caribbean countries*

Countries	*Area (Sq. miles)*	*Population[1] '000*	*GNP Per Capita[2] US $*	*Growth Rates (%)*	
				Population 1970–79	*GNP Per Capita (real) 1970–79*
South America					
Argentina	1,072,749	27,313	2,210	1.6	1.0
Bolivia	424,163	5,428	550	2.6	2.3
Brazil	3,287,195	116,539	1,770	2.3	6.1
Chile	286,396	10,917	1,890	1.7	0.8
Colombia	439,519	26,122	1,060	2.3	3.7
Ecuador	109,484	8,081	1.110	3.3	5.4
Guyana	83,000	790	630	1.1	0.0
Paraguay	157,047	2,974	1,140	2.9	5.3
Peru	496,223	17,149	850	2.7	0.2
Suriname	63,037	367	2,480	−0.5	6.4
Uruguay	72,172	2,904	2,500	0.3	2.9
Venezuela	352,146	14,453	3,440	3.4	2.7
Central America					
Belize	8,866	142	980	1.9	4.1
Costa Rica	19,575	2,162	1,630	2.5	3.2
El Salvador	8,061	4,410	640	2.9	1.4
Guatemala	42,042	6,811	1,010	2.9	3.1
Honduras	44,480	3,563	520	3.4	0.5
Mexico	760,337	65,509	1,880	3.0	1.9
Nicaragua	54,864	2,584	610	3.3	−1.6
Panama	28,753	1,794	1,550	2.3	1.3
Other Latin America					
Cuba	44,218	9,760	n.a.	1.4	n.a.
Dominican Republic	18,703	5,280	1,030	3.0	3.7
Haiti	10,714	4,921	230	1.7	1.8
Commonwealth Caribbean					
Bahamas	5,386	234	2,770	3.2	−4.7
Barbados	166	248	2,680	0.5	2.1
Grenada	133	109	650	1.8	−1.3
Jamaica	4,411	2,159	1,110	1.6	−3.7
Trinidad & Tobago	1,980	1,150	3,910	1.2	4.5

1 mid-1979 estimates.
2 1979.

Sources: World Bank *Atlas*; 1981; OAS *Introduction to the Latin American Nations*, 1968.

In Table 2.3 we present data which seeks to compare the growth experience with respect to GNP and real per capita GNP of the Latin American/Caribbean region with that of other parts of the developing world since 1960. Between 1960 and 1970 real GNP grew at an average rate of 5.5% which was higher than that of the industrial countries, but a few points lower than the average for all developing areas. In the 1970–80 period, the growth rate of 5.5% was also slightly lower than the average for all the developing region, but significantly higher than that of the 3.3% for the industrial nations. There is no doubt that one of

Table 2.2 *Latin America – annual cumulative rate of growth of selected variables, 1935–1961*

(Percentages)

Variable	*1935–1940*	*1940–1945*	*1945–1950*	*1950–1955*	*1955–1961*
Gross Domestic Product (GDP)	3.3	4.3	5.7	4.7	4.3
Gross Domestic Real Income	4.5	4.8	6.8	4.5	3.8
Population	1.9	2.1	2.5	2.7	2.8
Per Capita GDP	1.3	2.2	3.2	2.0	1.4
Per Capita Gross Domestic Real Income	2.5	2.7	4.2	1.7	1.0

Sources: UN, *The Economic Development of Latin America in the Post-War Period*, New York, 1964.

the main factors responsible for the difference in performance between the rich and poor countries in the 1970s would have been the higher prices charged for oil by the oil-exporting developing nations in the period following the Arab-Israeli war of 1973. Of course, this factor would also have been important in explaining the differences in performance among developing countries themselves, both in the hemisphere and elsewhere. When we look at the growth rate of real per capita GNP in the period 1960–70, the figure of 2.6% was lower than that of the average for both the industrial countries (4.0%) and for all developing regions (3.5%). However, in the decade 1970–80, a rate of 3.0% was achieved, which was lower than the average for poor nations as a whole but higher than that of the industrial countries. When compared to other developing areas in the 1960s and 1970s, the performance of the Latin American/Caribbean region (in terms of the growth of total real GNP and per capita GNP) was superior to that of Africa (south of the Sahara) and South Asia, and also of Southern Europe (including other Mediterranean countries) in the 1970s. The high income countries of the Middle East (including North Africa) and of East Asia and the Pacific were associated with higher growth rates, and their experience exerted a significant influence on the overall average.

Despite the impressive rates achieved by Latin America in the post-war period, data published by the World Bank show that in 1979 the per capita GNP of North America was 6.0 times (7.3 times in 1973) that of South America and 6.5 times (7.7 times in 1973) that of Central America. While the situation may differ with respect to each country, overall there has been a narrowing of the income gap in recent years. (See Table 2.4). It is also worth pointing out that while the per capita income gap between Latin America and Africa may have narrowed a

Table 2.3 *Real growth of GNP and GNP per capita in the developing and industrial countries, 1960–81*

(Percentage change per year)

	GNP					*GNP Per Capita*				
Areas	*1960–70*	*1970–80*	*1979*	*1980*	*1981*[a]	*1960–70*	*1970–80*	*1979*	*1980*	*1981*[a]
All developing regions[b]	*5.8*	*5.6*	*4.8*	*5.0*	*2.2*	*3.5*	*3.3*	*2.8*	*3.0*	*0.2*
Africa south of the Sahara	4.7	3.7	1.5	2.8	2.2	2.1	1.0	−1.1	0.0	−0.7
East Asia & Pacific	7.3	6.9	7.5	5.8	5.5	5.1	4.9	5.9	4.3	3.9
Latin America & The Caribbean	5.5	5.5	5.9	5.3	−0.4	2.6	3.0	3.5	3.0	−2.7
North Africa and the Middle East[c]	7.7	8.1	8.5	6.8	0.6	5.1	5.1	5.1	3.5	−2.3
South Asia	4.3	3.5	−3.1	6.6	5.9	1.9	1.2	−5.2	4.3	3.5
Southern Europe and Other Mediterranean Countries	6.6	5.1	2.5	1.2	2.4	5.0	3.3	0.9	−0.4	0.9
Industrial Countries[d]	*5.1*	*3.3*	*3.4*	*1.4*	*1.2*	*4.0*	*2.5*	*2.8*	*0.8*	*0.7*

a Preliminary
b The data include the high-income oil exporters minus Iraq.
c Excludes Iran and Iraq, as do the totals.
d The growth rates for the industrial countries refer to GDP rather than GNP.

Source: The World Bank, *Annual Report*, 1982.

little in recent years, in 1979 the per capita GNP of the former was still more than twice that of the latter. With respect to Asia (excluding Japan and the Middle East) the gap has widened from around 4 times in 1973 to over 5 times in recent years.

Table 2.4 *GNP per capita by major regions, 1973 and 1979*

	GNP Per Capita (US $)	
Regions/Country	*1973*	*1979*
North America	6,130	10,500
Japan	3,630	8,730
Oceania	3,400	7,000
Europe, excluding USSR	2,990	6,760
USSR	2,030	4,040
Middle East[1]	1,080	4,310
South America	840	1,730
Central America[2]	800	1,620
Africa	290	700
Asia, excluding Japan and Middle East	200	310
World		*2,430*

1 Consists of Bahrain, Iraq, Israel, Jordan, Kuwait, Oman, Qatar, Saudi Arabia, Syrian Arab Republic, United Arab Emirates, Yemen Arab Republic and People's Democratic Republic of Yemen.
2 Includes Mexico.

Source: World bank *Atlas*, various issues.

In many respects Latin America has reached an interesting stage of development. Assuming a growth rate of 6.1% per year (i.e. the actual rate of real growth of GDP between 1970–75), it is estimated that the domestic product of Latin America in 1990 will be around US$450 billion (in 1970 prices), a figure that is slightly lower than that of the EEC in 1970. Assuming an industrial growth rate of 7.1% per year (the actual average for the period 1970–75), the Latin American manufacturing product is expected to amount to some US$135 billion (1970 prices) – a figure 20% less than that of the EEC in 1970. Based on a growth rate of 11.2% (the annual average for the 1960–74 period) the gross value of the production of machinery and equipment in 1990 is expected to amount to some US$138 billion (1970 prices), which is higher than the figure (US$126 billion) recorded in 1970 for the EEC. Assuming a growth rate of 8.7% (the annual average for the 1950–75 period) the supply of electrical energy in 1990 will be close to 800 billion kWh – more than the supply of the EEC in 1970.[4]

It has long been recognised that it is possible for an economy to grow without any changes taking place in the basic structure, or without any improvement in the well-being of the average citizen. High prices for an export product (e.g. oil in the 1970s) can lead to unusual growth in total product of the countries concerned, while the resilience and functioning of the economy remains unchanged. Growth, of course, can also emanate from a broader range of factors related to structural changes taking place in the fabric of the economy. Whatever the source of growth, the pattern of income distribution would depend on the framework within which it is taking place and the kind of redistributive measures in force. Political perceptions play a crucial role in both these respects. In developing countries economic strategy is essentially a political exercise in which the state tends to be the key actor. In totalitarian states this is fairly obvious. In the so-called market or mixed-economy countries the state may not have the same powers to commandeer resources, but it is the state that operates the apparatus which influences private decision-making in crucial respects. The foreign exchange regulations, taxes, price and interest rates policies, labour laws, profit margins, exchange rates, re-investment of profits, local assets ratios, etc, are critical policy areas which influence the behaviour of investors. The greater the premium placed on growth the greater would be the tendency to orient regulations in this direction. Since in practice the measures which promote growth often tend to be in conflict with the measures aimed at redistribution, a certain amount of trade-off is necessary. The extent of this trade-off will be heavily influenced by the political framework which may be characterised by different degrees of sensitivity to public opinion. The less democratic a regime is, the more it can afford to tilt the balance in favour of growth. Of course, in a situation where the government can be changed by popular will, broad social and economic conditions cannot easily be ignored if the aim is to stay in power by legitimate means.

From the above, it is clear that the relationship between income growth and income distribution is not a simple one. There is a view which takes the position that growth must take place before redistribution. What is often not explicit is at what point in the process should emphasis start being placed on redistributive measures and policies, given the fact that by their very nature the latter could at any time be given an anti-growth interpretation, and thus exert an adverse effect on the investment climate. Another view advocates that re-distribution must take place simultaneously with growth. In other words the cake must be shared even while it is being made. The rationale here is that if social conditions are ignored they are likely to get worse and become increasingly more difficult to redress. Also, it is felt, by the time redistribution becomes an important concern the fruits of growth may have vanished.

We do not have very up-to-date information on the distribution of income in Latin America and the Caribbean. The data available suggests that the distribution of income has become increasingly worse in recent years. The figures given in Table 2.5 relate to seven countries (see footnote (a) of the Table), which represent nearly 80% of the population and 90% of the product of Latin America. As can be seen in the Table the share of income received by the poorest 40% of the population dropped from 8.7% in 1960 to 7.7% in 1975. The share of the richest 10% and of the 20% preceding the richest 10% increased slightly.[5] Looking at the distribution problem in slightly different terms, it is estimated that as late as 1970 some 40% of the Latin American population suffered from extreme poverty and almost half of these could be considered indigent (see Table 2.6).[6] This meant that in 1970 the poor of the region numbered almost 110 million of whom 54 million were indigent.[7] In Honduras, 65% of the households were below the poverty line, of which 45% were below the indigent line. In Brazil the comparative poverty percentage was 49%, in Mexico 34%, in Peru 50%, in Colombia 45% and in Venezuela 25%.

Table 2.5 *Latin America: household income distribution in the region as a whole in 1960 and 1975*[a]

Income Strata	*Share in Total Income*		*Income per Household*[b] *(1970 dollars)*	
	1960	*1975*	*1960*	*1975*
Poorest 20%	2.8	2.3	334	394
Next poorest 20%	5.9	5.4	707	902
Poorest 40%	8.7	7.7	520	648
30% following the poorest 40%	18.6	18.1	1,483	2,023
20% preceding the richest 10%	26.1	26.9	3,110	4,497
Richest 10%	46.6	47.3	11,142	15,829
Total	*100.0*	*100.0*	*2,389*	*3,348*

a CEPAL estimates on the basis of national surveys for seven countries (Argentina, Brazil, Chile, Colombia, Mexico, Peru and Venezuela).

b Corresponds to the concept of disposable income per household estimated on the basis of the national accounts of each country.

Source: Enrique V. Iglesias, 'Development and Equity, The Challenge of the 1980s', CEPAL *Review*, December, 1981.

Table 2.6 *Estimates of the incidence of extreme poverty in some Latin American countries around 1970*[a]

Country	*Percentage of Households below the Poverty Line*	*Percentage of Households below the Indigenous Line*
Argentina	8	1
Brazil	49	25
Chile	17	6
Colombia	45	18
Costa Rica	24	6
Honduras	65	45
Mexico	34	12

Table 2.6—*(Cont'd)*

Country	*Percentage of Households below the Poverty Line*	*Percentage of Households below the Indigenous Line*
Peru	50	25
Uruguay	...	...
Venezuela	25	10
Average of above	*40*	*19*

a The ten countries account for 84% of the population of Latin America.

Source: Enrique V. Iglesias, 'Latin America on the Threshold of the 1980s', CEPAL *Review*, December 1969.

Despite the growth in income and the structural changes which have taken place in the (Latin America/Caribbean economies) since the Second World War, the level of unemployment and under-development remains high in most countries of the region. While recent data on un-employment levels are not readily available, the ratios for the following countries do give indication of the magnitude of the problem: Chile, 11.8% (1980), Barbados 12.8% (1979), Jamaica 29.5% (1980), Trinidad & Tobago 11.0% (1980), El Salvador 16.8% (1980), Nicaragua 17.5% (1980) and Panama 8.1% (1978).[8] In Table 2.7 we present the distribution of the active labour force by sectors in 1950, 1970 and 1980 for 14 countries which represent 95% of the economically active population of Latin America.

As can be seen there, the percentage of the labour force employed in agriculture dropped from 53.8% in 1950 to 35% in 1980. The share in industry increased only marginally from 14.1% in 1950 to 16% in 1980. The most significant change was in services whose share changed from 15.1% to 25.0% between 1950 and 1970. When we compare the pattern of these movements with changes in the structure of the economy, an interesting point emerges. While the share of agriculture in GDP declined from about 25% in 1950 to about 10% in recent years, the manufacturing sector grew from about 20% to 25% over the same period. For some countries the growth of manufacturing was much more spectacular than this. Table 2.8 gives some indication of changes in the respective share of agriculture and manufacturing in GDP for selected countries in the period between 1960 and 1981.

One of the main criticisms often levelled against the manufacturing sector in the Latin American/Caribbean region has been its inability to absorb an increasing proportion of the labour force. The sector has received assistance in almost every conceivable form through a number of devices including protection from foreign competition, exemption from import duties on raw materials and equipments, income tax holidays, etc. This strategy has entailed certain costs for the economy, not only in terms of loss of revenue, but through its effects on other

Table 2.7 *Latin America: economically active population by sectors of activity, 1950, 1970 and 1980*

	'000 of Persons			*Percentages*			*Growth Rates*		
Sectors	*1950*[a]	*1970*	*1980*	*1950*	*1970*	*1980*	*1950–70*	*1950–80*	*1970–80*
Total	*51,969*	*78,874*	*103,094*	*100.0*	*100.0*	*100.0*	*2.1*	*2.3*	*2.7*
Agriculture	27,982	33,163	36,110	53.8	42.1	35.0	0.9	0.9	0.9
Mining	672	994	1,098	1.3	1.3	1.1	2.0	1.7	1.0
Industry	7,311	11,338	16,523	14.1	14.4	16.0	2.2	2.8	3.8
Construction	1,861	4,244	6,706	3.6	5.4	6.5	4.2	4.4	4.7
Transport	2,009	3,280	4,220	3.9	4.1	4.1	2.5	2.5	2.6
Electricity	155	300	385	0.3	0.4	0.4	3.4	3.1	2.5
Commerce	4,115	7,949	12,285	7.9	10.1	11.9	3.4	3.7	4.5
Services	7,864	17,516	25,767	15.1	22.2	25.0	4.1	4.0	3.9

Note: The total includes information from 14 countries which account for around 95% of the economically active population of Latin America: Argentina, Bolivia, Brazil, Chile, Colombia, Costa Rica, Ecuador, El Salvador, Guatemala, Mexico, Panama, Peru, Uruguay and Venezuela.

a In Peru, Uruguay and Venezuela the data correspond to 1960, since no information is available for 1950.

Source: Enrique V. Iglesias, 'Development and Equity.: The Challenge of the 1980s', CEPAL, *Review*, December, 1981.

Table 2.8 *Latin America and the Caribbean: share of manufacturing and agriculture in GDP, 1960–62 and 1979–81*[1]

	Manufacturing[2]		*Agriculture*[2]	
Country	*1960–62*	*1979–81*	*1960–62*	*1979–81*
Argentine	24.6	24.4	15.1	13.3
Barbados	12.7	15.9	25.0	10.0
Bolivia	12.7	15.9	22.6	17.2
Brazil	25.1	27.3	13.5	7.9
Chile	23.0	21.5	9.9	8.2
Colombia	17.5	18.7	30.3	25.5
Costa Rica	14.1	22.0	25.8	18.4
Dominican Rep.	15.4	18.2	30.2	16.8
Ecuador	12.3	19.4	28.2	15.2
El Salvador	14.9	17.1	31.9	25.3
Guatemala	13.1	16.4	29.8	25.1
Guyana	13.1	18.6	24.2	17.6
Haiti	13.5	16.6	43.2	32.5
Honduras	12.0	16.2	34.0	29.1
Jamaica	17.2	15.4	10.9	8.6
Mexico	19.7	24.9	16.0	9.0
Nicaragua	16.3	24.1	24.8	25.1
Panama	14.0	13.5	22.5	13.7
Paraguay	14.8	16.5	40.0	30.9
Peru	23.1	24.7	17.9	12.4
Trinidad & Tobago	25.0	10.2	7.0	2.9
Uruguay	22.5	25.0	14.6	11.3
Venezuela	14.5	17.6	7.1	6.2
All Countries	*21.3*	*24.0*	*16.0*	*10.6*

1 At constant market prices converted to US dollars of purchasing power of 1980.
2 Average for periods.

Source: IDB, Annual *Report*, 1980.

sectors of the economy. The general feeling was, however, that this was a necessary price to pay in order to bring about a greater degree of diversification and resilience in the economy. Replacing primary exports by manufactured goods was seen as one way of dealing with the deteriorating terms of trade facing the region. Given the initial perspectives and the present character of the industrial structure and orientation in the region, it would be instructive to go into a little more detail into the factors that have shaped Latin American/Caribbean industry.

In the period between 1950 and 1980, Latin American industry expanded at an average rate of 6.7% per year (5.0% if Brazil and Mexico are excluded) as compared to a rate of 5.9% for world industry. As a result of this performance, the region's industrial weight increased from less than 4% to close to 5%. Among Western market economies the manufacturing weight climbed from 4.7% to 8.4% as a result of Latin America's relatively rapid industrial growth and North

America's slow growth (3.6% annually) and the slow pace of Western Europe's growth (5.2% annually).[9] Of course, manufacturing output in the region is very unevenly distributed. Brazil alone accounts for about 40% of value added as compared to about 26% for Mexico, 10% for Argentina, 5% for Venezuela, and about 1% for Jamaica, Guyana, Barbados and Trinidad and Tobago taken together.[10]

While the significant expansion in the industrial sector took place in the post-war period, the beginnings of the sector go back many years.[11] By the end of the nineteenth century a number of countries (e.g. Argentina, Brazil, Chile, Colombia, Mexico and Uruguay) in Latin America had already taken some initial steps towards industrialisation. The process was encouraged by several developments during the early part of the twentieth century. One was the difficulties faced by traditional exports and their consequent inability to generate enough foreign exchange to pay for a growing volume of imports. 'In several countries of the region, exports, and consequently, the capacity to import reached their peak levels prior to the First World War, and later suffered considerable setbacks, so that per capita imports were higher in the years preceding the First World War than at the end of the twenties.'[12] The onset of the 1930s depression created even further difficulties for the Latin American economies which up to that time were still critically dependent on a narrow range of primary products for export earnings. The initiation (and in some cases the intensification) of the import substitution process in this period was not only a response to the problems faced by the external sector, but was also a consequence of other internal developments particularly of a socio-economic nature. One of the most important of these was the changing pattern of demand associated with rapid population growth, increasing urbanisation, income growth and increasing inequity in the distribution of income.

In the post-war period the process of industrial development gathered increased momentum in most countries of the region. The growth of the sector in this period, however, has become associated with certain features which have given rise to the view that continued industrialisation in the present form will not meet the social and economic needs of the majority of people in the region. One of these features is the critical influence which the demand patterns of the middle and upper income groups have exerted on the type of goods produced. The latter not only tend to be largely outside the range of the masses of the population, but often require technology which is unsuited to the local factor endowment situation. Again, as a result of the increasingly more complex range of goods produced over the years 'great horizontal diversification was achieved, but this was not accompanied by an equivalent degree of vertical integration and inter-sectoral complementation. The branches of greatest technological complexity and also of greatest dynamism thus remained somewhat behind, particularly in the case of those producing certain basic inputs such as chemical and metallurgical products, and those producing a wide variety of capital goods.'[13] One consequence of this trend is that the level of imports far from falling has tended to grow at a faster rate than product. Up to 1965 the average growth of imports was 0.4 times that of the product. Between 1965 and 1975 it is estimated to have grown to 2.4%.[14] There is evidence to indicate not only is the import coefficient of elasticity with respect to the product greater than unity, but it tends to increase as the growth rate accelerates.[15] While the proportion of consumer goods in total imports may have fallen as the import substitution process progressed, the dependence on intermediate and capital goods has correspondingly increased. The significance of this, of course, is that it is not easy to reduce the volume of these imports without affecting the level of domestic industrial activity. When earnings from exports are not sufficient to finance needed levels of imports, borrowing becomes inevitable, and this to some extent explains the increasing foreign debt position of many countries in the region, particularly the most industrialised.

The involvement of transnational corporations in Latin American/Caribbean development raises a number of issues which have a fundamental bearing on national decision-making and on the further growth of the region. A point to note here is that transnationals tend to be heavily concentrated in countries with the largest markets. In 1973, for instance, it was found that 21% of the branches of 7,500 transnational corporations in Latin America were located in Brazil, 19% in Mexico and 12% in Argentina.[16] One of the major features of their presence is their tendency to dominate the high growth sectors of the various economies. In Brazil, out of the total sales made by the 2,800 largest enterprises in 1975, foreign enterprises accounted for 76% in transport equipment, 71% in engineering products, 67% in machines and accessories including electrical machines, 66% in rubber products and 62% in chemical products. Figures relating to Mexico for 1970 attribute 40% of the industrial production to transnational corporations: 35% of the production of non-durable consumer goods, 30% of intermediate goods, 62% of durable consumer goods, and 36% of capital goods. In 1972 31% of Argentina's total manufacturing production corresponded to foreign enterprises.[17] There is an increasing body of evidence which indicates that transnationals contribute significantly to trade deficits in the region. This is the result of a high propensity to import[18] and an unwillingness or reluctance to export. Most transnationals enter regional markets with the aim of getting behind high tariff walls, where their operations often assume monopolistic positions in captured markets. Local branches and subsidiaries are often expressly forbidden by parent companies from exporting to other countries where they might have similar operations with which they would wish to avoid competition. As far as imports are concerned, the fact that a large part of transnationals' imports originate in other parts of the same firm abroad provide considerable scope for the juggling of prices which could be higher than prices for the same products on the open market. A number of studies has shown over-invoicing to be a popular medium for transferring funds abroad when other means are restricted.[19]

For a number of countries in the region, manufactured and semi-manufactured goods have formed an increasing proportion of total exports. In the case of Brazil for instance, industrial products accounted for over half of total exports in 1980 as compared to 24% in 1970. The corresponding figures for Argentina were 25% in 1980 and 14% in 1970. In the case of Mexico, non-traditional exports (7.3% of total) were overshadowed by exports of petroleum and related products (61% of total) in 1980. In 1970 when petroleum and petroleum products accounted for less than 3% of total exports, non-traditional goods contributed 15% to total export value. Despite this trend, a glance at Table 2.9 will show that the majority of countries in the region still depend critically on a narrow range of products for their export earnings. In a few cases (e.g. Barbados, Jamaica, Mexico) tourism makes a significant contribution to foreign earnings. For some of the smaller islands (not shown in the Table) in the Caribbean (e.g. Antigua, Bahamas) tourism is now the dominant activity in the economy.

Table 2.9 *Latin America/Caribbean: contribution of major commodities to total export value,[1] 1979–81*

Countries	*Products*	*Total %*
Argentina	beef (13.2%); corn (7.1%)	20.3[2]
Barbados	sugar (18.4%)	18.4
Bolivia	tin (42.7%); natural gas (25.6%); crude petroleum (3.7%)	72.0
Brazil	soyabeans (12.1%); coffee (10.1%)	22.2
Chile	copper (45.5%)	45.5
Colombia	coffee (57.7%)	57.7
Costa Rica	coffee (25.7%); bananas (22.0%)	47.7
Dominican Republic	sugar (34.6%); dore (19.7%); ferro nickel (11.1%); coffee (10.3%)	75.7
Ecuador	crude petroleum (56.0%); bananas (9.1%); coffee (7.0%)	72.1
El Salvador	coffee (60.2%); cotton (7.3%)	67.5
Guatemala	coffee (28.9%); cotton (10.3%)	39.2
Guyana	bauxite (35.3%); sugar (29.7%); rice (10.1%)	75.1
Haiti	coffee (30.0%); bauxite (10.6%)	40.6
Honduras	bananas (27.3%); coffee (24.7%)	52.0
Jamaica	alumina (54.5%); bauxite (18.8%)	73.3
Mexico	crude petroleum (60.3%)	60.3
Nicaragua	coffee (31.2%); cotton, (16.0%); beef (15.9%)	63.1[2]
Panama	petroleum products (22.7%); bananas (20.9%); shrimps (13.8%); sugar (14.3%)	71.7
Paraguay	cotton (36.6%); soyabeans (18.4%); timber (15.9%)	70.9

Table 2.9—*(Cont'd)*

Countries	*Products*	*Total %*
Peru	copper (18.0%); fish meal (5.3%)	23.3
Suriname	alumina (52.0%); bauxite (14.1%); aluminum (13.0%)	79.1
Trinidad & Tobago	crude petroleum and related products (90.0%)	90.0[3]
Uruguay	wool (17.9%); beef (17.0%)	34.9
Venezuela	crude petroleum (63.9%); petroleum products (29.6%)	93.5

1 For each country, products listed are those representing 10% or more of total exports in 1979–81.
2 Based on 1979–80 data.
3 1979 figure.

Source: IDB, *Annual Report*, 1982.

As indicated earlier, one of the main objectives behind the desire to attract private investment is that it would help to solve the problem of unemployment and under-development. 'Neo-classical models assume that factor markets (that is, the markets for land, labour and capital) are competitive. They assume that producers maximize profits and that consumers and workers maximize material well-being. They also assume that factors are inter-changeable, that there are known technologies that can use various combinations, not just one combination of land, labour and capital to produce a given amount of output. Given these assumptions, producers will choose the combination of resources that is the least costly. In technical terms, profits will be maximised when revenue product of one resource to the price of that resource is just equal to that same ratio for other resources. Thus for given marginal revenue products, the lower the price of any resource, the more that resource will be utilised in the production process.'[20] In the light of this reasoning why then do transnational firms operating in a labour-surplus situation use techniques that are labour-saving? Part of the answer lies in the fact that the technology transferred was designed in a situation where labour availability tends to be a constraining factor. It is also sometimes argued that the cost of labour may be far higher than the wage bill suggests when training is required to make labour usable in the production process. As far as maximisation of profits is concerned it is now well known that transnationals 'do not primarily maximise profits at the local level, but rather attempt to maximise global profits, to keep themselves dominant in as many local markets as possible, and to maintain their share of world markets. Thus firms may not necessarily operate in a particular local market up to the level that the marginal product of labour equals the wage rate.'[21]

Despite the impressive growth rates achieved by some countries of the Latin American/Caribbean region in the post-war period, a significant proportion of the population remains outside the mainstream of development. Social indicators relating to life expectancy at birth, infant mortality, adult illiteracy rates and the distribution of income all remain at levels for serious concern, as does the level of under-nourishment. 'Approximately 28% of the population above 9 years of age lack sufficient daily intakes of protein. No less than 56 per cent of children below the age of 9 are under-nourished, and below the age of 5 the figure is as high as 61%. The worst situations are found in Guatemala and Haiti where 80% of the children are chronically underfed. In all the Central American states, except Costa Rica and Panama, the nutrition levels deteriorated between 1965 and 1975. In Nicaragua, during the Somoza regime, the number of under-nourished children more than doubled between 1965 and 1975.'[22]

This situation could hardly be explained in terms of lack of resources. The region as a whole is well endowed with a wide range of resources capable of sustaining a highly diversified industrial sector at the local level. The development strategies used, however, have lacked both foresight and imagination in their main aim to emulate the experience of the centre countries.

Notes

1 Cuba did not manage to win independence status until the turn of the 20th century. It should be pointed out that a few of the present day Republics secured their independence from Spain as part of a larger grouping.

2 The status of 'Overseas Departments' allows these countries representation in the French Parliament. Since they are subject to French laws they are in effect an integral part of France.

3 To give one example: in the late fifties/early sixties when the Demarara Bauxite Company of Guyana (a local subsidiary of the Canadian based transnational Alcan) decided to build a small alumina plant in Guyana, it managed to obtain pioneer status from Britain (which was then responsible for the administration of the country).' The effect of this concession was that the plant paid virtually no taxes at all for the first ten years of its operations, beginning in 1961 when it was opened. See N. Girvan, *Corporate Imperialism: Conflict and Expropriation* (New York: M.E. Sharpe, Inc., 1976), p. 165.

4 See L.C. Marinho, 'The Transnational Corporation and Latin America's Present Form of Economic Growth' in CEPAL *Review*, August, 1981.

5 See Enrique V. Iglesias, 'Development and Equity, The Challenge of the 1980s' in CEPAL *Review*, December, 1981.

6 See Enrique V. Iglesias, 'Latin America on the Threshold of 1980s', CEPAL *Review*, December, 1969.

7 Ibid.

8 See ECLA, *Economic Survey of Latin America*, Various Issues.

9 See Hector Soza, 'The Industrialisation Debate in Latin America', CEPAL, *Review*, April, 1981.
10 IDB, *Annual Report*, 1982.
11 There are several studies which provide useful background material on the industrialisation of Latin America. Among them, see the UN, *The Process of Industrial Development in Latin America* (New York 1966, (Sales No.: 66 II. G4) and the IDB, *The Process of Industrialisation in Latin America*, (a publication based on a Round Table discussion held in Guatemala in 1969 to coincide with the IDB's Tenth Meeting of the Board of Governors).
12 UN, *The Process of Industrial Development*, op. cit., p. 4.
13 L.C. Marinho, op. cit., p. 15.
14 Ibid.
15 Ibid.
16 Ibid.
17 Ibid.
18 In fact the evidence for some countries indicate that the propensity of transnational to import tends to be higher than that of national firms. See Marinho, op. cit.
19 Ibid.
20 Jeannine Swift, *Economic Development in Latin America* (New York: St. Martin's Press, 1978), pp. 82–83.
21 Ibid. p. 69.
22 From the 1979 IDB Annual Report, quoted by C. Brundenins and M. Lundahl, *Development Strategies and Basic Needs in Latin America* (Boulder: Westview Press, 1983), p. 5.

3

Financing the Current Account Deficit

The extent of the current account deficit[1]

A glance at Table 3.1 shows that the Latin American/Caribbean region taken as a whole has tended to experience a consistent balance of payments deficit on current account in the post-war period. This deficit grew particularly large in the 1970s. For instance, in 1970 the figure was around $3 billion. By 1978 it had reached $16 billion and by 1981 an estimated $39 billion. In the space of three years (i.e. between 1978 and 1981) the deficit had more than doubled.

Table 3.1 *Latin America and the Caribbean:[1] selected balance of payments data, 1946–81*

US$ Billion

Year/Period	*(1) Current Account Balance[2]*	*(2) Merchandise Balance*	*(3) Non-Factor Services[3]*	*(4) Net Investment Income[4]*
1964–50[a]	−0.6	5.2	−2.1	−3.6
1951–55[a]	−3.3	5.2	−3.1	−4.8
1956–60[a]	−5.3	4.8	−2.5	−6.1
61	−1.3	0.8	−0.6	−1.5
62	−1.3	1.0	−0.7	−1.6
63	−0.4	1.8	−0.6	−1.6
64	−0.8	1.8	−0.8	−1.8
65	−0.6	2.0	−0.6	−1.7
66	−1.2	1.9	−0.8	−2.2
67	−1.9	1.3	−0.4	−2.4
68	−2.4	0.8	−0.4	−2.5
69	−2.3	1.1	−0.4	−2.4
70	−2.8	−0.8	−1.3	−2.9
71	−4.3	−0.3	−1.3	−3.2
72	−4.4	−0.2	−0.7	−3.3
73	−3.9	2.5	−1.3	−4.6
74	−7.3	3.8	−2.3	−5.4
75	−14.1	−5.9	−1.3	−6.0
76	−11.1	−1.8	−1.4	−7.6

Table 3.1—*(Cont'd)*

US$ Billion

Year/Period	*(1) Current Account Balance*[2]	*(2) Merchandise Balance*	*(3) Non-Factor Services*[3]	*(4) Net Investment Income*[4]
1956–77	−11.2	−0.1	−1.4	−8.8
78	−17.7	−2.8	−4.5	−10.5
79	−19.8	0.1	−5.8	−14.4
80	−28.7	−1.9	−8.7	−18.5
81[p]	−38.9	−2.4	−10.5	−27.5

1 Because of the unavailability of data, Cuba is not included in the figures from 1959 onwards. Jamaica and Trinidad and Tobago and Guyana are included from 1961, Barbados from 1964, Bahamas from 1973 and Suriname from 1979.
2 Goods, services and transfer payments.
3 Freight, insurance, transport and travel.
4 Profits and interest.
a Aggregate for period.
p Provisional.

Source: ECLA, *Economic Survey of Latin America*, Various Issues; UN *External Financing in Latin America* New York, 1965, Sales No.: 65, II. G. 4; IMF, *Balance of Payments Yearbook* Various Issues; Official Publications of Various Governments; UN, *Statistical Yearbook for Latin America*, 1979; IDB, *Annual Reports*, Various Issues.

Of course, the experience differs from country to country and from period to period, as Table 3.2 clearly shows. There has, however, been a clear tendency for the deficit to increase for most of the countries of the region, including some of the oil-exporting countries. The oil-exporting nations of the region include Bolivia, Ecuador, Mexico, Peru, Trinidad and Tobago and Venezuela. Of the estimated $38.8 billion deficit in 1981 these latter countries as a group contributed $11.5 billion (30%), and the non-oil exporting countries $27.3 billion (70%). Among the former group Trinidad and Tobago had a surplus of $0.6 billion, while Venezuela's was $4.0 billion. These favourable balances, however, were offset by the large deficit of almost $13 billion experienced by Mexico, and to a lesser extent by Bolivia ($0.3 billion) and Ecuador ($1.1 billion). The oil-exporting countries were favourably affected by the price increases for oil during the 1970s, but this was not sufficient to offset the rapidly increasing foreign payments for some of them. Mexico in particular, has been particularly hard-hit. Its current account deficit grew from an average of $83 million in the 1946–50 period to an average of $6 billion over the period 1977–81. Over the same periods the average deficits for Bolivia and Ecuador (two oil-exporters) grew from $9 million and $5 million respectively to average figures of $374 million and $618 million respectively. Peru, which also exports oil, had a similar experience with an average deficit of $484 million between the years 1977–81 as compared to an average deficit of $10 million in the early post-war years. The two other oil-exporters, viz. Trinidad and Tobago and Venezuela, appear to have had a more favourable experience in recent years. In the five year period 1977–81, the former experienced an average surplus of $170 million as compared to an average deficit of $47 million between 1958 and 1962. In 1980 and 1981 Venezuela had surpluses of over $4 billion, but because of a total deficit of over $8 billion in 1977 and 1978, the average surplus for the five year period 1977–81 was only $316 million. The average deficit in the early post-war years (1946–50) was $101 million.

Table 3.2 *Latin America and the Caribbean: balance of payments on current account of individual countries for selected periods, 1946–81*

$ million

	Average for Periods			
Countries	*1946–50*	*1958–62*	*1966–70*	*1977–81*
Argentina	85	−263	14	−1,188
Bahamas	n.a.	n.a.	−68[a]	39
Barbados	n.a.	n.a.	−25	−54
Bolivia	−9	−35	−40	−374
Brazil	9	−384	−382	−9,444
Chile	−37	−161	−97	−1,900
Colombia	−45	−55	−221	−367
Costa Rica	−8	−18	−58	−437
Cuba	83	n.a.	n.a.	n.a.
Dominican Republic	28	7	−81	−411
Ecuador	−5	−14	−79	−618
El Salvador	7	−6	−23	−95
Guatemala	−0.06	−32	−28	−240
Guyana	n.a.	−32[b]	−22	−110
Haiti	1	−10	−5	−117
Honduras	−5	−3	−37	−146
Jamaica	n.a.	−27	−93	−177
Mexico	−83	−241	−679	−6,051
Nicaragua	−3	−8	−49	−263
Panama	−17	−36	−44	−292
Paraguay	−2	−11	−28	−215
Peru	−10	−34	−99	−484
Trinidad & Tobago	n.a.	−47	−36	170
Uruguay	3	−42	0.0	−347
Venezuela	−101	195	−65	316

a 1970.
b 1960–62.
n.a. not available.

Source: ECLA, *Economic Survey of Latin America*, Various Issues; Official Publications of Various Governments; UN, *External Financing in Latin America*, (New York, 1965).

Besides the other demands on their foreign exchange earnings, the non-oil-exporting countries have been faced with the additional problem of huge increases in their oil bills since 1974. Argentina, for example, experienced a surplus in the early post-war years, which averaged about $85 million in the period 1946–50. By the late fifties, however, a deficit had emerged and this averaged $263 million in the period 1958–62. The situation improved during the mid-sixties, but by the late sixties a deficit had once more emerged and this tended to grow during the seventies. In 1981 there was an estimated deficit of over $4 billion while the estimated average for the 1977–81 period was $1,188 million. The deficit for Brazil experienced one of the fastest growth rates in the post-war period. From an average positive balance of $9 million between 1946–50, Brazil had an average negative balance of over $9 billion in the period 1977–81. The estimated figure for 1981 alone was over $11 billion. In the recent five years (i.e. 1977–81) Chile's current account deficit averaged almost $2,000 million as compared to under $40 million in the early post-war years. The data for the Bahamas (which depends largely on tourism) indicate that this country has experienced a favourable current account balance in recent years, despite its rapidly increasing foreign payments. Barbados, however, (which is also heavily dependent on tourism) has found itself facing an increasing (if fluctuating) deficit in recent years. Its current account deficit which averaged about $25 million between 1966 and 1970 reached $125 million in 1981. (The average for the 1967–81 period was $54 million.) The deficits for Guyana and Jamaica have also experienced a significant growth in recent years. With respect to the former, the deficit averaged over $100 million between the years 1978–81, as compared to about $6 million in 1964. In 1981 the estimated deficit was $214 million as compared to $126 million in the previous year. The current account deficit for Jamaica was estimated to be over $400 million in 1981 as compared to $167 million in 1974 and $28 million in 1960.

Factors affecting the current account balance

Essentially the current account of the balance of payments has three components: firstly, the goods or merchandise account; secondly, the services account; and thirdly the public and private transfers account. An examination of Table 3.1 shows that the merchandise balance (reflecting the differences between exports (f.o.b.) and imports (f.o.b.) for the region) has tended to be very erratic. This is not surprising given the high degree of variability to which the region's merchandise trade is subjected both with respect to volume and prices which tend to be affected by a wide range of internal and external factors. As we saw earlier, though non-traditional exports are beginning to feature in the export trade of a few countries of the region, generally individual countries are dependent on a narrow range of activities of a primary nature for their foreign exchange earnings. The latter can fluctuate widely from year to year as a result of a poor harvest, low production, or developments in foreign markets. Purchasing power, it should be noted, does not necessarily rise at the same rate as the volume of exports, since export prices could be falling or import prices rising at the same time. The negative effect of the terms of trade can offset part or all of the gains stemming from increments in the volume of exports, as has happened repeatedly in the region's history.

In the case of imports, there has been a steady upward increase both in value and volume terms. This is explained by the region's critical dependence on foreign sources for a wide range of consumer goods, food products, raw materials and capital goods. During the 1970s, while the oil-producing countries benefited from the significant increases in the price of petroleum, the payments problems of the oil-importing countries were further compounded by this additional cost. For the latter group, imports (c.i.f.) of crude petroleum and petroleum products amounted to $0.7 billion in 1970 or about 7% of total imports (c.i.f.). In 1981 the estimated comparable figures were $16.9 billion and 27%. Not all oil-importing countries were affected to the same degree. For example, in 1981 Argentina's oil bill was estimated to be $496 million ($59 million in 1970) or 5% of total imports (3.5% in 1970). Between 1970 and 1981 Barbados' expenditure on petroleum and petroleum products increased from $6 million (5% of total imports) to an estimated $72 million (13% of total imports). The impact on the other countries was far more severe. Brazil's oil bill, for instance, grew from $286 million (10% of total imports) in 1970 to $11,470 million (48% of total imports) in 1981. Over the same period oil payments for Guyana increased from $11 million (8% of total imports) in the earlier year to $138 million (34% of total imports) in the later year. In 1981 Jamaica was faced with an oil bill of around $490 million (33% of total imports) as compared to $33 million (6.3% of total imports) in 1970.

Between 1946 and 1970 the value of the region's merchandise exports tended to grow faster than the value of its imports. In this period the region incurred an accumulated trade (excluding non-monetary gold) surplus of some $26 billion dollars. Between 1971 and 1981, the annual average growth rate of imports tended to exceed that of exports by over 1%. In this latter period there was an accumulated trade deficit of over $4 billion. These aggregate figures tend to hide significant differences in the performance of individual countries, particularly in recent years. For instance, in 1980 the merchandise trade deficit for the region was estimated to be $1.3 billion. However the deficit for the non-oil-exporting countries was $9.8 billion as compared to a surplus of $7.6 billion for the oil-exporting countries. In the latter group, Venezuela's contribution amounted to $7.7 billion, but this was offset to some extent by Mexico's deficit of $2.3 billion.

An examination of Table 3.1 shows that the service component of the balance of payments on current account has exerted the most critical influence on the growth of the current account balance. The positive trade balances have tended to be cancelled out by the negative service balances, while trade deficits were further increased. The service account itself can be divided into factor, and non-factor payments. In the latter are generally included services relating to transport, insurance, travel etc., while the former includes investment income. The latter can be further sub-divided into profits (direct investment income and dividends) and interest on loans, public and private, Amortisation payments tend to be treated as part of the capital account. A glance at Table 3.1 shows that throughout the post-war period the region has incurred consistent deficits in both the factor and non-factor service accounts. Net payments relating to the former have tended to be larger than net payments relating to the latter. Between 1946 and 1981 the total non-factor services deficits amounted to an estimated $56 billion as compared to a total deficit for factor payments of $147 billion over the same period. With respect to the non-factor deficits, the main contributors have been payments relating to financial services and freight. For instance, data available for the period 1958 to 1969 point to an average annual deficit on these items of over $750 million. Between 1972 and 1977, the figure had risen to over $2,000 million. What this would indicate is that despite the efforts by some countries in the region to meet their trade needs in terms of the financial and transport services required, the region as a whole is still critically dependent on foreign agencies and carriers to conduct its foreign trade. The deficits incurred in the freight, insurance and other transport' account has been partly offset over the years by earnings from tourism. The latter account for the region as a whole has tended to be positive, the average surplus for the period 1958–69 being almost $300 million. The comparative figure for the period 1972 to 1977 was almost $800 million. Gross balance of payments earnings from the travel industry in 1977 was estimated to be around $4,525 million. Of this, Mexico's contribution alone was $2,120 million as compared to $407 million for the Bahamas, $111 million for Barbados, $284 million for Venezuela and $72 million for Jamaica. Several of the countries in the region, it should be noted, tend to experience large outflows in the travel account and this tends to offset some of the financial benefits derived from the tourism industry. In 1977 for example, travel payments for Mexico and Venezuela amounted to over $1 billion respectively.

As indicated earlier, net payments for factor services has been the most crucial element in the growth of the region's current account deficits, particularly in recent years. The item which is sometimes referred to as investment income in the balance of payments, as indicated earlier, includes payments of profit and dividends on direct investment and portfolio capital as well as interest on public and private loans. Net investment income increased from an average deficit of $721 million in the early post-war years to an estimated $27.5 billion in 1981. Of the estimated current account deficit (taking into account transfer payments) for the region of $38.9 billion in 1981, the merchandise trade deficit amounted to around 1%, non-factor services (trade, insurance, freight, etc.) 27% and net investment income 71%. The public and private transfers balance appeared to have been positive, and therefore provided a small offsetting inflow to the deficits in the other accounts. Data on the servicing (interest) on foreign loans and the payments of profits and dividends on private capital are not readily available separately for the entire period, and it is therefore not possible to make an unequivocal statement on the evolution of the two main elements in the investment income item. Available evidence, however, seems to indicate that the servicing of direct investment in the early post-war years exerted a heavier weight in the item than the servicing of loan capital. For instance, between 1946 and 1960 the net investment income deficit totalled approximately $15 billion, of which $13 billion related to the service of direct investments. In more recent years there appears to have been a reversal in this trend for a number of countries in the region, whose payments of interests on external loans now exceed payments of profits. For example, in the case of Brazil total payments of profits in the period 1975–79 amounted to $5,547 million while payments relating to interest amounted to $17,750 million in the period or more than three times as much as profits. In the same period Mexico paid out about $3,000 million in profits as compared to almost $10,000 million in interest payments. In the case of Jamaica interest payments also exceeded profit remittances by about $100 million in the period. The experience of Trinidad and Tobago was different. The relatively small amount of foreign borrowing undertaken coupled with the income received from the investment of its foreign reserves resulted in a net inflow of interest into the country. In the period 1975–79 this amounted to about $50 million as compared to profit remittances of almost $800 million. Generally, however, the trend for most of the countries was for interest payments to exceed profit remittances.

The financing of the current account balance

As we saw earlier, the Latin American/Caribbean region taken as a whole has been a net importer of capital in the post-war period. Using the International Monetary Fund's conventions, the capital account which shows the financing or disposal of the current account balance can be divided into two broad categories: one records what is referred to as compensatory financing items, while the other shows non-compensatory (or autonomous) capital movements. The latter, as the name implies, covers items which move independently of other transactions in the current account, and covers such transactions as direct investments (including new inflows and re-investment of profits), long and medium term loans (both public and private), grants and certain forms of short term operations, including portfolio investments. On the other hand the compensatory (or below the line) section shows how the overall balance (i.e. the net difference between current account and the automonous capital account taken together) is financed or disposed of. Essentially it records balance of payments loans and movements in the country's gold and foreign reserves account. It should be noted that in practice there tends to be differences in approach among countries with respect to the inclusion of certain forms of short term capital above or below the line. It should also be pointed out that, since some items escape recording for various reasons (e.g. secret capital movements, smuggling, etc.), or may not be entered correctly, an item called 'errors and omissions' is required to bring about equality between total receipts and total payments or to reconcile recorded details with changes in the country's external assets/liabilities position.

Balance of payments data are subject to errors from many sources, and this becomes particularly apparent when we try to measure capital flows.[2] The direct method used is simply to look at the balance of all movements in a country's external assets and liabilities (induced by capital transactions) over some period of time. A second approach basically uses the current account balance and certain known monetary flows to gauge the extent and direction of capital movements. Since the presence of errors or omissions in the balance of payments records does not usually permit the two estimates to come out equal, in practice an 'error and omission' item is inserted to bring about reconcilitation. This item can be positive or negative. A point to be borne in mind is that, since several factors may contribute to the particular figure, it is never easy to attribute proportions to particular transactions or omissions, and this obviously raises questions about the extent and role of flows that are identified, especially when the 'errors and omissions' figure is large. A negative correction figure, for instance, may suggest that we have either underestimated capital outflows, or overestimated inflows; but there might be other factors responsible upon which we can only speculate.

With these caveats in mind about the data we are using, we now proceed to examine how the current account deficit of the Latin American/Caribbean region has been financed in the post-war period.

Tables 3.3 and 3.4 give details of how the current account deficit has been financed over the years. Table 3.3 provides cumulative data, while Table 3.4 gives average figures for selected five-year periods and annual financing for recent individual years. The cumulative current account

Table 3.3 *Latin America and the Caribbean:*[1] *financing the current account deficit, 1946–81*
$ Billion (Cumulative Totals)

Year/ Period	Current Account Balance (1)	Net Autonomous Capital Movements (2)	Contribution of: Net Direct Investment (3)	Contribution of: Official Grants & Long-term Loans (4)	(2) as a % of (1) (5)	Compensatory Financing (6)	Net Errors & Omissions (7)
1946–50	−0.6	0.4	1.6	−1.0	66.6	0.5	−0.3
1951–55	−3.3	2.9	1.7	0.5	87.8	0.9	−0.5
1956–60	−5.3	6.7	4.5	1.2	126.4	1.4	−2.8
1961–65	−4.4	5.6	2.0	2.2	127.3	−0.1	−1.1
1966–70	−10.6	13.3	4.2	4.7	125.5	−2.3	−0.4
1971–75	−34.0	41.1	10.0	13.2	120.8	−3.8	−3.3
1976–80	−88.5	84.8	18.8	33.6	95.8	−1.9	5.6
1981p	−38.9	23.7	6.6	5.3	60.9	21.6	−6.4

Note: Because of coverage and slight differences in methodological compilation the figures previous to 1961 may not be strictly comparable with those after 1961.

1 Guyana, Jamaica and Trinidad and Tobago are included in the figures from 1961, while Barbados is included since 1964 and the Bahamas since 1973. From 1959 Cuba is not included.

p Provisional.

Source: Tables 3.4; ECLA, *Economic Survey of Latin America*, various issues.

Table 3.4 *Net inflow of external resources and compensatory financing to Latin American/Caribbean Region, 1946–1981*[1]

	Annual Averages										
	1946–50	*1951–55*	*1956–60*	*1961–65*	*1966–70*	*1971–75*[2]	*1976–80*[2]	*1978*	*1979*	*1980*	*1981*[a]
A. *Official grants and non-compensatory capital*	84	578	1,348	1,116	2,660	8,213	16,956	19,399	20,535	20,507	23,700
1. Official grants & long-term loans	−204	93	239	438	939	2,636	6,715	7,963	7,587	4,762	5,317
2. *Long-term private capital*				683	1,404	6,081	12,466	14,202	13,777	18,717	24,050
a. Direct investment	331	343	919	396	847	2,003	3,758	3,918	4,993	5,449	6,574
b. Loans and other items	−6	56	193	287	557	3,078	8,709	10,284	8,784	13,269	17,476
3. Short-term private capital	−37	87	−2	−5	318	496	−2,226	−2,766	−829	−2,973	−5,666
B. *Compensatory financing*	92	177	289	−13	−464	−762	−389	−6,625	−3,289	10,083	21,639
1. Transactions of the monetary sector	n.a.	n.a.	n.a.	−13	80	1,775	4,364	3,657	3,128	8,014	19,422
2. Net change in international reserves: (−) increase, (+) decrease)	76[b]	45[b]	114[b]	c	543	−2,537	−4,753	−10,299	−6,417	2,069	2,217

1 Figures up to 1960 refer only to the Latin American Republics (excluding Cuba in 1959 and 1960). Since 1961 the coverage includes all member countries of the IDB (except Canada, the US and Suriname). Data for Barbados are available since 1964 and for the Bahamas since 1973.

2 These averages are not strictly comparable with averages for the decade of the 1960s and 1950s. Beginning in 1971, transactions of Central Banks have been incorporated into the A-1 category. Category B-1 includes only transactions of deposit banks.

a IDB estimate; b only official monetary reserves; c included under transactions of the monetary sector.

Source: IDB, *Annual Report*, 1982; UN *External Financing in Latin America*, New York, 1965.

deficit in the period between 1946 and 1981 has been estimated to be around $184 billion. This represents the outflow of real resources from the region. Net autonomous capital movements amounted to roughly $179 billion or roughly 97%. If we were to deduct the total of 'errors and omissions' from autonomous capital movements, the latter would have amounted to about 91%.

The proportion of the current account deficit financed by autonomous capital movements and compensatory financing respectively varies from period to period. Between 1946 and 1960, for instance, autonomous capital movements (less 'errors and omissions') amounted to about 70% of the cumulative current account deficit. In other words compensatory financing amounted to about 30%. Between 1961 and 1975, autonomous capital movements amounted to 113% of the current account deficit. For the period 1976–80, the ratio was around 90%. In 1981, the estimated ratio was 44%. The increasing dependence on compensatory financing in recent years reflects the critical foreign exchange position being faced by many countries in the region.

Autonomous capital movements, as indicated earlier, has several components, and it would be interesting to look at the trends in the more important ones. Between 1946 and 1981 net direct investments amounted to about $50 billion or about 30% of cumulative net autonomous capital movements. The contribution of official grants and long terms loans over the same period was $60 billion or 34%. The financing of the current account deficit in the 1970s reveals a very interesting picture, as can be seen in Table 3.4. Between 1971 and 1975 autonomous capital movements averaged $8.2 billion as compared to −$0.8 for compensatory financing. Of the former, official grants and long term loans contributed $2.6 (32%), direct investment $2.0 billion (24%) and other private long term loans $3.1 billion (38%). In the period 1976–80 autonomous capital movements averaged $17.0 billions as compared to −$0.4 billion for compensatory financing. To the former official grants and long term loans contributed 39%, direct investment 22%, and other long term private capital 51%. Table 3.4 shows that the annual compensatory finance required was increasing from the early post-war years to the late 1950s. Looked at another way, we can say the overall deficits (balance on current account and autonomous capital movements) were growing larger. The trend was reversed during the 1960s and 1970s. The negative figures indicate an overall surplus in the balance of payments accounts for the region as a whole. In 1980 and 1981, however, there were overall deficits of $10.0 billion and $21.6 billion respectively. This corresponded with a noticeable slowdown in the inflow of official grants and long term loans. This latter item dropped from about $8.0 billion in 1978 to $7.6 billion in 1979 and to $4.8 billion in 1980. In 1981 the estimated figure was $5.3 billion. Direct investment flows, however, increased from $3.9 billion in 1978 to an estimated $6.6 billion in 1981. Other long term private capital dropped from $10.3 billion in 1978 to $8.8 billion in 1979, but increased to an estimated $17.5 billion in 1981.

Growth of the external debt

At the global level the oil-exporting developing countries experienced a cumulative current account surplus of $465 billion as compared to a cumulative deficit of $536 billion for the non-oil-exporting developing countries between 1973 and 1982. The cumulative deficit for the non-oil developing countries in the Western Hemisphere amounted to almost $200 billion in that period. Of this figure, the trade account contributed about $44 billion, while net services and private transfers accounted for the bulk of the remaining $156 billion. Net official transfers over the period were positive amounting to about $4.5 billion as compared to surplus net capital inflows (including SDR allocations) of $219 billion. There was an overall surplus of $24 billion for the period.

Earlier we gave some indication of the growth in importance of official grants and long term loans in the financing of the region's current account deficit. One of the central issues in relations between the developed and developing countries in the post-war period relates to the volume and terms of resource transfer from the developed to the developing countries. It is widely accepted that without foreign assistance to complement inadequate saving levels, many developing countries would be forced to lower their growth expectations. External resource transfers take many forms, and originate from several sources each of which tends to be associated by recipients and borrowers with its own peculiar advantages and disadvantages. At the official level governments may receive grants from other governments or organisations which they are not required to repay, but which may carry non-financial obligations. Governments also indulge in short term borrowing (the IMF is one source for such loans) to help finance balance of payments deficits. They also borrow long term to finance development programmes or to meet commitments of various kinds, e.g. to repay past loans. In this section we focus on one channel of the resource transfer spectrum, and that is long term government borrowing on which a great deal of attention has come to form in recent years.

At the end of 1950 the total outstanding external debt (disbursed and un-disbursed) of Latin American Republics taken together was estimated to be around $2.2 billion (see Table 3.5). By 1960, it had grown to just over $7 billion. At the end of 1970, the comparable figure for the Latin American/Caribbean region was around $21 billion, at the end of 1977 $97 billion, at the end of 1980 $160 billion and at the end of 1981 $181 billion. In other words between 1970 and 1980, the gross outstanding external debt of the Latin American/Caribbean region rose by $140 billion or by almost 8 times. In the space of one year (i.e. between 1980 and 1981) the total debt outstanding increased by about $20 billion. (See Tables 3.5 and 3.6.)

Table 3.5 *Latin American and Caribbean countries: external debt outstanding,*[a] *1950–81*

$ mn.

Countries	*1950*	*1960*	*1970*	*1981*
Argentina	400[b]	1,275	2,463	14,539
Bolivia	50[b]	179	549	2,773
Brazil	409	2,407	5,052	57,409
Colombia	158	377	1,850	7,630
Chile	355	562	2,534	4,948
Costa Rica	12[b]	55	227	2,620
Dominican Rep.	10[b]	6	299	1,836
Ecuador	32	95	352	4,257
El salvador	22	33	126	1,035
Guatemala	–	51	176	1,041
Haiti	8	38	45	464
Honduras	1	23	144	1,931
Mexico	509	1,151	3,792	47,519
Nicaragua	5	41	222	2,484
Panama	13	59	290	2,923
Paraguay	15	22	144	1,438
Peru	107	265	1,084	8,468
Uruguay	106	132	351	1,878
Venezuela	–	363	924	11,535
1. *Sub-Total*	*2,213*	*7,134*	*20,624*	*176,728*
Bahamas	n.a.	n.a.	50	228
Barbados	n.a.	n.a.	16	304
Guyana	n.a.	50	131	853
Jamaica	n.a.	n.a.	192	1,810
Suriname	n.a.	n.a.	6	27
Trinidad & Tobago	n.a.	21	122	794
2. *Sub-Total*	*n.a.*	*n.a.*	*517*	*4,016*
3. *Total = 1+2*	*n.a.*	*n.a.*	*21,141*	*180,744*

Note: Figures are rounded to the nearest million.

a disbursed and undisbursed.
b estimate.
n.a. not available.

Source: IDB, *Annual Report*, 1982; IDB, *Latin America's External Indebtedness*, Washington DC, May, 1977.

An examination of Table 3.5 will show that the growth rate of external indebtedness varies widely from country to country. Argentina's gross external debt outstanding, for example, grew from $2.4 billion at the end of 1970 to $14.5 billion at the end of 1981 – an

Table 3.6 *Latin America and the Caribbean: growth of external public debt outstanding[1] and debt service payments, 1965–80*

$ million

Year	*External Public Debt Outst.*[2] *(1)*	*Disbursement* *Loans (2)*	*Grants and Grant-Like (3)*	*Amortization (4)*	*Interest (5)*	*Net Transfer (6)*
1965	11,701	1,835	402	1,227	396	614
66	13,034	1,947	388	1,412	434	489
67	14,852	2,419	385	1,393	482	929
68	16,925	2,772	416	1,664	558	965
69	18,526	3,185	480	1,688	620	1,356
70	20,298	3,380	438	1,768	759	1,290
71	24,418	3,564	471	1,851	817	1,368
72	29,576	5,192	466	2,138	946	2,575
73	37,136	7,840	250	2,891	1,413	3,785
74	49,012	11,379	248	3,476	2,071	6,080
75	59,042	12,238	267	3,815	2,815	5,875
76	77,465	17,252	257	4,808	3,350	9,352
77	97,162	20,727	244	7,301	4,118	9,551
78	122,625	31,212	241	12,264	6,041	13,148
79	145,932	33,984	362	15,988	9,044	9,314
80	159,427	27,227	306	13,924	12,699	909

1 disbursed and un-disbursed.
2 The figures in this column may not agree with the figures in Table 3.5 for two reasons: (1) since the data come from two different sources, the position of individual countries may differ slightly; (2) the coverage may be less complete than that shown in Table 3.5.

Source: The World Bank *Annual Report*, Various Issues.

increase of almost 500%. Over the same period Brazil's external debt grew from $5.0 billion to $57.4 billion – a more than ten-fold increase. It should be noticed that even oil-exporting countries (Mexico, Venezuela, Peru and to a lesser extent Ecuador, Bolivia and Trinidad and Tobago) had increasingly to resort to external funds. Mexico's gross external debt outstanding, for instance, grew from $3.8 billion at the end of 1970 to $47.5 billion at the end of 1981 – an almost thirteen-fold increase. Over the same period Venezuela's external debt grew from $0.9 billion to $11.5 billion – a near thirteen-fold increase. Peru's external debt reached $8.5 billion in 1981 from $1.1 billion in 1970. Taken together, five countries (Argentina, Brazil, Mexico, Peru and Venezuela) accounted for more than 75% of the region's gross external debt outstanding at the end of 1981.

For most countries of the region the growth of the external debt corresponds very closely with the emergence of substantial deficits in the current account of the balance of payments. For instance, Brazil's increase in external indebtedness of $5 billion between 1980 and 1981 corresponds with an estimated current account deficit of $11.7 billion in 1981. In the case of Mexico, the external indebtedness increased by $8.5 billion between 1980 and 1981 while the current account deficit in 1981 was in the region of $13 billion. A few countries (e.g. Trinidad and Tobago and Venezuela) were increasing their external indebtedness during the 1970s even while experiencing favourable balances on their current account, and while external reserves were increasing. Recognising that the latter factor may have enhanced their borrowing capacity and credit worthiness, these countries sought to take advantage of the situation by trying to attract additional foreign funds to finance expanded development programmes. The rationale here seems to have been to borrow while you can and at the same time get your credit rating established, hoping the latter would be of help in less prosperous times.

It needs to be pointed out that a significant proportion of the proceeds of current borrowing tends to go into the servicing of past loans. In other words in order to get the net transfer of resources in any period we have to deduct amortization and interest payments from the volume of disbursements in that period. Table 3.6 gives some idea of the extent of the flows related to loan finance in recent years. Between 1965 and 1980 cumulative loan disbursements for the Latin American/ Caribbean region amounted to $186 billion. Over the same period amortization amounted to $78 billion and interest to $47 billion. Net transfer for the period therefore amounted to only $61 billion. Should there be any slowdown in the inflow of foreign funds in a situation where the current account deficit seems to be increasing, the servicing of the external debt could pose serious problems for most of the countries of the region. The data for 1980 indicate that, while loan disbursements totalled $27.2 billion in 1980, amortization and interest payments amounted to $26.6 billion, the net transfer amounting to less than $1 billion in that year. More recently, countries like Brazil, Mexico and Guyana have had to reschedule their debt obligations, because of the inability to service their foreign debt. This in itself would affect the ability of these countries to incur new loans.

It is difficult to gauge the significance of the external debt of any particular country by merely looking at the absolute figure outstanding at any point in time. The capacity of borrow and service debt varies from country to country, and for any particular country from period to period. Debt outstanding and debt servicing payments can be usefully looked at in relation to a number of other variables such as government revenue, national income, foreign reserves, or earnings from the export of goods and services. Each of these ratios can provide valuable insights into the position of the debt at different points in time, and consequently, give signals with respect to further borrowing or the need to reduce existing levels of indebtedness. In terms of the ability to service debt and to gauge the credit worthiness of borrowers, one of the most widely used indices is the ratio of debt service payments (amortization and interest) to earnings from the export of goods and non-factor services. As a measure of debt service burden, the debt service ratio (as it is commonly called) has several weaknesses, but because of its simplicity of calculation and the easy availability of the data on which it is based, the ratio tends to be widely used.

Table 3.7 provides information on the debt service ratio for individual countries in the region since the early 1960s. As can be seen there, the ratio varies widely from country to country and from period to period. While changes in debt service payments can influence the ratio, variations in the latter can also result from fluctuations in foreign exchange earnings. An increase in the ratio does not necessarily indicate greater debt service payments. For the region as a whole the ratio increased from about 14% in 1970/71 to 29% in 1979, but fell to about 24% in 1981. In the latter year seven countries (Bolivia, Brazil, Chile, Mexico, Nicaragua Panama and Peru) had ratios greater than the regional average. While it is difficult to use a particular figure to say whether a serious debt burden exists or not, there is no doubt that for many countries in the region servicing the external debt has become a critical issue. In 1981, 48% of Peru's foreign exchange earnings went into the servicing of its foreign debt. For Mexico the figure was 30% as compared to 57% in 1978 and 66% in 1979. Between 1978 and 1981 debt servicing absorbed about 35% (on average) of Brazil's foreign exchange earnings. The ratio for Jamaica in 1981 was 22% as compared to about 4% in 1970–71. Guyana's debt service ratio has also increased substantially since the early 1970s reaching 29% in 1979 and 18% in 1981.[3] Even for Venezuela (which is one of the region's major oil exporters) the debt service ratio has risen steadily from about 3% in 1970–71 to about 15% in 1981.

Table 3.7 *Latin America and the Caribbean: service payments*[1] *on the external debt as a percentage of goods and non-factor services, 1960–81*

	Average						
Country	*1960–61*	*1970–71*	*1980–81*	*1978*	*1979*	*1980*	*1981*
Argentina	21.4	21.1	19.8	28.2	16.1	19.9	19.7
Bahamas	n.a.	n.a.	1.5	1.5	0.4	1.3	1.7
Barbados	n.a.	1.0	2.8	2.5	2.8	2.5	3.0
Bolivia	25.6	11.6	25.8	49.8	30.3	26.2	25.4
Brazil	34.0	15.3	34.9	31.9	38.5	36.1	33.6
Chile	18.4	20.3	26.9	40.9	27.1	23.5	30.2
Colombia	13.5	13.0	14.3	10.0	14.5	11.2	17.3
Costa Rica	4.8	10.1	15.5	23.4	23.0	16.7	14.3
Dominican Rep.	0.7	6.6	15.1	10.8	21.6	12.8	17.3
Ecuador	7.8	10.9	16.5	12.1	30.0	14.4	18.5
El Salvador	2.4	4.8	3.9	3.0	2.4	3.5	4.3
Guatemala	2.3	7.7	3.6	2.2	2.7	3.7	3.4
Guyana	n.a.	3.2	17.6	15.6	29.2	16.9	18.3

Table 3.7—*(Cont'd)*

Country	Average 1960-61	1970-71	1980-81	1978	1979	1980	1981
Haiti	5.2	4.1	6.1	5.6	3.6	4.5	7.6
Honduras	3.3	3.1	11.7	8.7	12.9	10.2	13.2
Jamaica	n.a.	3.6	17.4	17.4	16.5	13.1	21.6
Mexico	14.9	23.7	31.4	56.7	65.6	33.2	29.5
Nicaragua	4.9	12.0	24.7	13.7	8.1	14.6	34.7
Panama	1.5	8.6	32.0	60.1	34.6	33.5	30.8
Paraguay	6.4	12.4	15.2	7.6	9.7	12.8	17.6
Peru	8.6	14.0	40.2	31.5	22.7	32.7	47.7
Suriname	n.a.	n.a.	n.a.	n.a.	n.a.	n.a.	0.5
Trinidad & Tobago	n.a.	3.1	3.3	2.0	2.4	3.1	3.4
Uruguay	5.4	22.2	11.4	46.8	10.4	12.3	10.5
Venezuela	4.6	3.4	14.8	7.7	10.3	14.8	14.7
All countries	*14.4*	*13.7*	*24.1*	*27.7*	*28.6*	*23.8*	*24.1*

1 interest and amortization payments
n.a. not available.

Source: IDB, *Annual Report*, 1982.

Table 3.8 *Latin America and the Caribbean: external public debt outstanding by type of creditor, 1970 and 1980*

Type of Creditor	1970 (end) US$ mn.	%	1980 (end) US$ mn.	%
Bilateral Official	6,605	32.5	20,652	13.0
Multilateral	5,026	24.8	27,694	17.4
Private				
Supplies	3,978	19.6	9,864	6.2
Financial Insts.	2,015	9.9	89,362	56.0
Other	2,674	13.2	11,855	7.4
Total	*20,298*	*100.0*	*159,427*	*100.0*

Source: World Bank, *Annual Report*, Various Issues.

The debt service ratios take on even more critical dimensions when seen against the substantial expenditures oil-importing countries incur in satisfying their domestic oil needs. The implications that these developments have for growth are not difficult to discern. Given the heavy dependence on outside sources for raw materials and capital goods, inability to obtain these critical imports would no doubt have an adverse effect on the rate of growth, and ultimately on the savings level.

As indicated earlier, foreign loan funds have several origins. They may come from bilateral sources (that is from other governments including their agencies), they may be provided by multilateral institutions (e.g. the World Bank, the IDB, the CDB, etc.) or they may originate in private sources such as commercial banks and other financial institutions. Table 3.8 shows that in relative terms the sources of foreign funds have changed radically in recent years. In 1970, for example, official bilateral assistance accounted for 33% of the region's total external debt outstanding. By 1980 this proportion had dropped to 13%. The share attributed to multilateral organisations also declined from 25% to 17% over the period. In recent years external borrowing has tended to shift significantly to private sources, and in particular to private financial institutions. In 1980 the latter accounted for 56% of the region's external debt outstanding as compared to about 10% in 1970.

This growing dependence by regional states (and for that matter by developing countries generally) on private sources for funds has taken place in a situation where over the years the terms on which private finance is made available have grown increasingly harder. Table 3.9 shows the average terms of loan commitments and the grant element of loans and grants from all sources from 1965. The four criteria used here tend to give some indication of the 'hardness' or 'softness' of loan funds. *Maturity* refers to the period for repayment of the loan; *grace* to the period between the granting of the loan and the beginning of repayment of the principal; *interest* represents the direct financial cost of the loan, while the *grant element* gives some indication of the proportion of the loan which is not repayable or which may carry no interest rate or rates below commerical levels. An examination of Table 3.9 shows that the maturity condition dropped from an average of 15 years between 1965 and 1970 to an average of ten years in the period 1975 to 1980. The grace period has remained more or less the same around three to four years. On the other hand, interest rates have increased steadily over the years, from an average of about 6% in the period 1965–70 to over 11% in more recent years. The grant element in loans has virtually disappeared, dropping from about 28% in 1965 to 3% in 1978 and to negative figures in 1979 and 1980.

Table 3.9 *Latin America and the Caribbean: average terms of loan commitments and grant element of loans and grants, 1965–80*

	Loan Commitments				
Year	*Maturity (Years)*	*Grace (Years)*	*Interest %*	*Grant Element*[(1)] *%*	*Grant Element of Loans and Grants*[(1)] *%*
1965	14.7	3.4	5.2	28	40
66	16.8	3.6	5.5	28	38
67	13.5	3.1	6.0	22	30
68	14.8	3.4	6.1	22	31
69	13.6	3.6	6.7	18	28
70	14.4	3.4	6.9	18	27

Year	*Loan Commitments* Maturity (Years)	Grace (Years)	Interest %	Grant Element[(1)] %	Grant Element of Loans and Grants[(1)] %
1971	13.5	3.6	6.7	19	27
72	13.0	3.4	6.6	18	23
73	13.5	4.2	8.3	9	11
74	12.3	3.6	9.2	5	7
75	10.1	3.1	8.3	8	9
76	10.3	3.3	7.4	11	12
77	9.2	3.5	8.0	8	9
78	10.1	4.2	9.5	2	3
79	10.1	4.2	11.2	−4	−3
80	10.2	3.9	11.3	−3	−2

Source: The World Bank, *Annual Report*, Various Issues.

Given this situation, how do we explain the growing shift towards private sources for finance. Generally, official funds (originating either in governments or multilateral agencies) tend to be made available on 'softer' terms than finance originating in private financial institutions. There can, therefore, be a number of explanations. One would certainly be the inadequacy of available official funds in terms of the requirements of regional states. A second may lie in the desire to escape the conditionality terms normally attached to financing made available by foreign governments and multilateral institutions. Let us examine each in turn.

Trends and patterns in resource flows from the developed countries

Financial resource flows to developing countries tend to take several forms. Broadly they can be divided into public and private transfers. A further sub-division is often made in terms of concessional and non-concessional finance. While there are no strict criteria to guide this latter division, the concessional category tends to include flows which are not motivated by profit making or market incentives. There is an element of assistance which may vary from one donor to another, and even from one transaction to another. The flow from donor to recipient may take place directly (i.e. on a bilateral basis), or through multilateral channels.

In 1961 when the first United Nations Decade was launched, it was proposed that the developed countries should aim at transferring 1% of their national income to developing nations as financial assistance.[4] The target (which incidentally covered both official and private capital flows) was subsequently adopted by the UNCTAD Conferences of 1964 and 1968[5] and by certain other forums. The Pearson Report,[6] for example, published in 1969 endorsed the 1% target and suggested 1975 as the date for meeting it. It, however, went further and recommended that development assistance should be increased from 0.39% of GNP in 1968 to 0.70% in 1975 'and in no case not later than 1980'. When the Second UN Development Decade was launched in 1970, it was urged that 'each economically advanced country should endeavour to provide annually by 1972, for the benefit of developing countries, resource transfers in the form of net disbursement of a minimum amount of 1 per cent of its gross national product at market prices, consideration being given to the special situation of countries which are not importers of capital.'[7] Within this overall target a proportion of 0.7% of GNP was set for official development (ODA) transfers. Since the target was first iniated, most of the Development Assistance Committee[8] (DAC) countries have accepted it in principle – some with a time frame, some without. A few countries (including the United States) have not committed themselves. The present position of DAC members with respect to the 0.7% aid target is as follows. Norway, Netherlands, Sweden and Denmark have already surpassed the target and have commited themselves to reaching or maintaining a proportion of at least 1% of GNP. France (excluding DOM/TOM[9]) has given 1988 as its target date while Austria, Canada, Finland and Italy have suggested 1988 or end of present decade. Australia, Belgium, Germany, Japan New Zealand and the United Kingdom have accepted the 0.7% figure, but have given no specific date for attainment. Switzerland and the US have not accepted the ODA aid target.[10]

Table 3.10 shows that total resource flows from DAC countries grew (in nominal terms) from $8.1 billion in 1960 to $88.0 billion in 1981 at an average annual rate of growth of 12.0%. Over the same period Official Development Assistance (ODA) of DAC countries increased from $4.7 billion to $25.6 billion – an average annual rate of growth of 10.9%. The 1981 figure represents a decline of 3% over the 1980 figure after adjustments are made for exchange rate and price fluctuations. ODA as a proportion of total resource flows increased from 58% in 1960 to 69% in 1963, but has shown a long term tendency to decline, reaching 29% in 1981. As a % of GNP, total resource flows surpassed the 1% target in 1975, reaching 1.17%. It has fluctuated since, the proportion for 1981 being 1.21%. ODA as a % of GNP has shown a different trend. (See col. 5 of Table 3.10). From an average of 0.53% in the 1960–63 period, the proportion declined to an average of 0.36% in the 1978–81 period.

Of course, the performance varies widely among the DAC donors. Data available for 1981 (see table 3.11) shows that only four countries (Netherlands, Norway, Sweden and Denmark) have surpassed the 0.7% ODA target. If we include French aid to the Overseas Departments and Territories the proportion for this country will also surpass

Table 3.10 *Development Assistance Committee: flow of resources to Less-Developed Countries (LDCs) and multilateral agencies, 1960–1981*

Year	*(1) Total Resource Flows $ bn*	*(2) Official Development Assistance $ bn*	*(3) (2) as a % of (1)*	*(4) (1) as a % of GNP*	*(5) (2) as a % of GNP*	*(6) Direct Investment*[1] *$ bn*
1960	8.1	4.7	58.0	0.89	0.52	1.7
61	9.2	5.2	56.5	0.95	0.54	1.8
62	8.5	5.5	64.7	0.81	0.53	1.5
63	8.6	5.9	68.6	0.77	0.52	1.6
64	9.1	6.0	65.9	0.75	0.49	1.8
65	10.4	5.9	56.7	0.78	0.45	2.5
66	10.3	6.1	59.2	0.71	0.42	2.2
67	11.3	6.7	59.3	0.73	0.43	2.1
68	13.1	6.4	48.8	0.78	0.38	2.9
69	13.6	6.7	49.3	0.74	0.36	2.6
70	15.9	6.9	44.2	0.79	0.34	3.7
71	17.4	7.9	45.4	0.78	0.34	3.3
72	20.2	9.2	45.5	0.78	0.36	4.2
73	22.4	9.1	40.6	0.72	0.29	4.7
74	22.5	11.6	51.6	0.65	0.34	1.2
75	44.8	13.8	30.8	1.17	0.36	11.5
76	46.0	14.0	30.4	1.10	0.33	8.6
77	51.5	15.7	30.5	1.09	0.33	9.6
78	70.6	20.0	28.3	1.24	0.35	11.8
79	75.4	22.8	30.2	1.17	0.35	13.4
80	75.4	27.3	36.2	1.04	0.38	10.3
81[e]	88.0	25.6	29.1	1.21	0.35	14.6

Col. 1 – Net Flow of Total Official and Private Financial Resources to Less Developed Countries.

Col. 2 – Net Flow of Official Development Assistance to Less Developed Countries.

1 The figures for the period 1960–70 refer to receipts from only DAC countries. The figures from 1971 onward covers receipts from all sources. DAC countries, however, tend to account for over 90% of direct investment flows of LDCs.

e estimate.

Source: OECD, *Development Cooperation* (or *Assistance*), various issues.

the 0.7%. An examination of Table 3.11 shows that in 1981 ODA as a % of GNP for some countries (e.g. Japan) was in fact less than half of the UN target. Even more surprising is the fact that the ratio for some countries has been falling over time. For example, the proportion for the US dropped from 0.53% in 1960 to 0.32% in 1970 and to 0.20% in 1981.

Table 3.11 *Official Development Assistance[1] (ODA) as a % of GNP, 1960–81*

Countries	*1960*	*1965*	*1970[2]*	*1975[2]*	*1980[3]*	*1981[3]*
DAC Countries[4]	*0.52*	*0.45*	*0.34*	*0.36*	*0.38*	*0.35*
Netherlands	0.31	0.36	0.61	0.76	1.03	1.08
Norway	0.11	0.16	0.32	0.66	0.85	0.82
Sweden	0.05	0.19	0.38	0.82	0.79	0.83
Denmark	0.09	0.13	0.38	0.58	0.74	0.73
France (Dom./Tom.)	1.38	0.75	0.66	0.62	0.64	0.73
France (excl. Dom./Tom.)	n.a.	n.a.	0.42	0.38	0.38	0.46
Belgium	0.88	0.59	0.46	0.59	0.50	0.59
Germany	0.33	0.38	0.32	0.40	0.44	0.47
UK	0.56	0.47	0.39	0.39	0.35	0.44
Portugal	1.45	0.57	n.a.	n.a.	n.a.	n.a.
Canada	0.19	0.19	0.41	0.54	0.43	0.43
Australia	0.38	0.52	0.62	0.65	0.48	0.41
Austria	n.a.	0.34	0.07	0.21	0.23	0.48
New Zealand	n.a.	n.a.	0.23	0.52	0.33	0.29
Japan	0.24	0.28	0.23	0.23	0.32	0.28
Finland	n.a.	n.a.	0.06	0.18	0.22	0.28
Switzerland	0.04	0.08	0.15	0.19	0.24	0.24
United States[5]	0.53	0.50	0.32	0.27	0.27	0.20
Italy	0.22	0.10	0.16	0.11	0.17	0.19
OPEC Countries[6]	*n.a.*	*n.a.*	*1.18*	*2.92*	*1.74*	*1.46*
of which						
Saudi Arabia	n.a.	n.a.	5.60	7.76	5.09	4.77
Kuwait	n.a.	n.a.	6.21	7.40	2.04	1.98
UAE	n.a.	n.a.	n.a.	11.69	3.38	2.88
Iraq	n.a.	n.a.	0.13	1.63	2.12	0.37
Quatar	n.a.	n.a.	n.a.	15.59	4.25	2.64
Other			0.28	0.66	0.18	0.08
CMEA Countries[7]	*n.a.*	*n.a.*	*0.14*	*0.07*	*0.14*	*0.14*
of which						
USSR	n.a.	n.a.	0.15	0.07	0.15	0.15
GDR	n.a.	n.a.	0.04	0.04	0.15	0.16
Eastern Europe, other	n.a.	n.a.	0.12	0.08	0.11	0.10

n.a. not available.
1 Net disbursements.
2 Excluding administrative costs.
3 Including administrative costs.
4 Development Assistance Committee.
5 Administrative costs are included in the US data for all years shown.
6 Organisation of Petroleum Exporting Countries.
7 Council for Mutual Economic Assistance.

Source: OECD, Development Cooperation (or *Assistance*), various issues.

Though DAC countries remain the most important single source of financial flows to developing countries in recent years their share of the total has been falling. An examination of Table 3.12 will show that total net receipts by developing countries from all sources increased from $19

Table 3.12 *Total net receipts of developing countries from all sources, 1970–81* $ billion at current prices

Source/Flow Type	*1970*	*1971*	*1972*	*1973*	*1974*	*1975*	*1976*	*1977*	*1978*	*1979*	*1980*	*1981*
1. *Official Development*												
Assistance/Bilateral	*8.08*	*9.36*	*10.06*	*12.43*	*16.46*	*20.09*	*19.65*	*20.36*	*27.22*	*30.61*	*36.36*	*(35.51)*
a. DAC countries	5.66	6.33	6.63	7.09	8.23	9.81	9.50	10.08	13.12	15.91	18.02	18.28
b. OPEC countries	0.39	0.44	0.66	2.03	4.15	5.68	5.17	4.28	6.90	6.58	8.26	6.91
c. CMEA countries	0.96	1.26	1.38	1.35	1.26	0.73	1.05	1.09	1.20	1.80	2.14	2.12
d. Other countries	..	..	..	....	...	0.03	0.06	0.08	0.10	0.12	0.20	(0.20)
Multilateral Agencies of	1.07	1.33	1.39	1.96	2.82	3.84	3.87	4.83	6.00	6.20	7.74	(8.00)
which OPEC financed	–	–	–	–	0.12	0.16	0.42	1.23	0.96	0.26	0.29	0.41
2. *Non-Concessional Flows*												
Bilateral	*10.92*	*11.80*	*13.29*	*19.75*	*19.71*	*34.34*	*38.57*	*43.39*	*56.08*	*54.94*	*59.31*	*(68.49)*
a. Direct Investment	3.69	3.31	4.23	4.72	1.89	11.51	8.64	9.59	11.83	13.42	10.36	(14.64)
b. Bank Sector[a]	3.00	3.30	4.80	9.70	10.00	12.00	15.00	15.50	22.87	19.67	(19.00)	(25.00)
c. Private Export Credits	2.09	2.71	1.44	1.15	2.40	4.42	7.22	9.11	10.22	9.49	12.20	(10.59)
d. DAC other official	0.15	0.28	0.43	9.90	0.65	0.56	0.57	0.48	1.27	1.14	2.24	(2.00)
e. OPEC countries[b]	0.20	0.19	–	0.14	0.92	1.50	1.61	0.89	(1.01)	(1.00)	(2.00)	(3.00)
f. Other countries[c]	0.11	–	–	–	0.79	0.04	0.12	0.09	0.87	3.20	(3.10)	(3.00)
g. CMEA countries	0.69	0.90	1.01	1.28	1.83	2.58	2.68	2.94	3.09	4.16	4.85	(5.00)
h. Other flows[d]	0.89	1.01	1.27	1.76	1.14	1.64	2.61	4.68	4.82	2.86	5.56	(5.26)
Multilateral	0.69	0.90	1.01	1.28	1.83	2.58	2.68	2.94	3.09	4.16	4.85	(5.00)
of which: OPEC financed	–	–	–	–	0.02	0.06	0.13	0.27	0.16	0.22	0.13	(0.27)
Total Receipts = (1) + (2)	19.00	21.16	23.35	32.18	36.17	54.43	58.22	63.77	83.30	85.55	95.67	(104.00)

Note: Figures concerning non-DAC Member countries are based as far as possible on information released by donor countries and international organisations and completed by OECD Secretariat estimates based on other published and unpublished sources.

a Excluding (i) bond lending and (ii) export credits extended by banks which are included under private export credits. Including loans by branches of OECD banks located in offshore centres, and for 1980 and 1981 participation of non-OECD banks international syndicates.

b Official flows only: no information is available on private flows.

c Includes Ireland, Luxembourg, Spain, Yugoslavia, India, Israel.

d Bond lending and official export credits.

.. not available; – nil or neglible.

( ) OECD Secretariat Estimate in whole or in part.

Source: OECD *Development Cooperation*, 1982 Review.

billion in 1970 to over $100 billion in 1981. Total ODA receipts increased from $8.08 billion (42.5% of the total) to $35.51 billion (34.1% of the total) over the same period. Of the former figure, DAC countries' bilateral contribution amounted to 70% (5.66 billion) as compared to only 51% ($18.28 billion) to the latter. One of the noticeable developments during the 1970s was the significant growth in ODA by OPEC countries. Their bilateral contribution increased from $0.39 billion (4.8% of the total) in 1970 to $6.91 billion (19.4% of the total) in 1981. The share of ODA receipts from CMEA (Council for Mutual Economic Assistance) countries fell during the 1970s decade, moving from 11.9% ($0.96 billion) in 1970 to 6% ($2.12 billion) in 1981. ODA receipts from multilateral agencies grew from $1.07 billion (13.2% of the total in 1971 to about $8 billion (22.5% of the total) in 1981. Despite this trend the data for recent years indicate a significant slowdown in ODA disbursements from multilateral organisations. One factor in this development has been the reduction in US contribution to these agencies. The sharp fall of 26% in real terms in ODA by the US in 1981 was due largely to the decline in US multilateral outflows. Contributions to IDA fell by $500 million and those to regional development banks by almost $700 million.[11]

When we examine the flow of non-concessional funds (NCF) to developing countries some interesting features emerge. Non-concessional receipts increased from $10.92 billion (57.5% of total flows) in 1970 to $68.49 billion (65.8% of total flows) in 1981. One of the most important factors in this growth during the 1970s has been the increasing resort by developing countries to private finance. In 1970 the latter source contributed $3 billion (27.5% of total NCF). By 1981, however, the figure had increased to $25 billion (36.5% of NCF). Over the same period direct investment grew from $3.69 billion (33.8% of NCF) in 1970 to $14.64 billion (21.4% of NCF) in 1981. Private export credits also showed a significant increase during the 1970s. The latter's contribution to total NCF flows in 1981 was $2.09 billion (15.5%) as compared to $10.59 billion (19.1%) in 1981. Non-concessional bilateral flows from CMEA countries appear to be much more significant than their bilateral ODA. The latter amounted to $2.12 billion in 1981 as compared to NCF of $5 billion in the same year. Non-concessional flows from multilateral agencies as a proportion of total flows from these agencies did not change significantly over the 1970s decade. In 1981 the proportion stood around 38.5% as compared to 39.2% in 1970.

There are many factors which motivate aid giving (particularly of a bilateral nature), and therefore actual flows to particular areas may bear little relationship to actual needs. Political and cultural ties, commercial and security interests tend to play a critical role in determining the geographical distribution of economic assistance. Differences in perception of aid needs both by country donors and multilateral agencies may also influence the volume and distribution of development assistance. Available data[12] indicate that the share of ODA[13] going to Asia declined from 35% in 1974/75 to 26% in 1979/80, while the share going to Sub-Saharan Africa increased from 18% to 23% over the same period. The proportion of North Africa and the Middle East declined from 23% to 22%, while Latin America's share dropped from 8.5% to 8.2%. As far as this latter group is concerned, it should be pointed out that over one-third of the concessional assistance going there (including the Caribbean) is directed to overseas dependencies.[14] Among the independent states, countries like Haiti, Bolivia, Nicaragua and Peru tend to be more favoured by aid donors than countries like Brazil, Mexico, Venezuela, Argentina and Trinidad and Tobago (to name a few) whose needs are seen to be less pressing than a large number of other developing countries, and who appear to be capable of meeting their external capital requirements by borrowing in international capital markets.

Earlier we made reference to the target of one per cent of GNP for all capital flows (and within that the 0.7% of GNP for ODA), which certain groups and agencies feel the developed countries should aim at in their efforts to help the less developed countries. It should be pointed out that there is nothing sacrosanct about these targets. In fact they crept into the literature quite accidentally, and do not necessarily bear any relationship to actual needs.[15] Estimated foreign capital requirements for developing countries vary from study to study depending on the kinds of assumptions that are made with respect to desired growth in total and per capita income, projected savings and foreign exchange earnings levels and even domestic and international rates of inflation. In the Brandt Report, for instance, we read the following statement: 'If present levels of assistance are merely continued, there cannot be much progress in meeting essential needs, and an annual growth in income per head of only one per cent in low-income Africa and only 2.8 per cent in low-income Asia would be possible. This, according to the World Bank's 1979 *World Development Report*, would actually widen the gap in living standards between the poor and the rich countries (from 1:40 in 1975 to 1:47 by 1990) even if the poor countries were to increase their savings sharply – an unacceptable situation.'[16] Based on a 6.5 per cent rate of GDP growth (3.5 per cent per capita) UNCTAD has estimated the external capital needs of all the least developed countries to be in the region of $11 billion during the 1980s, and $21 billion during the 1990s. It adds that for the poorest countries the assistance should be highly concessional.[17] According to another study done by the Overseas Development Council in Washington, 'countries with an income per head of below $520 (least developed, low income and lower middle-income) will need annual aid in the 1980s in the range of $40–54 billion (in 1980 dollars) either for achieving a 3.5 to 4 per cent growth in per capita income, or for obtaining resources equal to half the costs of meeting essential human needs, the other half being borne by the countries themselves. If 1980 aid were no higher in real terms than in 1977, it would fall short of adequacy for such objective by $21–35 billion.'[18]

The Issue of Conditionality

As indicated earlier, the increasing resort to private finance has also brought with it a reduction in the amortization period for loans. In 1966, 48% of the region's external debt outstanding had a maturity of up to five years, 23% between 5 and 10 years, 13% between 10 and 15 years and 15% with more than 15 years. By 1981 the proportion of outstanding debt with a maturity of up to five years had increased to 52%, while the proportion in the 5 to 10 year maturity period increased to 35%. Correspondingly the share in the category 10 to 15 years fell to 8%, while the proportion with a maturity of more than 15 years dropped to about 5%. Of course, the structure of the outstanding debt varies from country to country. In 1981, for instance, the proportion of Mexico's outstanding external debt with a maturity of up to five years was almost 60% as compared to 50% for Brazil, 42% for Jamaica, 33% for Guyana, 54% for Chile and 73% for Venezuela.

The accumulation of debt in the shorter maturity category implies increasing pressure on the servicing capacity of the countries concerned. In recent years, some countries in the region have had their debt rolled over, since they simply did not have the funds to pay. One of the main advantages associated with private finance is that the resources made available are not generally tied to individual projects, or do not have to be spent in a particular country, and are also generally not linked to the adoption of particular economic policies. In other words, borrowing countries have greater freedom of action with respect to the use of resources originating in private financial institutions. Some of the latter, of course tend to go towards balance of payments support.

Paradoxically, the absence of strict conditionality associated with bank credit, which developing countries favour, tends to be viewed with particular concern by the International Monetary Fund. In its 1977 Annual Report the Fund had this to say: 'As far as balance of payments finance is concerned, institutions in the private sector do not normally make a practice of applying comprehensive policy conditions when making balance of payments loans to governments. Access to private sources of balance of payments finance may, therefore, in some cases permit countries to postpone the adoption of adequate domestic measures. This can exacerbate the problem of correcting payments imbalances, and can lead to adjustments that are politically and socially disruptive when the introduction of stabilisation measures becomes unavoidable.'[19]

The issue of conditionality has been a source of great friction between the Fund and developing member countries in recent years. So distasteful are some of the conditions attached to Fund credit that many developing member states tend to use the conditional assistance of this institution as a last resort. Part of a communiqué issued after the 25th Meeting of the Ministers of the Group of 24 on International Monetary Affairs held in Toronto, Canada, in September 1982, read as follows: 'Ministers deplored the hardening of conditionality evident in the increasing resort to pre-conditions and the current tendency for the Fund to shift from three-year programmes to one-year programmes. They regretted the heavy emphasis on domestic demand management in the application of conditionality and felt that the mechanistic and narrow monitoring of performance criteria did scant justice to the structural nature of the problems faced by developing countries. They urged that in reviewing performance and in prescribing adjustment measures the Fund should pay adequate attention to the circumstances and factors beyond the control of countries and should make a case-by-case assessment of each country based on the concept of a sustainable balance of payments position over the medium term.'

The Fund for its part sees conditionality as an integral part of the adjustment process, 'Conditionality has sometimes been viewed as a penalty for the shortcomings of past policies or a quid pro quo for the financial assistance provided by the Fund. It is rather to be seen as an essential element of the contribution that the Fund makes to alleviating the balance of payments of member countries and to facilitating the international adjustment process. Indeed, in practice there is a large degree of complementarity between conditionality and financial assistance. Financing without the adoption of the policy measures required by conditionality would postpone necessary adjustments, and run the risk of prolonging an untenable situation. At the same time, corrective measures would render the process of adjustment more difficult and needlessly disruptive.'[20]

In the same article it is claimed that in helping countries to formulate 'programs that can be supported by its financial assistance as well as its general policy advice to members, the Fund does not rely on any particular model or approach' even though it tends to focus on certain aggregates and variables which are seen to be essential to the adjustment process.[21] Paradoxically, this is one of the major criticisms levelled against the IMF which is often accused of being too inflexible and orthodox in its approach to the adjustment problems faced by developing countries. While there may not be an explicit model on which the Fund bases its operations, its policies in practice do reflect (in essential respects) the economic philosophy and ideology embraced by the major contributors who were behind its establishment. Even at the technical level adjustment measures aimed at restoring external equilibrium, and which might be appropriate in the context of a smoothly functioning developed market economy, tend to be applied generally without apparently recognising the peculiar situation of many developing countries.

Against the charge that the Fund often interferes in the political affairs of members states with whose prevailing ideology or policies it may not be in agreement, the position is taken that this is quite unintentional, even if it is inevitable in some circumstances by the nature of the connection between economic and political variables. One official of the Fund assesses the position this way: 'Political considerations are not invariably isolated from economic considerations. The domestic, social or political policies of a member may produce consequences of an economic character that are within the scope of the Fund's purposes, and therefore within the concern of the Fund. It is then appropriate for the Fund not to object to the member's domestic, social or political policies, but to take cognisance of their economic consequences and their impact on decisions of the funds.'[22] In 1979 the Fund took a decision that with respect to use of its resources and standby arrangements, 'due regard' should be paid to the domestic, social and political objectives of member states.[23] The critical issue, however, still seems to be the perspective and economic philosophy embraced by the Fund, whether one chose to call this a model or not. Since it is against this framework that members' social and political objectives will be judged and their economic consequences appraised, there is need for a much broader consensus on the ideological and philisophical foundation of the Fund whose evolution has tended to lag too far behind international economic and political developments.

The World Bank, like the IMF, has also been subjected to severe criticisms by developing countries over the years both with respect to its terms of lending and general operational policies. As is widely known, the International Bank for Reconstruction and Development was originally set up to help in the reconstruction of Europe following the devastation of the Second World War. With the subsequent growth in its membership of developing countries, new issues arose which tended over the years to be addressed in a somewhat *ad hoc* manner. The original Charter itself has undergone no fundamental change. The Charter requires the Bank to lend only for productive purposes and must stimulate economic growth in the developing countries where it lends. The Bank is required to pay particular regard to the prospects for repayment, and loans can only be made to a government, or the loan must be guaranteed by the government concerned. Two further guidelines state that the loans cannot be restricted to purchases in any particular member country, and decisions to lend must be based on economic considerations.

IBRD loans generally have a grace period of five years and are repayable over twenty years or less. These loans are directed toward 'developing countries at more advanced stages of economic and social growth.'

Since a substantial part of its funds comes from borrowing in the world's capital markets, the cost of lending tends to be closely related to the cost of borrowing. In order to help its poorer members, the International Development Association (IDA) was formed as an affiliate in 1960 with the aim of providing assistance on less onerous terms than the IBRD. IDA credits are made to governments only, have ten-year grace periods, fifty-year maturities and no interest. A small annual service fee is charged on both the disbursed and un-disbursed portions of each credit. The bulk of the IDA's funds come from subscriptions, general replenishments from IDA's more industrialised and developed members, special contributions by IDA's richer members and transfers from the net earnings of the IBRD. At present, the countries that can qualify for assistance are those with annual per capita GNP of less than $731 dollars (in 1980 dollars).

Voting power in both the IMF and the World Bank is based on subscriptions, and this means that the countries which contribute most to the resources of these institutions exert the greatest influence on their policies and operations. Certainly there have been some changes in the operational policies and practices of these organisations over the years; but these clearly have not met the expectations of developing countries who tend to see the need for more fundamental changes in their structure and operations, if they are to serve the objectives of development.

There are several gaps in the existing spectrum of finance which need to be filled. Concessional assistance to the least developed countries who are unable to obtain finance in the commercial markets are not only inadequate, but appear to be decreasing. The severe burden of servicing the external debt by many countries who are able to borrow, and the slowing down in the rate of growth, point to the need for loans with longer maturities.

The question of reform of the international monetary and financial system revolves not only around the volume and kinds of finance required by developing countries. Recently the Brandt Commission Report has drawn attention to the need for a greater share of the responsibility for decision-making, control and management of existing monetary and financial institutions by developing countries.[24]

Bilateral aid is usually tied aid, and this often results in real benefits being less than what the nominal figures may suggest. Reservations over bilateral aid often stem from the political costs associated with it. Many countries prefer giving aid on a bilateral basis, because it can be used for greater leverage in the pursuit of national objectives, whatever these might be. In recent times, the Reagan administration in the United States has been putting greater emphasis on bilateral assistance which is seen as an important instrument in the pursuit of its foreign policy objectives. It has expressed dissatisfaction with some aspects of the Fund and World Bank operations, even accusing the latter of encouraging socialism in some countries.

Besides its participation in such international institutions like the World Bank and the IMF, the United States is also associated with regional organisations like Inter-American Development Bank (IDB) and the Caribbean Development Bank (CDB). These regional institutions obviously tend to be more in tune with the problems of the areas they serve than the global organisations, or even the officials agencies of many donor countries. The fact, however, that both the CDB and the IDB have shown a great deal of independence in the allocation of their resources may explain why the present US administration is now putting so much emphasis on bilateral aid. Of course, if the primary aim is to advance US security and ideological interest, then the latter approach may be the one to adopt. From the recipients' point of view, however, the aid conditions may not be in accordance with the dictates of economic development.

Notes

1 The data used in the first section of this chapter come from two main sources: (a) ECLA, *Economic Survey of Latin America*, Various Issues; and (b) UN, *External Financing in Latin America*, New York, 1965, (Sales No.: 65.II.G.4).
2 See UN *External Financing in Latin America*, op. cit., pp. 69–70.
3 In the case of countries like Guyana, Brazil and Jamaica, the actual ratio may be shown to be less than the scheduled ratio because of the inability of these countries to service their debt in recent years.
4 This followed the adoption of a similar resolution by the UN in 1960.
5 At the 1968 Conference the resolution specified 1% of GNP at market prices and not national income. 'Although the terms Gross National Product and National Income refer to the same common-sense notion, the GNP at market prices makes no allowance for the depreciation of capital and includes indirect taxes which do not constitute a part of anybody's income. It is on the average 25 per cent higher than national income. Thus, the effect of the UNCTAD action was to raise the target by about this amount, with the approval of all DAC members.' *Partners in Development: Report of the Commission on International Development* (Washington, DC: Praeger Publishers, 1969) p. 144.
6 *Partners in Development*, op. cit., pp. 147–9.
7 'International Development Strategy for the United Nations Development Decade', Resolution adopted by the 25th Session of the United Nations General Assembly, New York, 1970, A.Res/2626 (XXV).
8 The Development Assistance Committee (DAC) is one of the specialised committees of the Organisation for Economic Cooperation and Development (OECD) set up in 1960 and one of whose objectives is 'to contribute to sound economic expansion in member as well as non-member countries in the process of economic development.' The current members of the DAC are Australia, Austria, Belgium, Canada, Denmark, Finland, France, the

Federal Republic of Germany, Italy, Japan, the Netherlands, New Zealand, Norway, Sweden, Switzerland, the United Kingdom, The United States and the Commission of the European Economic Communities.

9 French abbreviations for Overseas Departments and territories.

10 See OECD 1982 Review, *Development Cooperation*, Paris, 1982, p. 64.

11 Ibid., p. 61.

12 Ibid., pp. 67–68.

13 Data refer to net ODA disbursement from bilateral and multilateral sources including OPEC, for 1979/1980 on average. Aid flows from CMEA countries are not included. China is also excluded.

14 OECD, *Development Cooperation* (1982), pp. 67–70.

15 While the idea of a 1 per cent of national income target floated around in the early 1950s it was 'first introduced for international consideration in 1958 in a statement adopted at a meeting of the World Council of Churches circulated to all United Nations delegations which stated that if contributing countries could divert at least 1 per cent of their national income to grants and concessional loans the international picture would be much more hopeful', *Partners in Development*, op. cit., p. 144. For a note on the concept see J.W. Bhagwati, *The Amount and Sharing of Aid*, Overseas Development Council Monograph, No. 2, (1970), p. 45.

16 *North-South: A Programme for Survival* (The Report of the Independent Commission on International Development Issues under the Chairmanship of Willy Brandt). Pan Booha Ltd (Paperback edition, 1980), p. 228.

17 Quoted in the above report, p. 228.

18 Ibid.

19 Annual report of the IMF, 1977, p. 39.

20 IMF *Survey*, Nov., 1982.

21 Ibid.

22 See Sir Joseph Gold, 'Non-political Character of the Fund', in IMF, *Survey*, May, 1983.

23 Ibid.

24 Brandt Report, op. cit., Chaps. 13 and 14.

4

The Growth and Pattern of US Direct Investment in Latin America and the Caribbean

Foreign investment in Latin America has its beginnings in the early part of the 19th century, and more particularly in the 1820s.[1] Even before the end of the independence struggles in the 1820s, the stage was already set for substantial British participation in the economic life of the region. Englishmen had taken a keen interest in the independence wars starting in 1910, providing both moral and material support for the revolutionary movements. Rippy makes the point that by the time independence was won by the Latin American Republics, and in some cases even before it was won, the new nations of Latin America were considerably indebted to British merchants, shipowners, soldiers, and army and navy officers.[2]

The period following the end of Napoleonic Wars in 1815 witnessed a significant acceleration in the flow of British capital to Latin America. There were several reasons for this. By the time peace came the British industrialisation process was well underway, giving her in manufacturers an overwhelming comparative advantage over foreign rivals.[3] Though Britain had emerged from the European Wars between 1793 and 1815 with a huge national debt, by this time she had already become the centre of an expanding international commerce.[4] She not only had a large surplus of capital – the only country in the world in such a position at the time – but the emergence of a wide range of financial institutions helped London to replace Amsterdam as a world financial centre.

London merchant banks and financial houses took an interest in Latin American countries as soon as they became independent. Most of the early investment in Latin America consisted of loans to governments, and these institutions were key instruments in the intermediary process. 'Concurrently with some commercial firms, they issued several series of bonds in 1822–25 on behalf of various Latin American Governments in need of funds with which to discharge substantial debts resulting from the acquisition of arms during the last stages of the wars of independence.'[5] Around the same time, a number of joint-stock companies were also formed with the aim of working the gold and silver mines that were believed to exist in the former Spanish colonies or exploiting the opportunities in various schemes such as those related to the opening of a canal in the Central American isthmus and the establishment of settlers in the River Plate countries.[6]

In the decade following 1815, Latin America absorbed a significant proportion of the total outflows of British capital. For instance, figures available for 1924 and 1925 indicate that of the nominal sum of £25,308,486 invested in the issues of foreign governments, more than two thirds were in Latin American government bonds. In the period 1824–25 alone more than forty-six joint stock companies were formed with the aim of operating mainly or entirely in Latin America.[7]

By the mid-1820s, however, the frenzy and speculation had come to an end – at least for the time. Government securities lost their attractiveness both to the British public as investments and to the Latin American Governments themselves, but for different reasons. With respect to the former, profit-making manipulations by merchant bankers and speculators led to frequent fluctuations in the value of the securities leading to capital losses for the holders. With respect to the latter, they received only a part of the funds raised, the other part being siphoned off in the form of commission fees, discounts, printing costs, etc. by financial institutions. Perhaps the more important factor was the inability of the Latin American Governments to service the bonds as a result of the poor performance of the export sector in the mid-1820s. The fate of government securities had an adverse effect on the shares and bonds of the joint stock companies, many of which were forced into early liquidation. The result of this experience was a drastic slow down in the flow of British capital to Latin America in the period 1825–50 – a period in which investments in other regions were increasing. In the entire period between 1826 and 1850 the nominal values of Latin American security issues on the London Stock Exchange amounted to 18,389 thousand pounds sterling as compared to 21,129 thousand pounds sterling in the few years between 1822–25. By 1850, however, conditions had again emerged which permitted an increased flow of British capital to Latin America. An enhanced foreign reserves position, (the result of a growing 'invisibles' surplus), greater domestic savings and more dynamic financial intermediation encouraged not only an expansion in the securities markets, but the search for investment outlets overseas as well. The nominal value of Latin American governments security issues on the London Stock Exchange amounted to 132,363 thousand pounds sterling in the period 1851–80. Investments in railways and other public utilities also began in this period. Early returns on the latter investment were estimated to be over 7%. Government securities, however, suffered the same misfortune as in the early 1820s. By the end of the 1880, 58% of the new Latin American public debt to Great Britain was in default.[8]

Table 4.1 *United Kingdom: geographical distribution of overseas investment, 1870, 1885 and 1913*

£ mn.

	1870		*1885*		*1913*	
Country or Region	*Total*	*% of Total*	*Total*	*% of Total*	*Total*	*% of Total*
British Empire	270	34.4	675	51.9	1,780	47.3
Europe and the Near East	230	29.3	175	13.5	471	12.4
Latin America	85	10.8	150	11.5	757	20.2
United States	200	25.5	300	23.1	755	20.1
Total	*785*	*100.0*	*1,300*	*100.0*	*3,763*	*100.0*

Source: UN *External Financing in Latin America*, New York, 1965.

Despite the investments made by British capitalists in Latin America in the third quarter of the 19th century, Continental Europe proved to be relatively more attractive to them in this period. Other European countries showed even less interest in getting involved in the economic activities of the region in this period. This situation, however, changed dramatically in the period between the mid-1870s and the First World War. British investment in Latin American securities increased from £179.4 million sterling (£123.0 million public and £56.4 million private) in 1880 to £999.4 million (£316.5 million public and £682.9 million private) in 1913. Table 4.1 shows that, while 10.8% of British overseas investment were in Latin America in 1870, this share had increased to 20.2% by 1913. Correspondingly, the share of Europe and the Near East dropped from 29.3% to 12.4% over the period. In terms of geographical distribution of the investment, Central America received about 20% while about 70% went into South American countries. In 1880 Argentina, Brazil, Mexico and Peru were responsible for 71% of Latin American securities issued to British investors as compared to 74% of the issues by the first three in 1913. In terms of sectoral distribution, Table 4.2 shows that loans to governments accounted for 68.6% of British investment in Latin America in 1880, as compared to 31.7% in 1913. The share of railways which amounted to 19.2% in 1880 increased to 45.8% in 1913. In the 40 years preceding the First World War the trend had clearly moved from the financing of revolutions and counter-revolutions (which was characteristic of the period immediately following the end of the Napoleonic Wars) to more productive investments, and particularly to railways which had brought good returns to British investors both at home and in Europe.[9]

Data on French and German early investment activities in Latin America in the period preceding the First World War have been even more difficult to obtain by historians than information on British.[10]

Table 4.2 *UK: sectoral distribution of investment in Latin America, 1880 to 1928* (millions of pounds sterling)

	1880		*1890*		*1900*		*1913*		*1928*	
Sector	*Total*	*% of Total*	*Total*	*% of Total*	*Total*	*% of Total*	*Total*	*% of Total*	*Total*	*% of Total*
1. *Government*	*123.0*	*68.6*	*194.3*	*45.6*	*228.0*	*42.2*	*316.5*	*31.7*	*340.9*	*28.4*
2. *Private Sector*	*56.4*	*31.4*	*231.4*	*54.4*	*312.0*	*57.8*	*682.9*	*68.3*	*857.6*	*71.6*
Railways	34.4	19.2	166.9	39.2	200.0	37.0	457.8	45.8	491.0	41.0
Public Utilities	11.1	6.2	19.9	4.7	30.0	5.6	...	...	...	...
Mining	3.4	1.9	12.6	3.0	10.4	1.9	22.2	2.2	22.5	1.9
Nitrate	–	–	5.4	1.3	9.2	1.7	...	...	...	...
Real Estate	0.5	0.3	7.9	1.9	10.8	2.0	...	...	...	...
Banking	3.0	1.7	3.6	0.8	11.7	2.2	18.5	1.8	41.9	3.5
Others	4.0	2.1	15.1	3.5	39.9	7.4	184.4	18.5	302.2	25.2
3. *Total*	*179.4*	*100.0*	*425.7*	*100.0*	*540.0*	*100.0*	*999.4*	*100.0*	*1,198.5*	*100.0*

... indicate data are not available or are not separately reported.

Source: UN *External Financing in Latin America*, New York, 1965.

Table 4.3 *Geographical distribution of US direct investment*[1] *in Latin America and the Caribbean, 1897 to 1981*

	1897		*1908*		*1914*	
Countries	*$mn*	*%*	*$mn*	*%*	*$mn*	*%*
Total = 1+2+3+4	*304.3*	*100.0*	*748.7*	*100.0*	*1,275.9*	*100.0*
1. *South America*	*37.9*	*12.5*	*104.3*	*13.9*	*325.2*	*25.5*
Argentina	0.7	0.2	1.0	0.1	1.2	0.1
Bolivia	a	a	a	a	2.0	0.2
Brazil	1.0	0.3	a	a	3.0	0.2
Chile	1.0	0.3	31.0	4.1	170.8	13.4
Colombia	9.2	3.0	10.8	1.4	24.0	1.9
Ecuador	3.0	1.0	6.0	0.8	7.6	0.6
Paraguay	a	a	a	a	5.0	0.4
Peru	7.0	2.3	23.0	3.1	58.0	4.5
Uruguay	a	a	a	a	a	a
Venezuela	2.0	0.7	3.5	0.5	6.5	0.5
Other S.A.	14.0	4.6	29.0	3.9	47.1	3.7
2. *Central America*	*221.4*	*72.7*	*454.3*	*60.7*	*676.7*	*53.0*
Mexico	200.2	65.8	416.4	55.6	587.1	46.0
Costa Rica	3.5	1.1	17.0	2.3	21.6	1.7
El Salvador	–	–	1.8	0.2	6.6	0.5
Guatemala	6.0	2.0	10.0	1.3	35.8	2.8
Honduras	2.0	0.6	2.0	0.3	9.5	0.7
Nicaragua	–	–	1.0	0.1	3.4	0.3
Panama	9.7	3.2	6.1	0.8	12.7	1.0
Other C.A.	–	–	–	–	–	–
3. *Other L.A.*	*45.0*	*14.8*	*190.1*	*25.4*	*274.0*	*21.5*
Cuba	43.5	14.3	184.1	24.6	252.6	19.8
Dominican Republic	1.5	0.5	1.0	0.1	11.0	0.9
Haiti	–	–	5.0	0.7	10.4	0.8
4. *Other W. Hemisphere*	*n.a.*	*n.a.*	*n.a.*	*n.a.*	*n.a.*	*n.a.*
Bahamas						
Bermuda						
Netherlands Antilles						
Trinidad & Tobago						
Others						

The annual amount of Latin American securities issued in France (after deduction of amortization and conversion) averaged 153.2 million francs in the period 1870–79, as compared to 338.2 million francs in the 1880–89 period, 104.1 million francs in the 1890–99 period and 505.2 million francs in the 1900–14 period. The outstanding amount of Latin American securities listed in the Paris Stock Exchange in 1880 amounted to 1,775.7 million francs, of which 99.4% related to bonds issued or guaranteed by the Latin American Governments, states and municipalities, and 0.6% of foreign corporations (including French) which had their main activity in Latin America. Because of losses, the figure dropped from 5,419.5 million francs (49.8% Government and

1919		*1924*		*1929*		*1936*	
$mn	*%*	*$mn*	*%*	*$mn*	*%*	*$mn*	*%*
1,977.6	*100.0*	*2,779.3*	*100.0*	*3,462.0*	*100.0*	*2,803.0*	*100.0*
664.6	*33.6*	*947.1*	*34.1*	*1,543.0*	*44.6*	*1,458.0*	*52.0*
2.5	0.1	4.5	0.2	332.0	9.6	348.0	12.4
22.0	1.1	29.5	1.0	62.0	1.8	18.0	0.6
4.0	0.2	4.5	0.2	194.0	5.6	194.0	6.9
307.0	15.5	331.5	11.9	423.0	12.2	484.0	17.3
45.0	2.3	84.0	3.0	124.0	3.6	108.8	3.9
7.6	0.4	7.6	0.3	12.0	0.3	5.0	0.2
6.0	0.3	7.5	0.3	11.0	0.3	5.0	0.2
110.5	5.6	140.5	5.1	124.0	3.6	96.0	3.4
a	a	a	a	28.0	0.8	14.0	0.5
20.5	1.0	103.5	3.7	233.0	6.7	186.0	6.6
139.5	7.0	234.0	8.4	–	–	–	–
756.1	*38.2*	*878.8*	*31.6*	*917.0*	*26.5*	*628.0*	*22.4*
643.6	32.5	735.4	26.5	682.0	19.7	480.0	17.1
17.8	0.9	13.5	0.5	22.0	0.6	13.5	0.5
12.8	0.6	12.2	0.4	30.0	0.9	17.0	0.6
40.0	2.0	47.0	1.7	70.0	2.0	50.0	1.8
18.4	0.9	40.2	1.4	72.0	2.1	36.0	1.3
7.3	0.4	6.8	0.2	12.0	0.3	5.0	0.2
16.2	0.8	24.3	0.9	29.0	0.8	27.0	1.0
–	–	–	–	–	–	–	–
556.9	*28.2*	*953.3*	*34.3*	*1,002.0*	*28.9*	*717.0*	*25.6*
518.1	26.2	877.2	31.6	919.0	26.5	666.0	23.8
21.5	1.1	58.2	2.1	69.0	2.0	41.0	1.5
17.3	0.9	17.9	0.6	14.0	0.4	10.0	0.4
n.a.	*n.a.*	*n.a.*	*n.a.*	*n.a.*	*n.a.*	*n.a.*	*n.a.*

50.2% foreign corporations) in 1880 to 2,969.2 million francs (83% Government and 17% foreign corporations) in 1900. This corresponded with a sharp reduction in the number of private corporations operating in Latin America, whose bonds and shares were quoted in Francs. Because of increasing interest by French investors in Latin America at the turn of the century, by 1913 the figure had climbed back to 8,150.9 million francs, of which 62.7% were government and 37.3% were foreign corporations. It has been assessed that the increase of 6,400 million francs (in book values) going to Latin America between 1880 and 1913 overstates the actual capital inflow since the Latin American securities were offered in Paris (as in London) at less than face value.

Table 4.3—*(Cont'd)*

Countries	*1943* *$mn*	*%*	*1950* *$mn*	*%*	*1964* *$mn*	*%*
Total = 1+2+3+4	*2,721.0*	*100.0*	*4,735.0*	*100.0*	*10,205.0*	*100.0*
1. *South America*	*1,541.0*	*56.6*	*2,957.0*	*62.4*	*6,612.0*	*64.8*
Argentina	380.0	14.0	356.0	7.5	882.0	8.6
Bolivia	13.0	0.5	11.0	0.2	997.0	9.8
Brazil	233.0	8.6	644.0	13.6	a	a
Chile	328.0	12.0	540.0	11.4	789.0	7.7
Colombia	117.0	4.3	193.0	4.0	508.0	5.0
Ecuador	11.0	0.4	14.0	0.3	a	a
Paraguay	9.0	0.3	6.0	0.1	a	a
Peru	71.0	2.6	145.0	3.1	464.0	4.5
Uruguay	6.0	0.2	55.0	1.2	a	a
Venezuela	373,0	13.7	993.0	21.0	2,786.0	27.3
Other S.A.	–	–	–	–	186.0	1.8
2. *Central America*	*569.0*	*20.9*	*727.0*	*15.3*	*2,282.0*	*22.4*
Mexico	286.0	10.5	415.0	8.8	1,034.0	10.1
Costa Rica	30.0	1.1	60.0	1.3	b	b
El Salvador	15.0	0.6	17.0	0.3	b	b
Guatemala	87.0	3.2	106.0	2.2	b	b
Honduras	37.0	1.4	62.0	1.3	b	b
Nicaragua	4.0	0.1	9.0	0.2	b	b
Panama	110.0	4.0	58.0	1.2	659.0	6.5
Other C.A.	–	–	–	–	589.0	5.8
3. *Other L.A.*	*611.0*	*22.4*	*761.0*	*16.1*	*b*	*b*
Cuba	526.0	19.3	642.0	13.6	–	–
Dominican Republic	71.0	2.6	106.0	2.2	b	b
Haiti	14.0	0.5	13.0	0.3	b	b
4. *Other W. Hemisphere*	*n.a.*	*n.a.*	*290.0*	*6.1*	*1,311.0*	*12.8*
Bahamas						
Bermuda						
Netherlands Antilles						
Trinidad & Tobago						
Others						

Source: UN *External Financing in Latin America*, New York, 1965; US Bureau of Commerce, *Survey of Current Business*, Various Issues.

The actual figure was nearer 4,800 million francs (or 900 million US dollars) which was roughly one third of the inflow of British capital estimates for the period. Of the estimated 8,375 million francs of French investment in Latin America in 1913, Argentina, Brazil and Mexico accounted for 89.5% as compared to 59.0% of the total (3,253 million francs) in 1902. In the latter year government securities accounted for 29.5% (railways for 4.8% and 'others' for 65.7%) as compared to 30.9% in 1913 (26.3% for railways and 42.8% for 'others').

1972		*1981*	
$mn	*%*	*$mn*	*%*
16,796	*100.0*	*38,883.0*	*100.0*
9,545.0	*56.8*	*18,109.0*	*46.6*
1,403.0	8.3	2,735.0	7.0
a	a	a	a
2,505.0	14.9	8,253.0	21.2
620.0	3.7	834.0	2.1
737.0	4.4	1,178.0	3.0
a	a	277.0	0.7
a	a	a	a
712.0	4.2	1,928.0	5.0
a	a	a	a
2,700.0	16.1	2,175.0	5.6
868.0	16.8	729.0	2.0
4,121.0	*24.5*	*11,675.0*	*30.0*
2,025.0	12.1	6,962.0	17.9
b	b	b	b
b	b	b	b
b	b	b	b
b	b	b	b
b	b	b	b
1,458.0	8.7	3,671.0	9.4
638.0	3.8	1,042.0	2.7
b	*b*	*a*	*a*
–	–	–	–
b	b	a	a
b	b	a	a
3,130.0	*18.6*	*9,099*	*23.4*
		2,987.0	7.7
		10,353.0	26.6
		−6,664.0	−17.1
		932.0	2.4
		1,491.0	3.8

Note: Totals may not add up due to rounding.
1 Book Value
a included in 'Other South America'.
b included in 'Other Central America'.

The data available for German investment in Latin America in the 19th and early 20th century are even more scanty than the British or French. The evidence available appears to put the beginning of German interest in the region somewhere in the mid-1890s – or more precisely just after the economic crisis of 1891–94. Estimates made by Wattershausen[11] put Germany's investment in Latin America and the West Indies at between 2,370 – 2,970 million marks (33.6 – 38.1%) of total German foreign investment in 1898. By 1904 the figures had already changed amounting to 2,880 – 3,350 million marks (or 35.8 – 36.2%) of the total.

Before the 1890s the United States' investment in Latin America was very small. In fact, until this time the US often found itself borrowing money in Europe to help pay for its imports and service foreign capital. 'Direct investment included only some silver and gold mines in Mexico, a few sugar plantations bought by American trading companies in Cuba during the political disturbances of 1876–78, a railroad in Panama and some trading firms in Peru, Argentina and Colombia.'[12]

While the US continued to import capital from Europe, the 1890s witnessed increased US investments in Latin America. The need for foreign markets, greater domestic savings and increasing domestic consumption of tropical fruit provided some of the explanation for this development. By the end of 1897, US investments in Latin America, however, still amounted to only US$304.3 million. The picture changed dramatically at the turn of the century. At the end of 1908 total foreign investments in Latin America amounted to US$1,062.9 million, of which US$748.8 million (70.4%) was direct investment. By the outbreak of the First World war, the figure had reached US$1,641.4 million, of which 77.7% was direct and the rest portfolio. At the end of 1914, the US share of the total estimated foreign private investment in Latin America of US$7,569 million was 18.4% as compared to 47.4% for the United Kingdom, 9.4% for France, 4.2% for Germany and 20.6% for others.[13]

A glance at Table 4.3 (see pp. 72–75) shows that at the end of 1897, Mexico alone accounted for 65.8% of US direct investment in Latin America, while Cuba accounted for 14.3% and the whole of South America for 12.5%. By the outbreak of the First World War, however, capital had began to flow to the other countries of the region in more substantial quantities. At the end of 1914, Mexico accounted for 46% as compared to 19.8% for Cuba, and 13.4% for Chile. Brazil accounted for only US$3.0 million or less than one per cent of the total.

In terms of the sectoral distribution of US direct investment, a glance at Table 4.4 shows that at the end of 1897, 42.6% were in railroads, 26% in mining and smelting, 3.5% in petroleum, and 18.6% in agriculture. By 1908, the share for railroads had dropped to 14.7%, and showed a steady decline in subsequent years.

The period between the two World Wars witnessed remarkable changes in the pattern and direction of capital movements. Table 4.5 shows that on the eve of the First World War, the UK owned about 40% of total World foreign investments, as compared to 20% for France, 13% for Germany and 12% for Belgium, Netherlands and Switzerland taken together. The data shows that the US owned about 8%, but since the value of foreign investments in the US was greater than that held by the US abroad, on balance the US was a debtor country. With respect to the geographical distribution of this investment, Africa accounted for

Table 4.4 *US direct investment in Latin America by sector, 1897–1950*

$mn.

Branch of Economy	1897		1908		1914		1919		1929		1943		1950	
	Total	%	Total	%	Total	%	Total	%	Total	%	Total	%	Total	%
Agriculture	56.5	18.6	158.2	21.1	238.5	18.7	500.1	25.3	877.3	24.1	385	14.1	a	a
Sugar	24.0		57.0		115.0		354.0		643.5					
Fruit	8.5		28.2		57.5		67.1		153.8					
Others	24.0		73.0		66.0		79.0		80.0					
Mining and Smelting	79.0	26.0	302.6	40.4	552.2	43.3	660.8	33.4	801.4	22.0	405	14.9	628	14.1
Precious Ores and Stones	58.0		141.6		176.2		144.5		164.3					
Industrial Minerals	21.0		161.0		376.0		516.3		637.6					
Petroleum	10.5	3.5	68.0	9.1	130.0	10.2	326.0	16.5	731.5	20.1	618	22.7	1,233	27.7
Production	3.5		55.0		107.0		286.0		654.0					
Distribution	7.0		13.0		23.0		40.0		77.5					
Railroads	129.7	42.6	110.0	14.7	175.7	13.8	211.2	10.7	230.1	6.3	b	b	b	b
Public Utilities	10.1	3.3	51.5	6.9	98.4	7.7	101.0	5.1	575.9	15.8	875	32.1	927	20.8
Manufacturing	3.0	1.0	30.0	4.0	37.0	2.9	84.0	4.2	231.0	6.3	325	11.9	780	17.5
Trade	13.5	4.4	23.5	3.1	33.5	2.6	71.0	3.6	119.2	3.3	a	a	a	a
Others	2.0	0.6	5.0	0.7	10.15	0.8	23.5	1.2	79.4	2.2	113	4.3	877	19.9
Total	304.3	100.0	748.8	100.0	1,275.8	100.0	1,977.6	100.0	3,645.8	100.0	2,721	100.0	4,445	100.0

a include in 'Others'.
b included in 'Public Utilities'.

Source: US Bureau of Commerce, *Survey of Current Business*, Various Issues; UN *External Financing in Latin America*, New York, 1965.

Table 4.5 *Approximate value of foreign investments by investing countries on the eve of World War I*

Country	*US$mn*	*%*
UK	18,000	40.9
France	9,000	20.5
Germany	5,800	13.1
US*	3,500	8.0
Belgium, Netherlands, Switzerland	5,500	12.5
Other Countries	2,200**	5.0
	44,000	100.0

* Foreign investments in the US amounted to some $6,800 million; on balance, therefore, the US was a debtor country.

** Rough estimates; includes the investments of Japan and Russia (e.g. in China), of Portugal (e.g. in Brazil) and of Sweden (e.g. in Russia).

Table 4.5A *Distribution of above investments by areas*

Foreign Long-Term Investment in:	*US$mn*	*%*
Africa	4,700	10.7
Asia	6,000	13.6
Europe	12,000	27.3
North America (north of Mexico)	10,500	23.9
Latin America	8,500	19.3
Oceania	2,300	5.2
	44,000	100.0

Source: Douglas, C. North, 'International Capital Movements in Historical Perspective', in R.F. Mikesell, ed. *US Private and Government Investment Abroad* (Oregon: University of Oregon Press, 1962).

11%, Asia 14% Europe 27%, North America 24%, Latin America 19%, and Oceania 5%.

World War I had a severe adverse impact on the foreign position of the three main creditor countries (viz., the UK, France, and Germany). While Germany lost almost all its foreign investments, the United Kingdom and France had to sell a large part of theirs to finance the war effort. In the aftermath of the war, the US emerged as the main international creditor.[14] Between 1919 and 1934, there was a net capital outflow from the US of almost 14 billion dollars. Capital funds, however, continued to flow out of the UK and France during the 1920s. With respect to the former there was a net outflow of 3.4 billion dollars betwen 1922 and 1929, while in the latter's case the figure was 2.6 billion for the same period.[15]

The depression years of the 1930s (particularly the latter part) witnessed a reversal of some of these trends. For instance, between 1934 and 1938 there was a net capital inflow into the US of some $6.0 billion. For the UK the inflow was $513 million. France, however, had a net outflow of $1.9 billion over the same period. During the 1930s decade many of the debtor countries were in fact exporting capital – the result of political instability and increasingly nationalistic policies.

With respect to the US a large part of this country's outflows consisted of direct investment. Of the US$10.4 billion long-term capital outflow from the US between 1919 and 1930, US$3.3 billion (31.7%) consisted of private direct investment, US$5.1 billion (49.0%) other private long-term capital and US$2.0 billion (19.3%) government funds. By the end of 1929, US direct investment abroad had reached $7.7 billion (of which 45% were in Latin America.) During the 1930s the outflow of direct investment capital slowed down considerably. The total outflow for the period 1931–40 amounted to only $109 million. Overall there was a net inflow of $1.4 billion (most of it other private capital) into the US over the period. By the end of 1940 US direct investment abroad was estimated to be just over 7 billion (of which about 40% were in Latin America.) The outflow of long-term funds in the 1940s (particularly after 1945) was dominated by Government transactions. Of the $17.4 net outflow of long-term capital between 1941–50, $13.3 billion (76.4%) consisted of Government funds. The reverse flow of direct investment capital observed in the late 1930s continued until the end of the War. Between 1941 and 1944, there was a net inflow of $235 million into the US. This situation, however, changed after the War. Between 1945 and 1950, for instance, there was a net outflow of $3.1 billion in direct foreign investment. Even before the war ended other forms of private long term capital had clearly started to flow out again. Between 1942 and 1950 the figure averaged about $124 million

Table 4.6 *Book value of United States direct foreign investment by industry, 1929 and 1946*

	1929		*1946*	
Sectors	*US$mn*	*%*	*US$mn*	*%*
1. Agriculture	880	11.7	545	6.2
2. Mining & smelting	1,185	15.7	1,062	12.0
3. Petroleum	1,117	14.8	1,769	20.0
4. Manufacturing	1,813	24.1	2,854	32.2
5. Public utilities, transportation and communication	1,610	21.4	1,277	14.4
6. Trade	368	4.9	740	8.4
7. Other	555[a]	7.4	607	6.8
Total	*7,528*	*100.0*	*8,854*	*100.0*

a excludes insurance

Source: R.F. Mikesell, (ed.) *US Private and Government Investment Abroad* (Oregon: University of Oregon Press, 1962), p. 55.

per year. At the end of 1945 total direct investment abroad totalled about $8.4 billion, of which $3.1 billion (or 37%) was in Latin America and the Caribbean.

In terms of the sectoral distribution of US total direct foreign investment a glance at Table 4.6 shows that between 1929 and the end of the Second World War some significant changes had taken place. Agriculture's share dropped from 11.7% in 1929 to 6.2% in 1946. The share of mining and smelting also fell from 15.7% to 12%, as did public utilities (including transportation and communication) from 21.4% to 14.4% over the period. On the other hand petroleum's share increased from 14.8% to 20% while that of manufacturing moved from 24.1% to 32.2%. In terms of the sectoral changes that took place in US direct foreign investment in Latin America in the inter-war period, Table 4.4 gives some indication of the trends. Agriculture's share increased from 18.7% in 1914 to 24.1% in 1929 but fell to 14.1% in 1943. The share for mining and smelting dropped from 43.3% in 1914 to 22% in 1929 and to 14.9% in 1943. The share for railroads and public utilities tended to increase over the period, moving from 21.5% in 1914 to 22.1% in 1929 and to 32.1% in 1943. Petroleum's share almost doubled between 1914 and 1929 but increased only slightly by 1943. In 1914 less than 3% of US direct foreign investment was in manufacturing. By 1929 the share had increased to 6.3% and by 1943 to 11.9%.

The post-war period

The decline of British overseas investment noted in the pre-war period continued after the war was over. It is estimated that British total overseas investments shrank from £3,490 million in 1939 to £1,960 million in 1948.[16] Over the same period British investments in South America fell from an estimated £665 million to £260 million, while in Mexico the figure dropped from £65 million to £30 million and in Cuba from £28 million to £24 million.[17] Corresponding with the decline of British capital abroad, the US foreign position has been increasing. In 1960, the stock of the United Kingdom's direct investment abroad was valued at $12 billion as compared to $32 billion for the US. West Germany's share was put at $0.8 billion and Japan's at $0.5 billion.[18] Table 4.7 shows that by 1967 the United States held about 54% of the total stock of direct foreign investment (DFI) attributable to the developed market economy countries. By 1976, however, the proportion had declined to about 48%. The United Kingdom's share dropped from about 17% in 1967 to about 11% in 1976. Over this period West Germany's share increased from 3% to 7%, as did Japan's from 1% to 7%. The proportion for France fluctuated around 4 to 5%, while Canada's averaged about 3 to 4%.

Table 4.7A *Stock of direct investment abroad of developed market economies/by major country of origin, 1967–76*

	US$ Billion					*Percentage Distribution*				
Country of Origin	*1967*	*1971*	*1973*	*1975*	*1976*	*1967*	*1971*	*1973*	*1975*	*1976*
United States	56.6	82.8	101.3	124.2	137.2	53.8	52.3	51.0	47.8	47.6
United Kingdom	17.5	23.7	26.9	30.8	32.1	16.6	15.0	13.5	11.9	11.2
Fed. Rep. of Germany	3.0	7.3	11.9	16.0	19.9	2.8	4.6	6.0	6.2	6.9
Japan	1.5	4.4	10.3	15.9	19.4	1.4	2.8	5.2	6.1	6.7
Switzerland	5.0	9.5	11.1	16.9	18.6	4.8	6.0	5.6	6.5	6.5
France	6.0	7.3	8.8	11.1	11.9	5.7	4.6	4.4	4.3	4.1
Canada	3.7	6.5	7.8	10.5	11.1	3.5	4.1	3.9	4.1	3.9
Netherlands	2.2	4.0	5.5	8.5	9.8	2.1	2.5	2.8	3.2	3.4
Sweden	1.7	2.4	3.0	4.4	5.0	1.6	1.5	1.5	1.7	1.7
Belgium-Luxembourg	2.0	2.4	2.7	3.2	3.6	1.9	1.5	1.4	1.2	1.2
Italy	2.1	3.0	3.2	3.3	2.9	2.0	1.9	1.6	1.3	1.0
Others (estimate)	4.0	5.1	6.3	15.1	16.8	3.8	3.2	3.1	5.7	5.8
Total	*105.3*	*158.4*	*198.8*	*258.9*	*287.2*	*100.0*	*100.0*	*100.0*	*100.0*	*100.0*

Source: UN, *Transnational Corporations in World Development: A Re-examination*, New York, 1978.

Table 4.7B *Development Assistance Committee (DAC) countries' stock of private direct investment[1] in the Latin American/Caribbean region by host country, end 1978*

Host Country	*US$ Million*	*%*	*Host Country*	*US$ Million*	*%*
Bahamas[2]	2,060	4.1	Argentina	3,340	6.6
Barbados[2]	180	0.4	Bolivia	140	0.3
Belize	75	0.1	Brazil	13,520	26.9
Bermuda[2]	4,300	8.5	Chile	1,440	2.9
Costa Rica	290	0.6	Colombia	1,510	3.0
Dominican Rep.	390	0.8	Ecuador	660	1.3
El Salvador	150	0.3	Guyana	230	0.4
Guadeloupe	55	0.1	Paraguay	110	0.2
Guatemala	290	0.6	Peru	2,150	4.3
Haiti	80	0.1	Suriname	420	0.8
Honduras	270	0.5	Uruguay	330	0.6
Jamaica	900	1.8	Venezuela	3,620	7.2
Mexico	6,000	11.9			
Neth. Antilles	2,500	5.0	*Total*	*50,330*	*100.0*
Nicaragua	(90)				
Panama[2]	3,140	6.2			
Trinidad & Tobago	1,300	2.6			
West Indies (Br.)	970	1.9			

1 Includes DAC Secretariat estimates for re-invested earnings.
2 Offshore Banking Centre.

Source: OECD, *International Investment and Multinational Enterprise: Recent International Direct Investment Trends*, Paris, 1981.

In 1964 the accounting value of total direct foreign investment in Latin America was estimated to be around $12 billion to $13 billion as compared to about $8.5 billion at the beginning of World War 1.[19] At the end of 1972 it was estimated that the stock of direct investment in Latin America and the Caribbean amounted to around $23 billion (about half the total for all developing countries).[20] Of this figure, the US held about two thirds. Despite the predominant position of the US, available evidence indicates that Japan and other Western European countries (see Table 4.8) have made substantial investments in Latin America in recent years. Between 1951 and 1969, Japanese direct investment flows to Latin America amounted to around $550 Million – almost a fifth of total direct Japanese investment abroad.[21] In terms of distribution, manufacturing absorbed 55%, mining 11%, fishing 2%, commerce 2.4% and construction 5.2%. Brazil was the chief recipient accounting for 56%. (See Table 4.9.) An examination of Table 4.8 indicates that in recent years Japan appears to be the most important of the non-US investors in Latin America. Between 1969 and 1978, the total flow of Japanese net direct private investment amounted to over $2.6 billion as compared to $1.5 billion for West Germany, $0.5

Table 4.8 *Total flow of direct private investment (net) by selected countries to Latin America in the period 1969–78*

US$ mn.

Country of Origin	*Argentina*	*Brazil*	*Mexico*	*Andean[1] Group*	*CACM[2]*	*Other[3] L.A.*	*Total*
W. Germany	93.87	1,069.23	212.94	61.09	9.67	52.08	1,498.88
Belgium	19.98	32.59	4.06	4.61	2.88	34.96	99.08
France	171.45	232.94	27.55	71.7	0.52	29.81	533.97
Italy	47.48	63.49	0.93	12.24	0.77	17.14	142.05
Netherlands	−1.60	114.38	10.89	2.89	-	37.08	163.64
UK	64.86	422.89	43.52	12.61	-	19.24	563.12
Japan	−5.03	1,776.47	155.64	449.55	36.55	193.63	2,611.84

1 Bolivia, Chile, Colombia, Ecuador, Peru, Venezuela (excluding Chile after 1977).
2 Costa Rica, Guatemala, Honduras, Nicaragua, El Salvador.
3 Chile (from 1977), Cuba, Dominican Republic, Haiti, Panama, Paraguay, Uruguay.

Source: Latin America Bureau, *The European Challenge*, London 1982. (Appendix 2). Original data supplied by the Commission of the European Communities, Directorate General for External Relations, Statistics Office.

billion for France and $0.6 billion for the UK. Though not shown in the Table, Canada's investment in the region has also been increasing. Canada's direct investment in Latin America and the Caribbean[22] increased from C$47 million in 1949 to C$267 million in 1967. Of this latter figure, 45% were in manufacturing and 51% in mining.[23] By the late 1970s the Latin American/Caribbean Region is estimated to have accounted for about half of the stock of private foreign investment in developing countries. (A distribution by host country is shown in Table 4.7B). The United States share was about two thirds which made her still the largest investor in the region.

Table 4.9 *Japanese direct investment in Latin America by sectors and countries as at March 30, 1969*

Sectors	*$mn*	*%*	*Country*	*$mn*	*%*
Agriculture & forestry	2.1	0.5	Brazil	230.2	55.7
Fishing	6.8	1.6	Chile	46.2	11.2
Mining	44.6	10.8	Peru	41.6	10.0
Manufacturing	228.5	55.2	Mexico	27.1	6.6
Construction	21.4	5.2	Argentina	20.7	5.0
Commerce	9.8	2.4	Others	47.8	11.5
Others	100.0	24.3			
Total	*413.6*	*100.0*	*Total*	*413.6*	*100.0*

Source: *Comercio Exterior de Mexico*, March 1972. Taken from Koichi Hamada, 'Japanese Investment Abroad', Third Pacific Trade and Development Conference, Sydney, August, 1970.

US Direct Investment in Latin America and the Caribbean in the Post-War Period

As indicated earlier, at the end of the Second World War, the US DFI in Latin America and the Caribbean amounted to $3.1 billion or about 37% of the total.[24] By the end of 1950, the figure had reached $4.6 billion or 39% of US total direct investment abroad. An examination of Table 4.10 shows that since 1950, US DFI in Latin America had grown in absolute terms, but as a proportion of US total direct investment abroad, the share has been falling steadily. At the end of 1981, the book value of US DFI in Latin America and the Caribbean amounted to $38.9 billion or to 17% of the total. Generally, US DFI in the developed countries had been growing at a faster rate than investment in the developing countries. In 1950, the former group accounted for 48% of total US DFI. By 1981, however, the proportion had grown to 74%.

In terms of the distribution of US investment by country, a glance back at Table 4.3 will show that there have been some significant changes since 1950. Argentina's share grew from $356 million in 1950 to $2.7 billion in 1981, but the proportion has remained around 7%. In absolute terms Brazil's share increased from $644 million to $8.3 billion, while the proportion grew from 14% to 21% over the period. Chile, which accounted for 11% ($540 million) of US DFI in the region in 1950, had only 2.1% ($834 million) of the total in 1981. The stock of US DFI in Colombia increased from $193 million to $1.1 billion over the period, but its share dropped from 4% to 3%. In Peru, US DFI stood at $1.9 billion (5% of total) as compared to $145 million (3% of the total) in 1950. While in dollar terms Venezuela's share increased from $993 million to $2.1 billion between 1950 and 1981, the proportion of the total declined from 21% to 6%. Other countries in South America (Bolivia, Ecuador, Paraguay and Uruguay) accounted for only about 2.7% of US total DFI in the region in 1981 as compared to 1.8% in 1950. In Central America the most important recipient of US direct investment capital in the post-war period has been Mexico. In 1981, the figure stood at almost $7 billion (18% of the region total) as compared to $415 million (9%) in 1950. Panama too appears to have been a fairly substantial recipient of US DFI. In 1981 the dollar value amounted to $3.7 billion (9.4% of the total) as compared to $58 million (1.2%) in 1950. Total US DFI in the Central American Common Market countries (viz., Costa Rica, El Salvador, Guatemala, Honduras and Nicaragua) reached $1.0 billion (2.7% of the regional total) in 1981. The comparable figure for 1950 was $254 million (5.3% of the total). The data in Table 4.3 indicate that US DFI in 'Developing Western Hemisphere' countries other than the Latin American Republics totalled $9.0 billion (23.4%) in 1981 as compared to $290 million (6.1%) in 1950. The breakdown of the 1981 figures shows that about $3 billion were located in the Bahamas, $10.4 billion in Bermuda,

Table 4.10 *The growth of US direct investment (book value) in the Latin American/Caribbean region, 1950–1981*

Year	*(1) Total US Direct Investment Abroad $mn*	*(2) US Direct Investment in LA*[1] *$mn*	*(3) Annual Change $mn*	*(4) Annual Change %*	*(5) (2) as a % of (1)*
1950	11,788	4,577			38.8
51	12,979	4,949	372	8.1	38.1
52	14,721	5,514	565	11.4	37.4
53	16,253	5,774	260	4.7	35.5
54	17,631	5,929	155	2.7	33.6
55	19,395	6,242	313	5.3	32.2
56	22,505	7,298	1,056	16.9	32.4
57	25,394	8,052	754	10.3	31.7
58	27,409	8,469	417	5.2	30.9
59	29,827	8,887	418	4.9	29.8
60	31,865	8,366	−521	−5.9	26.3
61	34,717	9,239	873	10.4	26.6
62	37,276	9,524	285	3.1	25.5
63	40,736	9,941	417	4.4	24.4
64	44,480	10,255	314	3.2	23.0
65	49,474	10,885	630	6.1	22.0
66	51,792	9,752	−1,133	−10.4	18.8
67	56,560	10,290	538	5.5	18.2
68	61,907	11,342	1,052	10.2	18.3
69	68,093	12,039	697	6.1	17.7
70	75,480	12,961	922	7.6	17.2
71	82,760	14,013	1,052	8.1	16.9
72	89,878	14,897	884	6.3	16.6
73	101,313	16,484	1,587	10.6	16.3
74	110,078	19,527	3,043	18.5	17.7
75	124,050	22,167	2,640	13.5	17.9
76	136,809	23,934	1,767	8.0	17.5
77	149,848	28,110	4,176	17.4	18.7
78	167,804	32,662	4,552	16.2	19.5
79	192,648	36,834	4,172	12.8	19.1
80	215,578	38,882	2,048	5.6	18.0
81	227,342	38,883	1	0.0	17.1

1 includes 'Other Developing Western Hemisphere'.

Source: Obie G. Whichard, 'Trends in the US Direct Investment Position Abroad, 1950–79', US Dept. of Commerce, *Survey of Current Business* Feb., 1981; Also his 'US Direct Investment Abroad in 1981', Survey of Current Business, Aug. 1982.

$932 million in Trinidad and Tobago and $1,491 million in other countries. The figure for the Netherlands Antilles is negative and this requires some explanation.

The Bahamas, Panama, Bermuda and the Netherlands Antilles are four of the tax havens in the Hemisphere and are widely used by American corporations in their international operations. Most of the investment in these countries tends to be for tax reasons. The size of the figures can be explained to some extent by the way 'direct investment abroad' data are computed by the US Bureau of Commerce. The US direct investment position is the book value of US direct investors' equity in, and net outstanding loans to, their foreign affiliates. (A foreign affiliate is a foreign business enterprise in which a single US direct investor owns at least 10 per cent of the voting securities, or the equivalent.) In other words the 'data reflect inter-company balances, i.e. the net of US parents' receivables from, and payables to affiliates. At year end 1981 payables were almost 70% as large as receivables.

In the last few years, US companies have borrowed substantially from their Netherlands Antillean affiliates which were largely set up to borrow in the Eurobond market, the proceeds from which are then re-loaned to the parents. Why the Netherlands Antilles? Because of a treaty between the latter and the US, interest payments which would normally be subjected US withholdings tax are exempt. It has been pointed out that although 'the US has treaties with several other countries that provide a similar exemption or a reduced withholding rate, the Netherlands Antilles is often chosen as a location because it does not have a withholding tax on interest payments to third countries and because most of its taxes on affiliates are structured so as to generate equal and offsetting tax credits for the US parents. To realise these tax advantages, the borrowing must be done through a bona fide foreign business entity that the US tax authorities will recognise as the issuer of the bonds, although the bond may be guaranteed by the US parent. To create such entities affiliates are separately incorporated in the Netherlands Antilles and are capitalised in accordance with generally accepted guidelines.'[25] Table 4.11 presents some selected data on transactions of US parents with their Netherlands Antillean affiliates. Capital stock and retained earnings (line 2) largely represent equity contributions by US parents to provide affiliates with the necessary capitalisation. The inter-company accounts (line 3) largely represent funds the affiliates raised abroad by issuing Euro-bonds, and then re-loaned to their parents. The figures represent what the US parents owe to the Netherlands affiliates. Since the negative inter-company accounts tend to offset the positive capital stock and retained earnings component, the direct investment position with respect to the Netherlands Antilles tend to be negative. Note that the figure of −$7,877 billion at the end of 1981 is different from that appearing in Table 4.3 because this figure reflects only transactions with and positions in incorporated affiliates established primarily to borrow funds abroad and re-lend them to their US parents.

Table 4.11 *US firms: selected transactions with, and position in, Netherlands Antillean finance affiliates*

	1977	*1978*	*1979*	*1980*	*1981*
Direct Investment Position	−1,215	−1,399	−2,664	−4,584	−7,877
Capital Stock and Retained Earnings[1]	1,006	1,117	1,614	3,222	4,813
Intercompany Accounts	−2,221	−2,506	−4,277	−7,806	−12,691
US Parents' receivables	152	234	362	380	383
US Parents' payables	−2,372	−2,740	−4,640	−8,185	−13,073
Equity and intercompany account flows (outflows +; inflows −)	441	−189	−1,348	−2,710	−3,647
Equity	136	96	423	818	1,238
Intercompany Accounts	305	−285	−1,771	−3,528	−4,885
US Parents' receivables	15	82	128	17	3
US Parents' payables	290	−367	−1,900	−3,546	−4,888
Income	−161	−101	−96	−127	−800
of which: interest	−130	−132	−178	−329	−1,188

1 Includes additional paid-in capital and valuation adjustments to the position.
Note: Table 4.11 shows only transactions with and positions in, incorporated affiliates established primarily to borrow funds abroad and relend them to their US parents.
Source: US *Survey of Current Business*, August, 1982.

With respect to the sectoral distribution of US direct investment in the Latin American/Caribbean region an examination of Tables 4.4 and 4.12 show a significant change in emphasis in the post-war period. The share of mining and smelting (excluding petroleum) fell from about 14% in 1950 to around 5% in 1981. Petroleum's share increased from 23% in 1943 to almost 40% in 1960, but has declined steadily since, reaching about 12% in 1981. The area where investment has increased most rapidly in recent years has no doubt been the manufacturing sector. In 1943 US DFI in manufacturing amounted to $0.3 billion of 12% of the total. By 1950 the figure had grown to $0.8 billion or 18% of the total and by 1981 to $15.8 billion or about 41% of the total. Of this 40%, 5% were in food industries, 10% in machinery, 3% in electrical equipment, 4% in transport equipment and 10% in other manufacturing activities. The 1981 DFI stock included 11% in trade, 10% in banking, 16% in finance (other than banking) and 6% in unspecified areas. This latter would include agriculture and the utilities-areas which ranked high prior to 1950 (see Table 4.4).

The trends described above reflect factors operating at both the national and global levels. A glance at Table 4.13 shows that petroleum's share in total US DFI dropped from 29% in 1950 to 22% in 1979. On the other hand the share of manufacturing increased from 33% to 43% over the period. The share of sectors other than petroleum and manufacturing declined slightly from 39% in 1950 to 35% in 1979.

Table 4.12 *US direct investment position (book value) in Latin America and the Caribbean at end of 1981* US$ Million

				Manufacturing											
Countries/Area	*All Industries*	*Mining*	*Petroleum*	*Total*	*Food*	*Chemicals*	*Metals*[1]	*Machinery*[2]	*Electric Equip*[3]	*Trans Equip*[4]	*Other*	*Trade*	*Banking*	*Finance*[5]	*Other*
1. *South America*	*18,109*	*1,482*	*2,714*	*9,391*	*1,192*	*2,089*	*928*	*1,165*	*564*	*899*	*2,553*	*1,514*	*1,021*	*1,241*	*746*
Argentina	2,735	69	483	1,570	264	360	67	223	48	308	301	202	276	28	107
Brazil	8,253	152	422	5,420	502	1,060	468	904	394	590	1,501	581	494	968	216
Chile	834	(D)	98	112	17	28	19	1	4	(D)	(D)	80	84	5	(D)
Colombia	1,178	(D)	318	574	89	181	22	10	48	19	204	98	16	24	(D)
Ecuador	277	0	(D)	107	27	15	(D)	0	(D)	4	36	45	(D)	2	−8
Peru	1,928	(D)	(D)	106	−2	30	21	1	15	10	32	76	(D)	4	21
Venezuela	2,175	(*)	126	1,156	276	397	65	24	34	−50	410	406	(D)	174	(D)
Other	728	1	192	347	19	17	(D)	3	(D)	(D)	(D)	25	75	37	52
2. *Central Amercia*	*11,675*	*126*	*960*	*5,860*	*654*	*1,423*	*586*	*418*	*541*	*848*	*1,391*	*1,637*	*323*	*1,726*	*1,042*
Mexico	6,962	77	189	5,140	436	1,130	564	417	503	846	1,242	878	(D)	176	(D)
Panama	3,671	(*)	601	302	90	175	0	(*)	1	0	37	672	186	1,532	377
Other	1,042	48	170	418	129	117	21	(*)	37	1	112	87	(D)	18	(D)
3. *Other W. Hemisphere*	*9,099*	*308*	*825*	*510*	*185*	*208*	*7*	*(*)*	*24*	*(*)*	*86*	*1,041*	*2,588*	*3,279*	*548*
Bahamas	2,987	(D)	289	39	5	33	0	0	2	0	−1	300	1,478	682	(D)
Bermuda	10,353	0	−609	15	(*)	12	0	(*)	(*)	0	3	573	(D)	10,190	(D)
Netherlands Antilles	−6,664	(D)	209	58	−1	(D)	0	0	2	0	(D)	17	(D)	−7,878	58
T'dad & T'go	932	0	808	102	7	(D)	(*)	0	3	0	(D)	12	(D)	(D)	(D)
Other	1,491	291	129	296	175	23	7	0	17	(*)	74	139	266	(D)	(D)
4. *1 + 2 + 3*	*38,883*	*1,916*	*4,499*	*15,762*	*2,032*	*3,719*	*1,521*	*1,871*	*1,130*	*1,747*	*4,030*	*4,192*	*3,933*	*6,246*	*2,336*
% Composition	100.0	4.9	11.6	40.5	5.2	9.6	3.9	4.8	2.9	4.5	10.4	10.8	10.1	16.1	6.0

1 Primary and fabricated metals.
2 Excluding electrical.
3 Including electronic.
4 Transport.
5 Excluding banking.
6 Less than $1,500,000 ±.
(D) Suppressed to avoid disclosure of data of individual companies.

Source: US Dept of Commerce, *Survey of Current Business*, August 1982.

Table 4.13 *US direct investment abroad: distributional changes and average annual rates of growth, 1950–1979*

Area/Sector	*$ million*		*Percentage Distribution*		*Average Annual Rate of Growth %*
	1950	*1979*	*1950*	*1979*	
1. *All Areas*	*11,788*	*192,648*	*100.0*	*100.0*	*10.1*
2. Petroleum	3,390	41,553	28.8	21.6	9.0
3. Manufacturing	3,831	83,564	32.5	43.4	11.2
4. Other	4,567	67,531	38.7	35.0	9.7
5. *Latin America*[1]	*4,577*	*36,834*	*100.0*	*100.0*	*7.5*
6. Petroleum	1,303	4,568	28.5	12.4	4.4
7. Manufacturing	781	13,220	17.1	35.9	10.2
8. Other	2,493	19,046	54.4	51.7	7.3
9. (6) as a % of (2)	38.4	11.0			
10. (7) as a % of (3)	20.4	15.8			
11. (8) as a % of (4)	63.3	28.2			

1 figures include 'Other Developing Western Hemisphere'.

Source: O.G. Whichard, 'Trends in the US Direct Investment Positions Abroad, 1950–79'. US Department of Commerce, *Survey of Current Business*, Feb., 1981.

In Latin America petroleum's share fell by more than half, while the proportion in manufacturing more than doubled in the period. Line (9) of the Table shows that, whereas petroleum investment in Latin America accounted for 38% of US global investment in this sector in 1950, by 1979 the proportion had fallen to 11%. Manufacturing's share also declined though by less, moving from 20% in 1950 to 16% in 1979. 'Other' sectors which accounted for over 60% of US stock of world-wide investments in this category in 1950, contributed only 28% in 1979.

One of the main factors behind the decline of US investment in the petroleum sector in the region has no doubt been the nationalisation policies adopted by certain of the oil-producing nations (e.g. Bolivia, Peru and Venezuela) who have sought to bring under national control what they consider a vital sector of the economy. This development, however, has been accompanied by substantial US oil investments in other parts of the world, particularly in the developed countries which accounted for about 75% of US worldwide investments in the petroleum sector in 1979, as compared to about 29% in 1950. As we saw earlier US investment in the manufacturing sector of the region has increased substantially in the post-war period, but this has been part of a general trend by US transnational corporations. The developed countries accounted for about 80% of the global stock of US investment in the manufacturing sector in 1979 as compared to about 78% in 1950. To the developing countries' share of 20% in 1979 Latin America contributed 82%. In 1950 22% of US foreign investment stock in manufacturing were located in developing countries, and of this Latin America accounted for 92%. Overall the Latin American region contained just over 75% of US DFI in developing countries in 1979 as compared to about 80% in 1950. It is clear that even though petroleum investments have declined, the region has maintained its attractiveness to US investors in other respects such as market potential, source of raw materials, locational advantage and in some cases cheap labour.

Notes

1 For a well documented study on early investment activities in Latin America see, J. Fred Rippy, *British Investment in Latin America, 1822–1949*, University of Minnesota Press, 1959. Other useful studies on British investment activities abroad include, A.K. Cairncross, *Home and Foreign Investment 1870–1913*, Cambridge University Press, 1953; C.K. Hobson, *The Export of Capital*, London 1914; L.H. Jenks, *The Migration of British Capital to 1875*, New York, 1927 and UN, *External Financing in Latin America*, New York, 1965.
2 J.F. Rippy, op. cit., p. 19.
3 See Douglas C. North, 'International Capital Movements in Historical Perspective' in R.F. Mikesell (ed.), *US Private and Government Investment Abroad* (Oregon: University of Oregon Books, 1962), p. 11.
4 Ibid.
5 *UN External Financing in Latin America*, op. cit., p. 5.
6 Ibid.
7 J. Fred Rippy, op. cit., p. 17.
8 See UN *External Financing*, op. cit., p. 6.
9 Ibid.
10 Details here have been taken from the above cited UN study.
11 Ibid., p. 13.
12 Ibid.
13 Ibid., p. 17.
14 See Douglas C. North, op. cit., p. 26.
15 Ibid., pp. 26–43.
16 Rippy, op. cit., p. 186.
17 Ibid., p. 191.
18 UN, *Multinational Corporations in World Development*, New York, 1973, p. 146.
19 OAS, *External Financing for Latin American Development*, Baltimore, The Johns Hopkins University Press, 1971, p. 63.
20 UN, *Transnational Corporations in World Development: A Reexamination*, New York, 1978, p. 260.
21 See *Comerico Exterior de Mexico*, March, 1972, p. 23. Figures are quoted from Koichi Hamada, *Japanese Investment Abroad*, Third Pacific Trade and Development Conference, Sydney, August 1970.
22 The figures exclude the investments of insurance companies and banks.

23 Figures of Canada's Dominion Bureau of Statistics cited by C.I. Bradford Jr and Caroline Pestieau in *Canada and Latin America: The Potential for Partnership* (Toronto and Montreal: Economic Policy Committee and Canadian Association for Latin America, 1971), pp. 164–165.

24 End of 1945 position.

25 Obie G. Whichard, 'US Direct Investment Abroad in 1981', US Dept of Commerce, *Survey of Current Business*, August 1982, p. 12.

5

Some Issues Related to US Foreign Investment in Latin America and the Caribbean

Between 1960 and 1969 total direct investment flows from Development Assistance Committees (DAC) members to developing countries amounted to US$20.7 billion or 53% of total private (net) capital flows and 20% of total flows.[1] Between 1970 and 1980 direct investment flows (at current prices) from all sources to developing countries totalled about $83 billion or roughly 23% of non-concessional finance and 14% of total flows.[2] Of the roughly $10 billion that was invested in developing countries by DAC countries in 1980, the US alone accounted for about a third.

Capital transfers in the 19th and early 20th century took the form largely of portfolio lending by private lenders to both public and private borrowers.[3] The direct investment that took place in this period was mainly in resource-based industries. In more recent years direct investment has tended to concentrate heavily in manufacturing. At the end of 1970 the book value of private direct foreign investment in developing countries was estimated to be around $40 billion (about a quarter of the world stock), of which $12.3 billion (31%) was in manufacturing and $13.0 billion (33%) in petroleum. (See Table 5.1).[4] By 1977 this figure

Table 5.1 *Estimates of regional and sectoral distribution of foreign direct investment in developing countries at end of 1970*

$ billion

	Latin America	*Europe*	*Africa*	*Middle East*	*Asia*	*Total*
Petroleum	4.8	0.4	3.3	3.2	1.3	13.0
Mining	2.1	0.1	1.4	–	0.4	4.0
Manufacturing	7.5	1.5	1.3	0.2	1.8	12.3
Other	5.4	0.5	1.6	0.1	2.1	9.7
Total	*19.8*	*2.5*	*7.6*	*3.5*	*5.6*	*39.0*

Source: Grant L. Reuber *et al.*, *Private Foreign Investment in Development* (London: Oxford University Press, 1973), p. 4.

had grown to over $85 billion.[5] In terms of geographical distribution, Latin America accounted for about half the stock in 1970, some 38% being in manufacturing. About 45% of the stock of total direct investment in manufacturing was of US origin, 33% of EEC (excluding the UK) origin, 15% of UK origin, and 5% of Japanese origin.[6]

The main agent of direct investment in the post-war period has been the transnational corporation. In 1971, of the 650 largest (by sales) industrial corporations (all transnationals) of the developed market economies, more than half were based in the United States.[7] Table 5.2 shows the expansion of US transnational corporations abroad since the turn of the century. The number of companies operating a foreign subsidiary increased from 23 in 1901 to 186 in 1967. The number of companies operating a foreign subsidiary in Latin America increased from 3 to 182 over the same period. It is clear from the table that the expansion has taken place largely in the manufacturing sector.

Table 5.2 *Expansion of United States multinational corporations abroad, 1901–1957*

	In all Areas	*Canada*	*Latin America*	*Europe*	*Southern Dominions*	*Asia and other Africa*
a. Number of companies operating a foreign subsidiary						
1901	23	6	3	22	2	0
1913	47	27	9	37	8	4
1919	74	54	16	45	14	8
1929	123	92	36	95	34	23
1939	153	123	72	116	63	33
1945	158	128	93	120	69	33
1957	183	167	155	160	105	83
1967	186	174	182	185	154	158
b. Number of companies operating a foreign manufacturing subsidiary						
1901	18	5	3	16	1	0
1913	39	24	6	26	3	1
1919	64	48	10	30	7	4
1929	110	79	24	76	20	15
1939	135	102	56	96	44	18
1945	138	107	73	96	50	17
1957	174	142	131	144	85	61
1967	185	161	171	183	135	134

Source: S. Hymer, 'United States Investment Abroad' in Peter Drysdale (ed.), *Direct Foreign Investment in Asia and the Pacific* (Toronto: University of Toronto Press, 1972). Original source: J.W. Vaupel and J.D. Curhan, *The Making of the Multinational Enterprise* (Boston: Harvard University Press, 1968).

The growth in the size and number of transnational corporations has not only made non-sense of traditional economic theory based on a large number of small competing firms, but has also given rise to concern by developing countries (and certain developed countries like

Australia and Canada) with respect to its implications for national economic and political development. The issues raised have been considered sufficiently important for the UN to set up a special centre to study the activities of transnationals. As far as the developing countries (particularly the smaller ones) are concerned, dealing with these corporations on an individual basis raises particular difficulties. While comparing company assets, sales, or liquid assets with a country's GDP, GNP or foreign reserves is not always a very meaningful exercise, the point that such comparisons seek to make is that the resources at the disposal of many of these companies put them in a powerful position *vis-à-vis* the governments of host countries, whose sovereignty is often challenged in a *de facto* if not legal sense. It is now well established that constitutional independence and economic independence are not the same thing. The domination of key sectors by transnationals means that their behaviour can affect such critical variables like tax revenues, exports, capital formation, employment etc. TNCs make their decisions in the context of their global operations, and not necessarily with reference to the situation prevailing in one particular location. They are not charitable organisations. They are driven by the profit motive, and react to any decisions which affect this. While they benefit from development in host countries, national aspirations relating to economic diversification, creation of employment, increasing the level and types of exports, etc, are not necessarily their concern.

The goals of national governments, be they of the right or the left, elected or unelected, often come into direct conflict with the interests of TNCs. Governments, for instance, may insist that a greater proportion of their raw materials exported be processed locally in order to create jobs and increase income, and generally strengthen the national economy. TNCs may see this as an unnecessary cost and loss of business for their refining plants established elsewhere. Governments may demand that foreign enterprises use a greater amount of local inputs in their production to accelerate the process of linkage creation in the economy. TNCs, on the other hand, may see this as adversely affecting the pattern of intra-firm transactions already neatly established within the existing network of plants. In order to increase revenue for national development governments often try to increase their tax take, particularly from companies operating in the mining sectors where the resource involved often cannot be replaced (i.e. it is a wasting asset which may run out at some point in time). Since paying greater taxes may mean less profits, companies tend to use a variety of devices to reduce their tax payments. With respect to this issue, the *modus operandi* of TNCs and the limited information at the disposal of host governments often put the latter in a very disadvantageous position. Again, while host governments may wish to increase the number of job opportunities available, the TNC may insist on using a technology readily available to it, even though the local factor situation may call for a different one. With respect to exports, TNCs are often reluctant to export since this may mean competing with a sister plant elsewhere, and may even infringe an agreement with the parent firm whose strategy has generally been to penetrate countries individually, producing a relationship with direct linkage to the centre and little or none among the satellite operations.

The areas listed here do not exhaust the range of issues which bring foreign enterprises in conflict with host governments. There are some concerns which have a larger and more explicit political content. Governments, for instance may seek to increase local ownership of the economy in order to reduce its foreign dependence and strengthen the framework for national decision-making. Sometimes such a desire comes straight from a political objective that may be related to the ideological stance adopted. At other times, it may be a reaction to dissatisfaction with the contribution foreign enterprises are making to national development and a perception that such enterprises are not assisting in the attainment of national goals. There are instances, of course, where both set of factors have been at play.

Many of the issues which bring foreign enterprises into conflict with host governments are intimately related to the cost and benefits arguments associated with foreign investment. In the following section we take a critical look at some of the main areas around which controversy still rages.

Impact on the balance of payments

A study published by the United Nations[8] in 1955 drew attention to the fact that over a period of some 25 years private investors had taken out more than they put into Latin America.[9] In the context of a situation where the developed nations were being urged to increase the flow of resources to developing countries, this revelation created quite a stir in many quarters. It also gave rise to a controversy which is still very much alive, and which comes up every time the pros and cons of private foreign investment are discussed. This is the effect on the balance of payments. Let us look at the data for recent years.

Between 1946 and 1960, it is estimated that the net outflow of direct investment income from Latin America amounted to almost $13 billion. Direct investment inflows in this period totalled about $8 billion.[10] The available evidence indicates that this trend has continued into more recent years. Table 5.3 shows the experience of the US (which is the largest investor in the region) since 1960. Between 1960 and 1981, total US direct investment (net) in the Latin American/Caribbean region amounted to around $30 billion. It should be noted that this represented the sum of changes in book value. Direct investment

Table 5.3 *US: selected financial flows associated with direct investment in Latin America,[1] 1960–1981*

	Outflow to Latin America						
	Annual Direct Investment						
Year	*Equity & Inter-company*	*Re-investor Earnings*	*Valuation & other Adjustments*	*Total*	*Inflow[4] Direct Investment Income[2]*	*Fees & Royalties from Affiliated Foreigners*	*Fees and Royalties from un-affiliated Foreigners*
1960	149	278	−948	−521[3]	919	91	n.a.
61	219	279	+375	873	1,009	98	n.a.
62	29	308	−52	285	1,070	117	n.a.
63	235	182	–	417	983	124	n.a.
64	113	250	−49	314	1,145	134	n.a.
65	271	345	414	630	1,214	162	n.a.
66	303	309	−1,745	−1,133	1,423	176	n.a.
67	311	202	−25	538	1,392	192	n.a.
68	708	361	−17	1,052	1,579	283	44
69	385	331	−19	697	1,608	302	42
70	579	453	−110	922	1,510	318	46
71	696	373	−17	1,052	1,497	336	45
72	272	645	−33	884	1,560	259	47
73	654	991	−58	1,587	2,511	269	48
74	2,244	1,109	−310	3,043	3,145	341	63
75	1,245	1,621	−226	2,640	3,224	389	67
76	439	1,323	+5	1,767	3,480	298	63
77	2,422	1,582	+172	4,176	3,988	337	71
78	2,204	1,918	+430	4,552	4,779	372	98
79	1,454	2,924	−206	4,172	6,521	422	89
80	−631	3,366	−687	2,048	6,969	581	101
81	−3,312	3,254	+59	1	5,845	669	131

1 includes 'Other Developing Western Hemisphere'.
2 includes interest, dividends, branch earnings and re-invested profits of foreign incorporated affiliates of US firms.
3 reflect exappropriation of US investment in Cuba.
4 US direct investment income from investments in Latin America.
n.a. not available.

Source: US, Department of Commerce, *Survey of Current Business* various issues.

income (made up of interest, dividends, branch earnings, and re-invested profits of foreign incorporated affiliates) on the other hand came up to $57 billion. During 1981 alone direct investment income amounted to $5,845 million. Although $2,591 million of this was re-invested, the fact that capital outflows from the region amounted to $3,312 million meant that the book value of US direct investment position in the region at the end of 1981 was virtually the same as it was at the end of the 1980, after valuation adjustments were made. Some insight into the experience of individual countries can be gained from Table 5.4.

According to balance of payments accounting procedures, re-invested earnings are not only treated as an outflow (i.e. as part of direct investment income), but also as an inflow (i.e. as new invest-

Table 5.4 *Latin American countries: total direct investment inflows compared with direct investment income to foreigners for period 1970–80*

Countries	*Net Direct Investment Inflows $mn*	*Direct Investment Income $mn*	*Re-invested Earnings as a % of New Investment*
Argentina	1,391	1,121	50[a]
Bolivia	62	111	n.a.
Brazil	13,234	3,550	36[b]
Chile	−39	364	n.a.
Colombia	652	851	n.a.
Costa Rica	458	113	21
Dominican Republic	636	538	n.a.
Ecuador	784	735	42[c]
El Salvador[1]	108	115	70
Guatemala	701	216	32
Haiti	78	62	n.a.
Honduras	1,031	293	8
Mexico	7,911	3,972	46
Nicaragua[1]	120	219	50
Panama[1]	208	129	36
Paraguay	188	187	n.a.
Peru[1]	659	872	n.a.
Uruguay[1]	411	14	n.a.
Venezuela	−967	6,707	n.a.

a relate to the period 1977–80.
b relate to the period 1973–80.
c relate to the period 1968–78.
1 1969–79.
n.a. not available.

Source: IMF, *Balance of Payments Statistics*, Various Issues.

ment). In other words not all new investment is financed by foreign savings. As an examination of Table 5.5 will show re-invested earnings by American corporations form a significant part of new investments. The actual proportion varies from year to year, and may be influenced by regulations relating to remittance of profits, tax laws, opportunities for investment, etc. Capital expenditure, of course, can also be financed from locally-raised funds. In fact it is often contended that in order to escape exchange risks and the high costs that may be associated with external finance, TNCs tend to resort to domestic resources to underwrite local operations wherever this is possible. Their reputation, name and size of assets may serve to give them easy access to local credit in preference to domestic borrowers, particularly in situations where the lending institutions themselves may be based in the home country of the TNC.

Table 5.5 *The finance of annual direct investment*[1] *in Latin America*[2] *by US incorporated affiliates, 1951–81*

(Percentages)

Year	*Equity and Inter-company*	*Re-invested Earnings*	*Valuation and Other Adjustments*	*Total*
1951	50.3	56.4	−6.7	100.0
52	57.0	46.9	−3.9	100.0
53	54.6	54.2	−8.8	100.0
54	34.2	81.9	−16.1	100.0
55	54.0	60.1	−14.1	100.0
56	72.0	22.3	+5.7	100.0
57	161.8	43.7	−105.5	100.0
58	78.9	45.8	−24.7	100.0
59	63.6	54.1	−17.7	100.0
60	a	a	a	a
61	25.1	31.9	+43.0	100.0
62	10.2	108.4	−18.6	100.0
63	56.4	43.6	0.0	100.0
64	36.0	79.6	−15.6	100.0
65	61.4	54.8	−16.2	100.0
66	a	a	a	a
67	57.8	37.5	+4.7	100.0
68	67.3	34.3	−1.6	100.0
69	55.2	47.5	−2.7	100.0
70	62.7	49.1	−11.8	100.0
71	66.1	35.4	−1.5	100.0
72	30.8	73.0	−3.8	100.0
73	47.7	62.4	−10.1	100.0
74	73.7	36.4	−10.1	100.0
75	47.1	61.4	−8.5	100.0
76	24.8	74.9	+0.3	100.0
77	58.0	37.9	+4.1	100.0
78	48.4	46.0	−5.6	100.0
79	34.8	62.0	−3.2	100.0
80	−30.8	164.3	−33.5	100.0
81	a	a	a	a

1 year-end to year-end change in current book values.
2 includes 'Other Developing Western Hemisphere'.
a there was a decline (or little or no change) in book value in the year.

Source: US Department of Commerce, *Survey of Current Business*, various issues.

There is a widely-held view which argues that foreign capital inflows may help ease balance of payments problems in the short term, but they lay the foundation for reverse flows in the form of interest and dividends in the future. To offset these outflows, countries may find themselves in certain circumstances having to attract more and more foreign capital, a policy which increases the foreign presence in the economy. Streeten, for example, argues that 'since foreign investment must grow at a rate above the rate of return on foreign investment if profit remittances are not to exceed new capital inflows, and since the rate of return on the existing foreign capital stock is almost certainly greater than the rate of growth of the host country, the host country faces a choice of between on the one hand, slow rate of growth of foreign investment - and consequent balance of payments problems; and on the other, a more rapid rate of growth of foreign investment - and increasing alienation of the country's stock to foreigners.'[11] Some writers see direct private investment as a relatively expensive way to acquire foreign capital. 'There is little doubt that the rate of profit of TNCs is significantly higher than the long-term rate of interest in international capital markets and that TNCs are more profitable than other firms.'[12] They conclude that 'host economies do not gain much financial benefit from foreign direct investment and would be seen to gain even less if hidden remittances in the form of transfer pricing were fully known.'[13]

There are some observers on the other hand who think this is a highly simplistic view of the situation. Even the UN study cited earlier cautioned that 'comparison of particular items in the balance of payments are of limited significance. . . . The basic questions are how a given amount and composition of foreign investments affect the country's output and international payments position.'[14] Frank argues that the outflows of profits and the inflows of private foreign capital in a particular period are logically unrelated.[15] The 'outflow of profits in a given year is related to investments in prior years, not to the inflow of capital in the same year. Furthermore, as a statement of the balance of payments effects of foreign direct investment, it is grossly misleading to look at only one item of receipts (capital inflows) and compare it with one item of payments (profit remittances). It is necessary to look instead at the impact of foreign investment on all items in a country's balance of payments, including the effect on the volume of imports and exports.'[16] Reuber and others also take the view that some of the arguments which seek to assess the costs and benefits of foreign investment solely in terms of profit remittances and capital inflows rest on 'special and highly implausible assumptions'.[17] The 'economic gains of foreign investment for the host country abstracting from distributive effects are measured in terms of the value added to production less the opportunity cost of local factors used in production and the after-tax profits and dividends paid to the foreign investor, plus or minus any external effects. To suggest that such gains cannot be reconciled with a viable balance of payments position implies that price and income elasticity coefficients approach zero, or price (including foreign exchange rates) and income adjustments are precluded, or both.'[18]

Certainly foreign investment in the resource industries has had a favourable effect on the export sector of many developing countries which have had neither the finance nor the technology to exploit and develop their natural resources. There has also been some impact on employment and tax revenues. Generally, however, the contribution to national development has been of a limited nature. Raw materials have been exported largely in a raw and semi-refined form for processing abroad where the multiplier effects in terms of the generation of income and employment are felt. The resource industries in developing countries have evolved essentially as 'enclave' sectors integrated to operations abroad within the vertical organisation of transnational corporations, and have little production linkages with the rest of the local economy. Since attaining independence many developing countries have sought to revise old agreements made between the colonial powers and foreign companies which virtually gave away their resources, but the practice of transfer pricing used by transnationals still acts as a serious constraint on the formulation of more equitable tax arrangements. The highly capital intensive nature of the technology employed has made an insignificant impact on the employment problem in host countries which are basically labour – surplus economies. The manufacturing sector's contribution to exports, employment and tax revenue, as we discussed earlier, has been extremely limited. In fact given the high import orientation of manufacturing activities, the existence of this sector in many countries tends to depend on the foreign exchange earnings of traditional sectors of the economy.

In the light of the foregoing, it is not surprising that the relationship between outflows relating to the servicing of past investment and foreign capital inflows tend to attract such attention. As we saw earlier, with few exceptions deficits in the current account of the balance of payments tend to be the norm for Latin American/Caribbean countries. Foreign capital inflows may have helped in financing the current account deficit; but they also may have diverted attention away from some of the fundamental issues reflected in the trends in the current account, and the need for policies which could have imparted a more dynamic element to the domestic economy, and particularly to the export sector.

Besides the media we have discussed for the outflow of funds from the domestic economy, the export of capital can take more subtle forms. Economic theory assumes that transactions between firms are done at arms length. The evidence, however, indicates that a high proportion of the international flows in the markets for goods and services (including those of capital, management and technology) takes place within firms.[19] It is estimated that in the period between 1966 and 1975 about 37% (on average) of US imports from Latin America originated in majority-owned affiliated companies.[20] Transnational corporations dominate such key sectors of the economy as engineering products, machines and accessories, rubber products, chemicals and pharmaceuticals.[21] In 1972 imports from the United States, Germany and Japan by branches of transnational corporations of those countries operating in Mexico represented 74%, 81% and 94% respectively of the total imports of such branches.[22] Imports of raw materials by US branches in Brazil and Mexico from their own parent firms in 1972 amounted on average to 58% of the total of such imports in the first case and about 50% in the second.[23] Such arrangements, of course, offer considerable scope for overcharging of foreign inputs of goods and services. The transfer prices used may bear no relationship to market prices, but instead may reflect the interests of transnationals in the context of their world wide operations. According to an UNCTAD study transfer pricing may be established within a transnational corporation in order 'to reduce to the minimum payments in respect of dividends and taxes to local shareholders and authorities; to take maximum advantage of State subsidies and bonuses; to evade national controls on the repatriation of profits; to permit foreign exchange protection or speculation or accumulate cash balances in given countries; or to use such prices as a marketing policy instrument in order to eliminate local competition.'[24] In a study of the Colombian pharmaceutical industry it was found that of the total remittances abroad by branches of transnational corporations 'declared profits' represented 3.4%, royalties in respect of technical assistance 14%, and over-invoicing 82.5%.[25]

A glance back at Table 5.3 will give some indication of the extent of payments made by United States affiliates in Latin America for use of patents, management services, etc. in recent years. Between 1960 and 1981 over $96 billion was paid out for such services. This figure excludes fees and royalties paid out by unaffiliated firms. Between 1968 and 1981, such payments by the latter amounted to almost one billion dollars. In a number of cases governments have entered into contracts with foreign firms to run nationalized companies or to supply certain needed skills and know-how. Payments under such arrangements tend to be guaranteed and are free from the kinds of risk normally associated with equity investments. The point is even though an enterprise may be nationalised, certain kinds of foreign payments may continue to be a feature of its operation. Effective control as distinct from *de jure* control may still be in foreign hands.

Rate of return on investment

Earnings on total US direct investments in Latin America ranged from 11.2% of book value in 1945 to 21.0% in 1948 and 20.5% in 1951. This represented a significant increase over the estimated 6% in 1929.[26] One explanation for the higher returns in the early post-war years was the higher proportion of investment in mineral extraction and manufacturing. The rate of return tends to vary widely from sector to sector. The

Table 5.6 *Rate of return[1] on US foreign direct investment by areas and sectors, 1977–81*

	All areas				*Developed Countries*				*Latin America*			
Years	*All Sectors*	*Petroleum*	*Manuf.*	*Other*	*All Sectors*	*Petroleum*	*Manuf.*	*Other*	*All Sectors*	*Petroleum*	*Manuf.*	*Other*
1977	14.0	18.8	11.7	14.0	11.4	8.8	11.8	12.9	15.3	19.4	11.4	17.2
78	16.1	18.1	15.4	15.9	14.3	9.9	15.6	15.6	16.1	14.7	14.5	17.4
79	21.9	38.7	17.6	18.0	19.2	25.1	18.4	16.5	19.6	39.6	12.7	20.2
80	18.4	30.4	13.1	17.4	16.5	26.5	12.4	15.7	18.8	23.0	15.8	20.0
81	14.4	26.4	9.0	13.0	11.5	19.8	8.2	10.6	15.0	23.8	11.2	15.9

1 income divided by the average of the beginning and end-of-year direct investment positions.

Source: US Department of Commerce, *Survey of Current Business*, various issues.

highest yields are to be found in the petroleum industry where the average return was 31.1% during the period 1948–51, as compared to 28.1% for distribution, and 1.9% for public utilities.[27] The trend has continued into recent years where petroleum is still the most lucrative sector. In the five year period 1977–81, the rate of return in the latter averaged about 24% as compared to 13% for manufacturing and 18% for other sectors.

In making charges of exploitation against US investors, observers often draw attention to the fact that the rate of return on their investments in Latin America generally tends to be of a larger magnitude than that on investments made at home or in other developed countries. This often tends to be the case not only in the high yielding petroleum industry, but in other sectors as well, as can be seen in Table 5.6. For instance, in 1981, the rate of return on manufacturing investments in the developed countries was 8.2% as compared to 11.4% in Latin America. The main argument often advanced to justify this situation is that the risks in developing countries tend to be higher, and investors need to recover their investments as quickly as possible. This, however, does not explain the situation where high rates of return persist in cases where capital investment has evidently long been recovered.

The question of denationalisation

Foreign enterprises sometimes penetrate local economies not by setting-up new plants but by acquiring (in part or in whole) existing ones which may be either locally or foreign-owned. Thus, not all foreign investments represent the initiation or introduction of new producing facilities. In some cases, however, the acquisition may be accompanied by the introduction of new products or changes in design, engineering, etc. One author estimates that as much as a third of foreign subsidiaries in developing countries have been established through the acquisition of an on-going business.[28] A glance at Table 5.7 will show that the percentage of new US manufacturing affiliates established by acquisition in Mexico and Brazil has been growing over the years. Between 1946 and 1973 the total percentage for Brazil was 33% while that for Mexico was even higher – 43%.

A situation where one resident foreign-owned firm is sold to another foreign-owned firm is quite different from one where a locally-owned firm is sold to a foreign enterprise. The latter situation represents a displacement of local enterprise and an increasing foreign control of the local economy. This process of denationalisation (which implies increasing loss of control of national decision-making) could be taking place while the economy is experiencing relatively high rates of growth. The explanation often advanced for increasing denationalisation is that

Table 5.7 *Acquisition as a mode of entry into Brazil and Mexico: percentage of new US manufacturing affiliates established by acquisition*

	Brazil		*Mexico*	
Date of Formation	*% of New Affiliates Established by Acquisition*	*Total No. of Newly Established Affiliates*	*% of New Affiliates Established by Acquisition*	*Total No. of Newly Established Affiliates*
Prior to 1945	0	28	9	35
1946–50	9	11	6	18
1951–55	22	22	11	18
1956–60	33	36	39	54
1961–65	38	16	43	60
1966–70	52	46	64	77
1971–73*	61	18	75	32
Total, all periods	*33*	*177*	*43*	*294*

* The terminal data for Mexico is 1972.

Source: P. Evans and G. Gereffi, 'Foreign Investment and Dependent Development: Comparing Brazil and Mexico' in S.A. Hewlett and R.S. Winert, *Brazil and Mexico: Patterns of Late Development*; Philadelphia, 1982. Original Source: R.S. New farmer and W. Mueller, *Multinational Corporations in Brazil and Mexico: Structural Sources of Economic and Non-Economic Power*, a Report to the Sub-Committee on Multinational Corporations Committee on Foreign Relations, US Senate, Washington, DC, 1975.

the small local firms with their limited resources are unable to compete with the large foreign firm with greater access to credit, technology and markets. Not only do monopoly positions tend to grow out of such a situation with all the implications this has for prices and resource allocation, but the objective of developing local entrepreneurial talent recedes further into the background. Very often, foreign participation in local enterprises is motivated by the need for the knowledge and skills of the local firm or enterprise rather than the desire to share know-how, techniques and other assets with local entrepreneurs.

The transfer of technology

Contrary to the assumption of classical and neo-classical theory which states that technology is constant, or if changing is equally available to all countries, in the real world technology is far from static and is certainly not equally available to all members of the world economy. In practice technological development takes place largely within the big transnational corporations whose power often rests on the control of certain modern production processes. Since access to a particular process developed by one company could affect its position *vis-à-vis* competitors, a large part of modern technology is available only in package form (i.e. technology, capital, management, etc.) on terms and conditions dictated by the owner(s). In other words, it is often difficult to have one component without the others. In this situation many countries which may wish to pursue a policy of tighter control over ownership of the domestic capital stock often find themselves giving free rein to transnationals in order to secure certain types of technology in order to give themselves an edge over other countries. The need for technology thus plays a crucial factor in the dependency relationship between transnationals and host countries.

Of course, there is a growing body of technology which could be bought (and adapted to local conditions) on the open market, mainly in the form of capital goods. Processes, of course, can also be rented, as can managerial skills. Because of this, some writers[29] have argued that there is no need for direct foreign investment in package form which allows investors to reap large profits. Against this it may be argued that the most modern technology (if this is what is desired) may not be available in separate components since this may put its owner(s) at a disadvantage *vis-à-vis* competitors.

In most developing countries the process of adaptation has generally made little headway, and the reason may well lie in the scant attention paid to Research and Development (R & D). Governments and local firms devote very little of their resources to research or training programmes which would assist in transforming imported technology into something more relevant to local conditions. Local businessmen often find it easier simply to act as conduits rather than exercise any initiative in securing relevant techniques which could make better use of local resources and reduce the costs (direct and indirect) to the domestic economy.

The charge often levelled against transnationals that the processes they transfer to developing countries do little to help the unemployment situation reflects a considerable amount of naïveté. The companies tend to use technology that their own situations dictate and may only embark on adaptation if local regulations so require and the desire to enter the local economy far outweighs the costs and inconvenience of technological adaptation. The fact of the matter is that not only has national policies in many instances contributed little towards a greater appreciation of science and technology in development, but the tendency by developing states to negotiate individually with transnationals may not have allowed them to obtain the best possible arrangements from the point of view of local conditions. In the absence of an international code of behaviour, a more fruitful approach (particularly for countries in the same area or region) may require the observance of certain common guidelines and the exchange of information with a view to preventing manipulation of an exploitative nature.

Nationalisation

In recent years the governments of many developing countries have sought to bring under local control key sectors of the economy, which for a long number of years were in foreign hands. This policy has often been termed the regaining of the 'national patrimony'. The process of localisation has operated at two main levels. At one level foreign enterprises in certain sectors have been urged (or required) to form local companies and dispose of a certain minimum proportion of their stock to citizens of the country concerned. A minimum stipulation of 51% is quite common. It should be pointed out, however, that, while the aim here may be that control should pass into local hands, this may not in fact take place since control can be exercised in a variety of ways. At the other level, government itself may decide to take over (nationalise) certain industries which are thought to have significant importance for national development. These have been in the areas of public utilities, large agricultural holdings and the extractive industries where the investments are large. The term 'nationalisation' is used where the process of take-over is based on negotiations with reference to the terms of ownership transfer. On the other hand, the term 'expropriation' (which is a form of nationalisation) is used to describe a situation where the take-over (seizure) is done without prompt and adequate compensation.

There are few concerns which affect relations between the United States and Latin America as much as the issue of nationalisation. While take-overs have become more widespread in recent years, the seizure of American assets in the region pre-dates the Second World War. In fact one may even go further back to the Mexican Revolution of 1910–20, in which one of the main concerns was the increasing control by foreigners over the land and other resources of the country. Table 5.8 gives some examples of take-overs since the 1930s. There are several others one can add to this list. For example, Cuba under Fidel Castro expropriated US assets totalling some $1,809 million in 1960. In the 1970s the Guyanese Government of Forbes Burnham nationalised the assets of the two foreign bauxite companies operating in that country: the Demerara Bauxite Company (a subsidiary of the Canadian based Alcan) in 1971, and the US based Reynolds Metal Company in 1975. Under Salvador Allende, Chile was less selective, and in 1971 nationalised a number of foreign concerns with total assets estimated to be between $747 million and $833 million. Of the total, the assets of the US copper mining companies amounted to between $537 million and $623 million including notes repudiated by the Marxist coalition government.[30] In 1976 Venezuela (under Carlos Andres Perez) also nationalised its iron and oil industries.[31]

There is no set pattern or framework into which one can cast the process of nationalisation in the region. The motivating factors have been

Table 5.8 *Delayed, negotiated settlements on US properties in Latin America* (as of March 1974)*

Country		*Year of Takeover*	*Year Settled*
Mexico	Plantations and Ranches	1936	1941
	Sinclair Oil Group	1938	1940
	Standard Oil Co. (NJ)	1938	1942
	Other oil companies	1938	1942
Brazil	American and Foreign Power Co.	1959	1964
	International Tel. and Tel. (ITT)	1962	1967
Argentina	Standard Oil Co. (NJ)	1963	1967
	10 other oil companies	1963	1967
Bolivia	Gulf Oil Co.	1969	1971
	Mina Matilda Corp. (US Steel and Phillip Brothers)	1971	1972
Peru	W.R. Grace and Co. (sugar plantation)	1969	1974
	W.R. Grace and Co. (industries)	1974	1974
	Cerro de Pasco (agricultural estates)	1969	1974
	Cerro de Pasco (mines and smelters)	1974	1974
	9 other companies	1974	1974

* This table does not include settlements with Chile.

Source: E.N. Baklanoff, *Expropriation of US Investments in Cuba, Mexico and Chile* (New York: Praeger Publishers, 1975). Original source: US State Department, *Nationalisation, Expropriations, and Other Takings of United States and Certain Foreign Property since 1969*, Bureau of Intelligence and Research, (30 November 1971): Chs. 3, 6, and Appendix A.

diverse and complex. Take-overs have been carried out by regimes on the right and the left responding to both internal imperatives and external factors. With the exception of Cuba (and to a lesser extent Chile under Allende) where all foreign property was nationalised in 1960, the nationalisations have tended to be of a selective nature. Public utilities and resource industries have been high on the list and this in itself may tell a story. From the second half of the 19th century there has been a tendency for many governments in the region to assume an increasing responsibility for guiding national development. At first, intervention took the form largely of enacting laws and regulations designed to influence economic behaviour. In more recent years state ownership of key sectors (which are seen to have a critical influence on the rate of development of other activities and on the economy as a whole) has come to be seen as an almost indispensable pre-requisite to further national development. Mixed economies are now the rule rather than the exception among developing countries, and it is important to understand the factors at play here in the context of international economic relations and policies.

As indicated earlier, the textbook models of international trade function at a plane far removed from conditions obtaining in the real world. The economic and political environment prevailing in the post-war period is far different from that of earlier years. The assumptions of trade theory in fact may never have had any counterparts (in a strict sense) in the real world. The idealism reflected in many theories, however, seems able to exert an influence on policy-making even when the politico-economic structural framework on which they were presumably based no longer obtains. There may be a lot in the saying that all policies have their origin in some defunct theory or economist. The United States frowns upon state ownership and the use of regulations which have the effect of interfering with the free movement of goods and services among countries. Institutions like the World Bank and the IMF take a similar position. Implicit here is an economic ideology with political connotations. Not only is private enterprise associated with efficiency (and the state with inefficiency), and the better allocation of resources at the domestic level, but state encroachment is seen to interfere with the political rights and freedom of individuals of the society. This position ignores completely the history of these countries and the social and economic structures which have emerged as a result of past policies and relationships. In a situation of unfettered competition the high concentration of wealth and power in the hands of small groups in the society tends to lead to further dispossession of the masses and a general worsening of their economic conditions. This has happened even in cases where there has been some minimal state intervention and ownership. The problem one suspects is the tendency in recent years to attribute to ideology the inefficiency associated with bureaucratic mismanagement and corruption which may be related to far broader issues of a more political nature. With respect to pressures to keep trade restrictions to a minimum, the argument is that this would facilitate the optimal allocation of resources at the global level, thus leading to the maximisation of world income. Again here, nothing is said about the distribution of these benefits. Even in the developed countries powerful interest groups are at work to protect employment, wage levels, etc. which would be threatened by a policy of free competition. Clearly the developing countries do not enjoy the same freedom for action as the developed countries do. This can also be seen to some extent in the developed market economies of Western Europe where state intrusion into the private sector is not interpreted in the same way as in the developing countries, where it is seen as part of an East-West ideological struggle for the very soul of these countries.

In assessing the factors which give rise to nationalisation, the need to have crucial sectors of the economy under local control would rank very high. While there may be a psychological element involved in this basic factor, other concerns may be no less important in the decision. For instance, there might be a genuine feeling that a particular foreign enterprise far from assisting in the attainment of national economic objectives might be working against them. In relation to the basic factor it is often possible to discern what might be termed more immediate motives or influences related to ideology or nationalism and the prevailing political or economic situation. For example, a regime may embrace an ideology or philosophy which simply finds foreign ownership of any part of the economy an intolerable situation. Nationalisation of a 'conspicuous' or obviously powerful enterprise could also be prompted by the prevailing political climate in which a government may find it necessary to have an 'external enemy'. 'A well-documented theory in international relations is that a government in trouble may attempt to unify the country behind it through use, even creation, of an external threat. The expropriation of a foreign corporation can attest to the patriotism of the government or can divert public attention from other difficulties facing the country.'[32] The prevailing economic situation may also be a precipitating force. 'The expropriation may be brought about because the government seeks to divert public attention from the economic problems through a scapegoat or because government control of a particular foreign corporation or industrial area is seen as a cure for the country's economic ills.'[33] With respect to US property, some observers cite the state of relations between the United States and the host government as a factor which may influence national attitudes towards the takeover of American property.[34] A regime which perceives itself to be pressured by the US or places little importance on existing economic ties or aid flows is more likely to develop a hostile posture towards US interests than one which places a high premium on US assistance, trade ties or military support.

Recent nationalisations in the region have no doubt been assisted by changes in the international environment, and in some instances by developments in the internal economic and political situation of some countries. The formation or strengthening of producer organisations, and the resultant transformation in bargaining strength in some cases, has reduced the willingness to tolerate historically unacceptable arrangements with foreign companies. The increasing availability of certain components of direct investment (e.g. management and technical skills) on the open market and the growing body of trained nationals now tend to encourage governments to get involved in areas which hitherto they perceived to be outside their area of competence. Increasing self-assertiveness in the context of a growing body of independent nations often lending support to each other, and an enhanced domestic position in some cases may also have contributed to a climate of nationalisation.

As indicated earlier, the take-over of US assets in the region is not a new phenomenon. The nationalisation process, however, continues to be a very complex and often emotional one. There are no fixed or universally acceptable rules to be followed. Every take-over is in a sense a new experience since the context and environment change rapidly.

Most Latin American nations for their part practise the Calvo doctrine,[35] i.e. they take the view that foreign investors should be treated no differently from local investors. Thus, they tend not to recognise any right of appeal to foreign courts. This may be one reason why they have not generally acceded to membership of the International Centre for the Settlement of Investment Disputes (ICSID.) (See Annex 5.1 for list of members.) The United States for its part insists on its right to look after the interests of its companies abroad. In cases of nationalisation, it takes the position that all nations should observe the principle of 'prompt, adequate and effective' compensation.

While the right to nationalise foreign property is now widely accepted as a sovereign right[36] this latter condition has resulted in a great deal of friction between the United States and Latin American countries. Given the financial position of many of the nationalising countries, the requirement of 'prompt' payment is not one they are easily able to satisfy. What constitutes 'adequate and effective' compensation often tends to give rise to even further controversy. While foreign investors may insist on 'book' or 'market value', the nationalising government may insist that compensation takes into account the huge profits reaped over the years, which may have amounted to several times the original investment. It is this latter consideration that often leads to expropriation, i.e. nationalisation without adequate compensation.[37]

Many of the countries in the region that have nationalised foreign assets in certain industries are not necessarily opposed to foreign investment which they feel should only be channelled into specified areas and under specified terms. For this reason, and in order not to attract retaliation from the US, they generally make every effort to reach accommodation with the owners of the nationalised assets. It is worth pointing out here that very often host governments do not seek to take over an entire industry. Recognising the difficulties arising from marketing, technology transfer, refurbishing of equipment, management, etc. some governments have only sought enough equity to give them control of the enterprise, or at least substantial participation in what is perceived to be a key industry.[38] There are instances where such overtures have been met with near contemptuous reaction thus forcing the host government to nationalise the entire enterprise or industry.

Despite the nationalisations which have taken place in the region, and despite the criticism in the US from some quarters that companies which invest abroad are exporting jobs and income, US firms have continued to expand their activities abroad in search of markets and raw materials. Such activities are often important to US domestic economic well-being and even its national security which may depend on access to certain raw materials abroad. One measure which the US government has instituted in order to deter nationalisation of US assets is the so-called Hickenlooper Amendment which allows it to retaliate by imposing economic sanctions or cutting off aid. This may not be possible in cases where the country concerned may have great strategic or military importance to the US, and therefore the US government has tended to use other means and avenues to protect its investors. Besides the protection afforded its corporations through normal diplomatic espousal (and in some cases by treaties of friendships, commerce and navigation (FCN) that commit the respective governments to assure reciprocal treatment of each other's investments and to provide fair compensation in the event of nationalisation),[39] the US also operates the Overseas Private Investment Corporation (OPIC) which basically provides insurance against certain types of political risks, which is not normally available in private insurance markets. Another agency which has assumed prominence in the context of international investment activities is the International Centre for the Settlement of Investment Disputes (ICSID) which was set up in 1965 for the international arbitration of investment disputes. It functions as an autonomous agency of the World Bank group and is intended to be of assistance to both investors and host countries as a neutral arbiter. 'The arbitration process of ICSID is standard. Each party selects an arbitrator from panels of prominent economists, jurists and bankers of many countries maintained by ICSID. The two selectees agree upon a third, who acts as president of a tribunal that hears arguments from both parties and renders a decision binding upon both.'[40] Failure to abide by an ICSID decision could attract retaliation from the World Bank.

Some countries in the region like Jamaica, Barbados, Trinidad and Tobago and Guyana have chosen to become members of ICSID. The intention no doubt is that this decision would provide an incentive to foreign investors, who so to speak, could make appeal to a higher neutral court. It would appear that for ICSID to intervene both parties would have to agree to arbitration. The Latin American countries tend to see membership of ICSID, as we said earlier, as a threat to their sovereignty and have refrained from joining, thus making the institution one of limited relevance in the region.

Annex 5.1
List of contracting states and signatories of the Convention (as of June 30, 1982)

The 88 States listed below have signed the Convention on the dates indicated. The names of the 81 States that have deposited instruments of ratification are capitalised, and the dates of such deposit and of the attainment of the status of Contracting State by the entry into force of the Convention for each of them are also indicated.[1]

State	Signature	Deposit of Ratification	Entry into Force of Convention
AFGHANISTAN	Sep 30, 1966	Jun 25, 1968	Jul 25, 1968
Australia	Mar 24, 1974		
AUSTRIA	May 17, 1966	May 25, 1971	Jun 24, 1971
BANGLADESH	Nov 20, 1979	Mar 27, 1980	Apr 26, 1980
Barbados	May 13, 1981		
BELGIUM	Dec 15, 1965	Aug 27, 1970	Sep 26, 1970
BENIN, PEOPLE'S REPUBLIC OF	Sep 10, 1965	Sep 6, 1966	Oct 14, 1966
BOTSWANA	Jan 15, 1970	Jan 15, 1970	Feb 14, 1970
BURKINA FASO	Sep 16, 1965	Aug 29, 1966	Oct 14, 1966
BURUNDI	Feb 17, 1967	Nov 5, 1969	Dec 5, 1969
CAMEROON	Sep 23, 1965	Jan 3, 1967	Feb 2, 1967
CENTRAL AFRICAN REPUBLIC	Aug 26, 1965	Feb 23, 1966	Oct 14, 1966
CHAD	May 12, 1966	Aug 29, 1966	Oct 14, 1966
COMOROS	Sep 26, 1978	Nov 7, 1978	Dec 7, 1978
CONGO, PEOPLE'S REPUBLIC OF THE	Dec 27, 1965	Jun 23, 1966	Oct 14, 1966
Costa Rica	Sep 29, 1981		
CYPRUS	Mar 9, 1966	Nov 25, 1966	Dec 25, 1966
DENMARK	Oct 11, 1965	Apr 24, 1968	May 24, 1968[2]
EGYPT, ARAB REPUBLIC OF	Feb 11, 1972	May 3, 1972	Jun 2, 1972
El Salvador	Jun 9, 1982		
Ethiopia	Sep 21, 1965		
FIJI	Jul 1, 1977	Aug 11, 1977	Sep 10, 1977
FINLAND	Jul 14, 1967	Jan 9, 1969	Feb 8, 1969
FRANCE	Dec 22, 1965	Aug 21, 1967	Sep 20, 1967
GABON	Sep 21, 1965	Apr 4, 1966	Oct 14, 1966
GAMBIA, THE	Oct 1, 1974	Dec 27, 1974	Jan 26, 1975
GERMANY, FEDERAL REPUBLIC OF	Jan 27, 1966	Apr 18, 1969	May 18, 1969[3]
GHANA	Nov 26, 1965	Jul 13, 1966	Oct 14, 1966
GREECE	Mar 16, 1966	Apr 21, 1969	May 21, 1969
GUINEA	Aug 27, 1968	Nov 4, 1968	Dec 4, 1968
GUYANA	Jul 3, 1969	Jul 11, 1969	Aug 10, 1969
ICELAND	Jul 25, 1966	Jul 25, 1966	Oct 14, 1966
INDONESIA	Feb 16, 1968	Sep 28, 1968	Oct 28, 1968
IRELAND	Aug 30, 1966	Apr 7, 1981	May 7, 1981
Israel	Jun 16, 1980		
ITALY	Nov 18, 1965	Mar 29, 1971	Apr 28, 1971
IVORY COAST	Jun 30, 1965	Feb 16, 1966	Oct 14, 1966
JAMAICA	Jun 23, 1965	Sep 9, 1966	Oct 14, 1966
JAPAN	Sep 23, 1965	Aug 17, 1967	Sep 16, 1967
JORDAN	Jul 14, 1972	Oct 30, 1972	Nov 29, 1972
KENYA	May 24, 1966	Jan 3, 1967	Feb 2, 1967
KOREA, REPUBLIC OF	Apr 18, 1966	Feb 21, 1967	Mar 23, 1967
KUWAIT	Feb 9, 1978	Feb 2, 1979	Mar 4, 1979
LESOTHO	Sep 19, 1968	Jul 8, 1969	Aug 7, 1969
LIBERIA	Sep 3, 1965	Jun 16, 1970	Jul 16, 1970
LUXEMBOURG	Sep 28, 1965	Jul 30, 1970	Aug 29, 1970
MADAGASCAR	Jun 1, 1966	Sep 6, 1966	Oct 14, 1966
MALAWI	Jun 9, 1966	Aug 23, 1966	Oct 14, 1966
MALAYSIA	Oct 22, 1965	Aug 8, 1966	Oct 14, 1966

Annex 5.1—*(Cont'd)*

State	*Signature*	*Deposit of Ratification*	*Entry into Force of Convention*
MALI	Apr 9, 1976	Jan 3, 1978	Feb 2, 1978
MAURITANIA	Jul 30, 1965	Jan 11, 1966	Oct 14, 1966
MAURITIUS	Jun 2, 1969	Jun 2, 1969	Jul 2, 1969[4]
MOROCCO	Oct 11, 1965	May 11, 1967	Jun 10, 1967
NEPAL	Sep 28, 1965	Jan 7, 1969	Feb 6, 1969
NETHERLANDS	May 25, 1966	Sep 14, 1966	Oct 14, 1966[5]
NEW ZEALAND	Sep 2, 1970	Apr 2, 1980	May 2, 1980[6]
NIGER	Aug 23, 1965	Nov 14, 1966	Dec 14, 1966
NIGERIA	Jul 13, 1965	Aug 23, 1965	Oct 14, 1966
NORWAY	Jun 24, 1966	Aug 16, 1967	Sep 15, 1967
PAKISTAN	Jul 6, 1965	Sep 15, 1966	Oct 15, 1966
PAPUA NEW GUINEA	Oct 20, 1978	Oct 20, 1978	Nov 19, 1978
Paraguay	Jul 27, 1981		
PHILIPPINES	Sep 26, 1978	Nov 17, 1978	Oct 17, 1978
ROMANIA	Sep 6, 1974	Sep 12, 1975	Oct 12, 1975
RWANDA	Apr 21, 1978	Oct 15, 1979	Nov 14, 1979
SAUDI ARABIA	Sep 28, 1979	May 8, 1980	Jun 7, 1980
SENEGAL	Sep 26, 1966	Apr 21, 1967	May 21, 1967
SEYCHELLES	Feb 16, 1978	Mar 20, 1978	Apr 19, 1978
SIERRA LEONE	Sep 27, 1965	Aug 2, 1966	Oct 14, 1966
SINGAPORE	Feb 2, 1968	Oct 14, 1968	Nov 13, 1968
SOLOMON ISLANDS	Nov 12, 1979	Sep 8, 1981	Oct 8, 1981
SOMALIA	Sep 27, 1965	Feb 29, 1968	Mar 30, 1968
SRI LANKA	Aug 30, 1967	Oct 12, 1967	Nov 11, 1967
SUDAN	Mar 15, 1967	Apr 9, 1973	May 9, 1973
SWAZILAND	Nov 3, 1970	Jun 14, 1971	Jul 14, 1971[7]
SWEDEN	Sep 25, 1965	Dec 29, 1966	Jan 28, 1967
SWITZERLAND	Sep 22, 1967	May 15, 1968	Jun 14, 1968
TOGO	Jan 24, 1966	Aug 11, 1967	Sep 10, 1967
TRINIDAD AND TOBAGO	Oct 5, 1966	Jan 3, 1967	Feb 2, 1967
TUNISIA	May 5, 1965	Jun 22, 1966	Oct 14, 1966
UGANDA	Jun 7, 1966	Jun 7, 1966	Oct 14, 1966
UNITED ARAB EMIRATES	Dec 23, 1981	Dec 23, 1981	Jan 22, 1982
UNITED KINGDOM OF GREAT BRITAIN AND NORTHERN IRELAND	May 26, 1965	Dec 19, 1966	Jan 18, 1967[8]
UNITED STATES OF AMERICA	Aug 27, 1965	Jun 10, 1966	Oct 14, 1966
WESTERN SAMOA	Fab 3, 1978	Apr 25, 1978	May 25, 1978
YUGOSLAVIA	Mar 21, 1967	Mar 21, 1967	Apr 20, 1967
ZAIRE	Oct 29, 1968	Apr 29, 1970	May 29, 1970
ZAMBIA	Jun 17, 1970	Jun 17, 1970	Jul 17, 1970

1 The Convention was signed on behalf of the Republic of China on January 13, 1966, and ratified on December 10, 1968. At its Fourteenth Annual Meeting on October 2, 1980, the Administrative Council considered a communication received from the People's Republic of China, decided that the Republic of China be removed from the list of Contracting States and noted that, pending study by the Government of the People's Republic of the possibility of becoming a party to the Convention, China is not a Contracting State.

2 Denmark excluded, by a notification received on May 15, 1968, the Faroe Islands; by a notification received on October 30, 1968, Denmark extended the application of the Convention to the Faroe Islands as of January 1, 1969.
3 Germany declared, on depositing its instrument of ratification, that the Convention would also apply to the Land Berlin.
4 Until Mauritius attained its independence on March 12, 1968, it was covered by the ratification of the United Kingdom.
5 On depositing its instrument of ratification, the Netherlands restricted the application of the Convention to the Kingdom in Europe; by a notification received on May 22, 1970, the Netherlands withdrew that restriction and thus extended the application of the Convention to Suriname and the Netherlands Antilles; Suriname having attained independence on November 25, 1975, the Convention ceased to be applicable to Suriname as of that date.
6 On depositing its instrument of ratification, New Zealand, pursuant to Article 70 of the Convention, excluded from its coverage the Cook Islands, Niue and Tokelau.
7 Until Swaziland attained its independence on September 6, 1968, it was covered by the ratification of the United Kingdom.
8 The United Kingdom, pursuant to Article 70 of the Convention, excluded from its coverage the following territories for whose international relations it is responsible: Jersey, Isle of Man, Brunei, British Indian Ocean Territory, Pitcairn Islands, British Antarctic Territory, Sovereign Base Area of Cyprus, and New Hebrides. By a notification received on June 27, 1979, the United Kingdom extended the application of the Convention to Jersey as of July 1, 1979.

Notes

1 OECD, *Development Assistance*, (1970 Review), p. 30.
2 OECD, *Development Cooperation*, (1982 Review), p. 51.
3 See UN Department of Economic and Social Affairs, *Foreign Capital in Latin America*, in M. Bernstein, (ed.) *Foreign Investment in Latin America* (New York: Alfred A. Knopf, 1966), pp. 29–33.
4 See Grant L. Reuber *et al.*, *Private Foreign Investment in Development* (London: Oxford University Press, 1973), p. 4.
5 See I. Frank, *Foreign Enterprise in Developing Countries* (Baltimore: The Johns Hopkins University Press, 1980), p. 13.
6 G.L. Reuber *et al.* op. cit., p. 4.
7 UN *Multinational Corporation in World Development* (New York, 1973), p. 127.
8 UN *Foreign Capital in Latin America*, op. cit.
9 See Comments by H.W. Balgooyen, 'Problems of United States Investments in Latin America', in M.D. Bernstein, op. cit., p. 220.
10 UN *External Financing in Latin America*, op. cit.
11 Quoted in G.L. Reuber *et al.* op. cit., pp. 37–38.
12 Lall and Streeten, op. cit., p. 54.
13 Ibid.
14 Quoted by H.W. Balgooyen, op. cit.
15 I. Frank, *Foreign Enterprise in Developing Countries* (Baltimore: Johns Hopkins University Press, 1980), p. 30.
16 Ibid.
17 Reuber *et al.* op. cit., p. 38.
18 Ibid.

19 G.K. Helleiner, *Intra-firm Trade and the Developing Countries* (London: Macmillan Publishers Ltd, 1981), p. 3.
20 Ibid., p. 18.
21 See Marinho, op. cit., p. 14.
22 Ibid., p. 17.
23 Ibid.
24 UNCTAD, *Intra-firm Transactions and Their Impact on Trade and Development*, Geneva, Seminar Programme Deport Series, No. 2, May 1978. Quoted in Marinho, op. cit.
25 See Marinho, op. cit.
26 See UN study, *Foreign Capital in Latin America*, op. cit., quoted in Bernstein, op. cit., p. 59.
27 Ibid., p. 60.
28 R. Vernon, *Storm Over the Multinationals: The Real Issues* (Cambridge, Mass: Harvard University Press, 1977), p. 72.
29 See, for example, R. Ffrench-Davis, 'Foreign Investment in Latin America: Recent Trends and Prospects', in V.L. Urquidi and R. Thorp (eds.), *Latin America in the International Economy* (London: Macmillan Publishers Ltd, 1973).
30 See Eric Baklanoff, *Expropriation of US Investments in Cuba, Mexico and Chile* (New York: Praeger Publishers, 1975), p. 110.
31 For an interesting background analysis to this act, see J. Petras *et al.*, *The Nationalisation of Venezuela Oil* (New York: Praeger Publishers, 1977).
32 G.M. Ingram, *Expropriation of US Property in South America* (New York: Praeger Publishers, 1974), p. 2.
33 Ibid., p. 3.
34 Ibid., p. 3.
35 Named after the 19th century Argentine diplomat and publicist Carlos Calvo, this doctrine consists essentially of two fundamental principles: 'sovereign states have the right to freedom from any kind of interference by other states, and foreigners are not entitled to any rights and privileges that are not accorded to nationals and consequently may not seek redress of grievances except before the local authorities'. See H.K. Wright, *Foreign Enterprise in Mexico, Laws and Policies* (Chapel Hill: The University of North Carolina Press, 1971), p. 99.
36 In international law this is conditional on the following: (a) There is no discrimination; (b) There is a public purpose; and (c) There is fair compensation (unless there is a 'confiscation' in connection with penal action under criminal law). See I. Delupis, *Finance and Protection of Investments in Developing Countries* (New York: John Wiley & Sons 1973), pp. 67–68.
37 For example the Chilean approach under Salvador Allende was influenced by this view.
38 As one example of this one can cite the Guyanese case when Alcan was first approached.
39 See M.T. Mays, 'The Protection of Overseas Investment', in P.M. Boarman and H. Schollhammer, *Multinational Corporations and Governments* (New York: Praeger Publishers, 1975), p. 61.
40 W.H. Jacoby, 'Multinational Corporations and National Sovereignty', in ibid., p. 11.

6

Foreign Investment Policy and Experience: Selected Cases

The dependence on foreign capital (whether based on actual need or perception) varies widely from country to country in the region. This is perhaps the major explanation for the differences in approach and policy adopted by various states. As we saw earlier, private capital, which accounts for a large part of total inflows, gives rise to certain issues which are not associated with official assistance. While it is widely recognised that the benefits to recipient states from private investment could be increased if there were to be greater co-ordination in the treatment of foreign capital, with the exception of the Andean Group of countries there has been little effort in this direction elsewhere in the region. In this chapter we propose to look at the policies and experience with respect to direct foreign investment of certain countries and group of countries in the region. The selection is aimed at highlighting some of the different approaches taken and the consequences flowing from the policies pursued.

Capital inflows into Latin America prior to the First World War were virtually free of government controls (including the absence of exchange restrictions) either on the part of capital-exporting countries or the capital-importing countries. The legal framework operated by Latin American countries was generally simple and non-discriminating. Sometimes special assurances were given to investors in the form of a guaranteed yield on capital invested in railways and public utilities.[1] Taxes and royalties were kept at fairly low levels. These policies were generally continued after the War until the depression of the 1930s when the governments of both the creditor countries and of the borrowing countries found themselves having to institute a number of measures to deal with the problems created by the crisis. These measures included trade and payments agreements, the introduction of exchange control regulations, the licensing of imports and restrictions on the entry of foreign nationals for gainful employment. Several countries introduced 'saturation laws' whose aim was to limit the expansion of investment in specified industries. Brazil and Mexico adopted legislation prohibiting foreign investment in certain sectors of the economy. Our aim in this chapter is not to go into details of specific regulations but rather to explore the general policy framework and experience in order to bring out some of the salient differences in approach.

Brazil

As we saw earlier, Brazil alone (with an area of over three million square miles and an estimated population of around 120 million in 1980) accounts for almost half the land area of South America and a similar proportion of its population. Its physical size is almost as large as that of the United States (1980 population, 230 million), 22 times that of Japan (1980 pop. 120 million) 34 times that of West Germany (1980 pop. 60 million), 35 times that of the United Kingdom (1980 pop. 56 million) and 16 times that of France (1980 pop. 55 million). Besides the factor of size and population, the country is well endowed with agricultural and mineral resources and has one of the world's largest potential for hydro-electric power.

Despite all this, Brazil's industrial development is of a relatively recent origin. For most of its history the economy of Brazil has rested critically on the export of a narrow range of primary products with certain key staples holding a dominant position at various points in time. Before the rise of coffee in the 19th century, Brazil wood, sugar and rubber (among others) played a lead role at some stage in the country's history. In late 1920s coffee accounted for about 70% of the value of exports, while cotton, cocoa and sugar accounted for another 6%.[2] By 1962 coffee still contributed about half of merchandise exports earnings, while cotton, cocoa and sugar contributed another 14%. In 1920 about 70% of the gainfully employed population were in the primary sector (agriculture, fishing, etc.) as compared to 14% in the secondary sector (minerals and manufacturing industries) and 17% in the tertiary sector. In 1940[3] 71% were still in the primary sector, 9% in the secondary sector and 20% in the tertiary. After the second World War secondary activities began to assume greater importance and available data indicate that by 1950 this sector provided employment for 13% of the gainfully occupied population as compared to 64% for the primary sector and 23% for the tertiary sector.

As a colony Brazil's role was confined to producing food and raw materials, earnings from which paid for the imported manufactured goods supplied by the European metropole, largely Britain and Portugal. Independence was achieved from Portugal in 1822, but by the end of the 19th century, Brazil was still a country 'dominated by a plantation society based on slave labour, producing agricultural staples and raw materials for export'.[4] From the 1850s there were some small spurts of industrialisation, but nothing on any significant scale to change the basic agricultural economy. These spurts became stronger in the early twentieth century partly as a result of protective measures, and partly as a result of factors affecting supplies or insufficient availability of foreign exchange to pay for imports. A number of new industries sprung up during the First World War, but these were largely of a consumer type. In 1920, textiles (including textile products and footwear) and food products (including beverages and tobacco) accounted for almost 70% of value added in the industrial sector. In the 1920s because of the poor quality and high prices associated with local products, and the absence of a well-articulated protective policy, these infant industries found themselves struggling to survive against lower priced superior imports, particularly from the United States. The onset of the depression in the 1930s, however, introduced conditions which served to give a further filip to the growth of the industrial sector. The drop in export earnings in the early years of the decade resulted in the introduction of a series of measures (including the depreciation of the currency) designed to restrict imports. This provided further incentive for the establishment of import competing industries and expansion in the capacity of existing ones. As the 1930s progressed not only was there an increase in the output of consumer goods, but certain types of capital goods began to make an appearance. Despite this development, however, the data indicate that in 1940 textiles (including textile products and footwear) and food products accounted for 57% of value added in the industrial sector as compared to 6% (2% in 1920) for machinery and 10% (6% in 1920) for chemical and pharmaceutical products.[5]

Throughout the twentieth century external developments were a major factor in the emergence of the Brazilian manufacturing sector. The shortages created by the Second World War were another instance where an outside stimulus played a crucial role in the expansion of the industrial structure. The War also had the effect of removing some of the foreign competition which was seen locally as an adverse factor on local production. During the 1940s certain manufactured goods (e.g. textiles) began to assume an increasingly prominent role in Brazil's export trade. The strides made in industrial development are reflected in the fact that industry's contribution to national product increased from 17% in 1939 to 22% in 1947. Over the same period agriculture's share dropped from 33% to 28%. The continued domination of the latter sector, however, could be seen in the fact that in 1950 64% of the gainfully occupied population was in agriculture (excluding forestry and fishing) as compared to only 12% in manufacturing (including civil engineering and the utilities).[6]

The period since the Second World War has witnessed remarkable changes in Brazil's economic structure. The growth performance achieved has generally ranked among the best in the world. Between the end of World War II and 1961 Brazil's annual growth rate averaged around 7% which was reputed to be the highest in Latin America and among the best rates achieved internationally. This was followed by a severe decline in economic performance in the following few years. The growth rate plummetted from 10.3% in 1961 to 5.3% in 1962 and to 1.3% in 1963. 'With the population growing at an estimated 3 per cent per year, the 1.5 per cent growth rate meant a decline in per capita income for a population whose average annual per capita income did not exceed $300. At the same time the steady inflation of 20 per cent turned sharply upward, unemployment rose to record levels, and the heavy accumulation of foreign debts brought the country close to international bankruptcy.'[7] The economic difficulties experienced in this period gave rise to political turmoil which eventually resulted in the overthrow of a democratically elected president in 1964 and the establishment of a military oligarchy which has exercised political control since through several military presidents. The economy resumed growing in the late sixties and is estimated to have achieved a real average annual growth rate of more than 8% between 1963 and 1981.[8] The period between 1969 and 1973 was particularly prosperous with growth rates exceeding 11% per year, inflation (as measured by the GDP deflator) declining to under 20 per cent a year, and the current account deficit of the balance of payments averaging less than 2 per cent of GDP.[9] Brazil is a large net importer of oil, and the oil price increases of 1973–74 took its toll. 'In the following five years the average annual rate of growth of real GDP fell to 7 per cent, and the rate of inflation doubled to almost 40 per cent; the current account deficit of the balance of payments rose to 5.3 per cent of GDP in 1974, then declined to 3.3% in 1978.'[10] The oil price increases in the late 1970s served to compound further the difficulties that were being experienced on both the internal and external fronts. Inflation rose rapidly to an annual average of over 80% in 1980 and to almost 100% in 1982 as compared to an average of 40% in the period 1975–79 and around 20–25% in the late sixties/early seventies. The higher cost for oil was only one factor affecting the external imbalance. The slackening in external demand for the country's exports coupled with falling prices for some of its main products resulted in a decline of some of $20 billion in export earnings in 1982. Though the value of imports also fell in 1982 as a result of some of the demand management measures instituted, the cost of servicing foreign capital (the accumulated foreign debt alone amounted to $81 billion at the end of 1982) has been rising significantly. Net service payments on foreign capital rose from $5.5 billion in 1979 to over $15 billion in 1982 in which year the current account deficit reached an estimated $14½ billion or 4½% of GDP. Service payments alone in 1982 amounted to 85% of exports of goods and services. Net capital inflows in 1982 amounted to $5½ billion or nearly 38% of the current account deficit. There was therefore a loss of reserves of some $9 billion in 1980.[11]

A significant part of the growth experienced by Brazil in the post-war period is attributable to the expansion of the manufacturing sector. In 1960 manufacturing accounted for 23% of GDP; by 1970 this had grown to 25% and by 1980 to over 30% (at 1970 prices). In 1970 industrial products accounted for 24% of the f.o.b. value of goods exported, while commodities accounted for 75% (coffee beans alone, 34%) and other products 1%. By 1980, however, industrial products had increased their share to about 57% as compared to 42% for commodities and 1% for other goods. While Brazil produces some of the raw materials for its industrial output, the country is critically dependent on outside sources for many key imports. Over 80% of its fuel requirements come from abroad. In 1980 fuels and lubricants accounted for about 45% of total (f.o.b.) imports, other intermediate goods 31%, capital goods 19% and consumer goods only 6%.

The strategy pursued since the mid-1960s has succeeded in raising per capita GNP from $240 in 1966 to an estimated $2,000 in 1980. The growth rate of 6.1% in real per capita GNP between 1970 and 1979 was among the highest in the world. Despite this performance, however, the Brazilian 'model' is far from being universally accepted as a standard to emulate. Large areas of the country and large sections of the population remain outside the mainstream of economic development. Data available for the 1960s decade indicate that the distribution of income may have worsened. The share of income received by the poorest 40% of the population is reported to have fallen from 10.5% in 1960 to 7.1% in 1970.[12] The richest 10% of families is estimated to receive 50% of the income.[13] While the structure of domestic production and exports may have changed in recent years, the increasing dependence on foreign factors of production is seen in some circles as a case of 'dependent development', that is, a situation where a certain kind of development is taking place within a growing network of dependency relations that tend to reinforce basic underdevelopment.

Earlier, we made reference to the fact that an increasing proportion of foreign exchange earnings in recent years has been directed towards the servicing of foreign capital – both official and private. Private capital inflows on a large scale into the manufacturing sector is largely a post-war phenomenon. As we saw earlier, the earliest involvement of foreign private capital was mainly in the utilities – transport, electric power, telephones, etc. American investment began to assume substantial proportions in the 1930s, corresponding with the withdrawal of British capital from Latin America. The import substitution device in the 1940s and 1950s continued to attract some foreign capital, but until 1964 there was no clear policy on the role of foreign investment in Brazilian development. This can be attributed to the presence of a number of opposing considerations stemming from both political factors and the dictates of economic strategy. On the one hand there was a political recognition that Brazil needed foreign capital, but the accumulation of foreign investments (particularly US investment) during the 1950s became a matter of concern for the local business groups who saw themselves threatened by the foreign invasion. The 1950s and early 1960s were generally a nationalistic period in Brazilian history, and given the need to build up a local entrepreneurial class the introduction of some control on foreign investment was not only feasibile, but was seen to be economically desirable.

Paradoxically, though most of these curbs (including a law controlling the remittance of profits) were supported by the local business elites, they were seen by the Castello Branco regime (1964–67) (and foreign investors) as one of the main reasons for the economic decline in the early 1960s. The mid-1960s marked the beginning of a deliberate effort to attract foreign capital, though significant inflows did not begin until about 1969.

The stock of direct foreign investment in Brazil grew from about $2.9 billion in 1965 to $4.4 billion in 1969 and to $14.8 billion in 1975. While Japan and other European countries have shown greater interest in recent years, the United States has been the main source of capital flow. As we saw earlier, US investments in Brazil increased from about $644 million in 1950 to about $1.1 billion in 1965 and to $8.3 billion at the end of 1981. In 1973 foreign private enterprises are estimated to have accounted for 37% of the sales and 22% of the net book value of the 1,000 largest companies.[14] Foreign involvement in Brazilian industry, however, is far greater than the book value suggests. Brazilian companies 'depend heavily on foreign sources for licensing of patents and industrial technique, for technical help in designing, building and operating manufacturing plants, and for the use of internationally known brand names with already established consumer acceptance.'[15] It is worth pointing out that the significance of private foreign inflows may lie not in the absolute figures themselves, or even in the relation to total savings and investment, but in the fact that they tend to be concentrated in key sectors of the economy, which provide the dynamic for the overall economy.

The strategy adopted by the military establishment in 1964 not only had economic growth as its foremost objective, but assigned a key role to foreign capital. A certain kind of atmosphere was therefore needed to help the process of rapid industrial development. The political climate had to be accommodating, and nationalistic posturing could not easily be tolerated. Political activities were repressed while trade union power had to be curtailed and wages controlled. Laws controlling profit remittances were modified or abolished and investors determined their own form of operation and their own profit margins. Social development took a secondary place in the overall strategy, and the lack of effective redistributive policies resulted in a very uneven division of gains, as we saw earlier. In many developing countries there has been an intensive debate on the need for balance between growth-oriented policies and the need for redistributive measures. The two do not always survive well together. 'In the early 1970s many Brazilian economists argued that the "cake had to grow before it could be redistributed" but the rapid economic growth would trickle down to the poor and help solve Brazil's social problems almost automatically.'[16] There was some 'trickle down' but not nearly enough to solve Brazil's social problems. In fact, Brazil's economic growth has been achieved at tremendous social cost. Generally there was little effort to encourage technology more suited to the factor situation in Brazil, with the result that the capital/employment ratio was extremely high. The policy of controlling wages in the face of high rates of inflation (and often in the face of rising productivity) helped in redistributing income in favour of the business classes. The concentration of wealth in the hands of small sections of the population also tended to influence the kinds of foods produced for the local market. Domestic agriculture also suffered in a strategy which put overwhelming emphasis on export agriculture. 'Although Brazil has the potential to feed its people well, expand agricultural exports rapidly and have sufficient land left to produce a substantial portion of its liquid fuel requirements from bio-mass, the fact is that, between 1966 and 1979, the output of domestic food crop has hardly kept up with population.'[17]

While Brazil has generally pursued an open door policy towards foreign capital since the mid-1960s, local business groups have been able to exert a considerable influence on the policy framework in a way designed to protect and enhance their own interests. Over the years a number of regulations have emerged aimed at affecting the behaviour of foreign companies in a particular way. For example, at present (under law 4131) 'transnationals are charged a withholding tax of 25% on all remittances of up to 12% of registered equity capital. The remittance is calculated as a three-year rolling average, net of withholding tax. In the case of double taxation agreement, the tax is reduced to 15%, or even 10% in the case of Japan. If the annual remittance is over 12% of the investment, a supplementary tax of up to 60% is charged.'[18] There are also restrictions relating to payment of technical assistance and royalties as well as foreign participation in the stock market. Decisions are also being increasingly taken with the aim of reserving certain areas (e.g. micro and mini computers and their peripheral equipment) for local firms and encouraging companies to produce a greater proportion of their components locally.[19] Faced with a serious foreign exchange problem the government is under increasing pressure to modify some of these policies in order to attract a greater flow of private foreign capital which is perceived in some quarters (including the international lending agencies) as part of the solution to the current balance of payments problems. In the present context, the expression of social discontent may invite political retaliation, but there is no guarantee that the policies pursued since the mid-1960s could be as effective in the middle and late 1980s, even in terms of the limited accomplishments of previous years.

Mexico

Mexico is now one of the most industrialised of the developing countries. Its accomplishments in the post-war period justify the label of 'semi-industrialised' or 'semi-peripheral' which is often used to describe it. With a land area of 760,337 square miles (1980 population: 67 million) it is the third largest of the Latin American nations in terms of land space. Per capita GNP in 1980 was estimated to be over $2,000 as compared to less than $500 in 1966. In nominal terms per capita GNP grew by 3.7% between 1970 and 1979 and by 1.9% in real terms.

One of the major factors in Mexico's post-war growth has been the rapid strides made by the manufacturing sector which in 1980 contributed almost 25% to GDP (at 1970 prices) as compared to an estimated 3% for mining and 9% for agriculture. Non traditional exports in 1980 amounted to over $4 billion as compared to less than $2 billion for the main traditional exports and about $10 billion for petroleum and petroleum products. The post-war strategy pursued recognised the need for foreign private capital (including technology and management), but the approach was selective, and over time became increasingly restrictive. Before examining the general policy towards foreign capital, it would be instructive to look at the position of foreign reserves in relation to overall financing. Between 1946 and 1960 total inflows of net official donations and non-compensatory capital amounted to $1.8 billion or roughly 2.6 times the accumulated deficit on current account. In the absence of adequate data, it is difficult to establish a relationship between foreign capital and national savings or investment in this period. Some statistics available for the 1960s and 1970s do give us an indication of the significance of foreign inflows. Between 1960 and 1970 net long term public borrowing averaged about 8.1% of gross internal savings (measured at current prices) per annum, while direct investment averaged 6.1%. Taken together these two categories of inflows averaged about 14.8% of gross internal savings in the period. Direct foreign investment averaged only about 7.6% of total private investment in the 1960–70 period and 4.9% of total gross fixed investment. The significant role played by domestic resources in the financing of development seemed to have continued in the 1970s when national savings accounted for over 80% of total investment.

During the 20th century, policies of accommodation to foreign capital have alternated with periods of fierce nationalism. The present attitude towards foreign investors can be said to have its roots in the Revolution of 1910–20 which ended the dictatorship of Porfirio Diaz which began in 1876. The Diaz era was not without accomplishments. In fact it marked the beginning of modern industrialization in Mexico. With the help of foreign capital the infrastructure of the country (including the critical area of railway transport) was improved. By the early years of the twentieth century the country had become a leading producer of silver and copper, and by 1910 the third largest oil producer in the world. The period, however, witnessed a serious deterioration in social conditions. In his attempt to accommodate foreign investors, little attention was paid to the plight of the Mexican worker. Labour was exploited, unions suppressed and land resources alienated. Towards the end of the Diaz regime foreign interests 'controlled two-thirds of Mexico's capital, excluding capital in the agricultural and handicraft sectors of the economy, and owned 72 million acres of land (representing one-seventh of the country's land surface). Several thousand Mexican families controlled the remaining arable land.'[20] A close examination of Table 6.1 will show that in 1911 railroads and mining alone accounted for 67% of direct investment, as compared to less than 5% for manufacturing. It would appear from the Table that the US was the largest source of direct investment capital accounting for 42% of the total, while Britain and France held 31% and 20% respectively.

Table 6.1 *Foreign investment in Mexico in 1911*

$ Millions

	Total	*USA*	*UK*	*France*	*Other*
Total	*1,700*	*646*	*495*	*454*	*105*
Indirect (public debt)	249	30	41	164	14
Direct	1,451	617	454	290	91
Railroads	565	267	201	58	39
Mining	409	250	58	90	11
Public Services	119	7	106	5	1
Real Estate	97	41	46	8	3
Banks	83	17	9	50	7
Manufacturing	66	11	5	36	14
Commerce	61	5	–	40	16
Petroleum	52	20	29	3	–

Note: Because of rounding details may not add to totals.

Source: Harry K. Wright, *Foreign Enterprise in Mexico, Laws and Policies* (Chapel Hill: University of North Carolina Press, 1971), Table 3. Original Source: Luis N. D'Oliver, 'Las inversiones extranjeras', in *Historia moderna de Mexico*, ed. Daniel Cosio Villegas, Vol. 7, 'El Porfiriato: La vida economica' (Mexico, D.F.: Editorial Hermes, 1965), Tables 65 and 66.

During the course of the 1910–20 phase of the Revolution (which, incidentally, Mexicans feel still to be in progress) a new Constitution was adopted in 1917, which among other things, severely restricted foreign ownership of Mexican resources. Article 27 of the 1917 Constitution takes the position that the Mexican nation held the original ownership of all land, as well as the subsoil and waters, and granted its use. In order to restore peasant ownership to lands seized, it permitted private property to be seized for public use. Only Mexican citizens could own land, subsoil and mineral rights. The Mexican Government could, however, grant certain of these rights to foreigners under prescribed conditions. Foreigners could not own land or water within 30 miles of the sea or 60 miles of the border. Banks were permitted to own only the property they used to transact business, though temporary ownership was allowed where real property used as collateral reverted to them as a result of default on the part of a client.[21]

The large foreign debt appears to have been one of the main concerns during the 1920s. Social and economic reforms receded into the background until the inauguration of Lazaro Cardenas in 1934. Cardenas saw the take-over of certain foreign interests as essential to the success of his economic policy. In the mid-1930s foreign interests in Mexico controlled 95% of the nation's oil production and refining, 95% of mining production, 79% of the railways and street cars, and 100% of both electric power and telephone service.[22]

In 1936 a number of plantation and livestock companies were expropriated. The remaining foreign-owned railways followed in 1937, and petroleum (including oil lands and refineries) in 1938. Foreign direct investment in Mexico fell from $1.5 billion in 1935 to $480 million in 1940.[23] With the accelerated flow of foreign capital into Mexico during the war years, there was fear that Mexican enterprises would be displaced and foreign control would once more assert itself. An emergency decree was issued on June 29, 1944 with the aim of restricting foreign investment on a broad front, and, though this was intended to be a temporary measure (even its constitutionality has been often been challenged), it has survived. In subsequent years, however, the decree has proved to be inadequate in terms of serving governmental objectives and policies, and this has given rise to the use of specific statutory restrictions in selected industries as the need or desire arose.[24] In 1958 a group of Mexican businessmen took controlling interest in Telefonos de Mexico and in 1960 the electric power companies were nationalised. Since 1961 the government has used penalties and incentives to encourage foreign companies in mining and other areas to sell the majority of their stock to Mexican shareholders. The Mining Law of 1961 provided that only firms with a majority of Mexican capital may obtain new mining concessions. 'In the exploitation of government-owned reserves, Mexican participation must represent not less than 66% of the corporate capital. To provide an incentive for "Mexicanization", the mining code was revised in 1963 to allow any company to obtain a production and export tax reduction of 50–75%, with a 50% decrease being automatic on "Mexicanization".'[25]

Until recently there was no general law or code governing foreign investment in Mexico.[26] This was a deliberate policy in that it permitted flexibility and allowed the various administrations to use their own particular approach in dealing with the problem. Over time a number of laws and decrees have been passed or issued with the aim of controlling the extent and pattern of foreign capital inflow, and these laws form part of the overall framework under which private enterprise in Mexico functions. The basic principle informing Mexican policy on foreign enterprise is that the latter should operate on a minority basis with Mexican interest. Besides the explicit regulations obtaining in certain areas, devices such as tariff and quantitative restrictions, the granting of import licences and tax concessions are used to promote the principle. Enterprises that support Mexican aspirations tend to receive more favourable treatment by the authorities than those that do not.

The Mexican policy on foreign investment has been influenced by two main considerations. One is a recognised need for foreign capital in the context of the goal of rapid industrialisation and modernisation. The other is the desire to maintain its economic sovereignty. With respect to the latter a guiding principle is that the foreign enterprises should be treated no differently from Mexican enterprises. The use of the 'Calvo Clause' more than anything else reflects this sentiment. This Clause (widely used in Latin America and named after the 19th century Argentine diplomat and publicist Carlos Calvo), requires a foreigner who wishes to own property or engage in business in Mexico to enter into an express agreement with the federal government (through the Ministry of Foreign Relations) under which he agrees to be considered a Mexican national and to give up the right to diplomatic protection from his home government.[27] As a Mexican 'national' the foreigner would have recourse to local law. The thrust of the Calvo principle is to discourage intervention by foreign governments on the pretext of protecting the citizens against unfair treatment – a salient practice in Latin American history.

It does not mean that foreigners who agree to the Calvo requirement have automatic access to any area of the economy. There are certain basic sectors (e.g. the petroleum industry, electric power generation, railroads) which are largely reserved for the state. The petroleum industry includes 'the exploration, production, refining, transportation, storage, distribution and firsthand sales of petroleum, gas and products that are obtained from the refining thereof, and the manufacture, storage, transportation, distribution, and firsthand sales of articificial gas and petroleum derivations that are susceptible to serving as basic industrial raw materials.'[28] This, however, does not prohibit Petroleos Mexicanos (the state enterprise set up after the 1930s nationalisation to run the oil industry) from obtaining certain services (e.g. construction, drilling, technical services) from private enterprise on a cash basis. Payments, however, cannot take the form of royalties or participations.

Mexican-controlled private enterprise tends to be favoured, but where such companies cannot provide the service required, foreign companies are usually contracted. There are certain areas from which foreigners are totally excluded. One of these is the storage, transportation and distribution of liquid petroleum gas.

Investment in the petro-chemical industry is governed by the petroleum law of 1958 and its 1959 regulations.[29] The regulations stipulate which categories of products will be produced by the state and which by private enterprise alone or in collaboration with the state. The wording of some of the regulations is not quite clear, and a considerable amount of confusion has resulted from their application. For instance, Article 27 which deals with products reserved for the state names two categories of products. Those that result from 'petroleum processes based on the first important chemical transformation or the first important physical processing', and those that 'have a fundamental social economic interest for the State'. These definitions often give rise to a considerable amount of disagreement as to what should be on the reserve list. As worded, the definitions also permit the list of products reserved for the state to undergo constant change.

As indicated earlier, investment in mining is governed by the mining law of 1961 (and subsequent amendments) which virtually excludes all foreigners from major participation in the industry. As pointed out earlier also, Article 27 of the 1917 Constitution which vests ownership of all subsurface minerals in the state provides the main plank of the policy on mining. When private persons and companies do engage in mining it is on the basis of concessions granted by the government. Only Mexican citizens and Mexican companies with a majority of Mexican ownership can obtain ordinary mining or mill concessions. 'Foreign governments and sovereigns are absolutely prohibited to acquire concessions or other mining rights or to hold ownership interests in mining companies.'[30] In the case of special concession on national mining reserves, for companies to be considered for concession they must be at least 66% owned by Mexicans. There are also requirements with respect to the management of Mexican mining companies.

With respect to banking, insurance and other financial operations special authorisation is required and in the case of foreign enterprise this tends to be granted mainly in situations where the service cannot be provided by Mexicans. The laws permit branch operations of banking and insurance institutions but investment and bonding companies have to use Mexican corporations. There are stipulations with respect to the form of organisation, minimum invested capital and management. While branch banking is permitted by foreign concerns, only one concession has been granted. Several banks maintain a less active presence in the form of agency and representative offices. Foreign insurance companies have generally been excluded from insuring Mexican risks. 'This prohibition applies to insurance of persons when the insured is in

Mexico at the time of execution of the contract, insurance of property that is transported from or to Mexican territory when the risks are on persons domiciled in Mexico, insurance of hulls of ships or aircraft or any type of vehicle of Mexican registry or owned by persons domiciled in Mexico, insurance of debt when the insurance is subject to Mexican law, insurance against civil liability resulting from events that may occur in Mexico, and other insurance against risks that may occur in Mexico.'[31] Permission to use foreign insurance companies tend to be given where authorised institutions cannot provide the coverage required.

Electric power for public service is seen to be a state responsibility, and the law is operated accordingly. Radio and television are reserved for Mexican (persons or companies owned by Mexicans). While the law does not expressly prohibit foreign involvement in fishing, forestry, communications, transport or shipping, the policy in practice favours Mexicans and Mexican-controlled companies. As we saw earlier, the growth of foreign investment in the industrial sector reflects a more liberal Mexican policy towards foreign capital in this area. In recent years, however, the tendency to impose restrictions in certain areas of manufacture has become stronger. In 1970, President Diaz Ordaz issued a decree to the effect that at least 51% of the capital stock of companies formed to engage in the steel, cement, glass, fertiliser, cellulose or aluminum industry should be held by Mexicans or Mexican companies whose articles of incorporation contain a clause prohibiting foreign ownership. Where a larger percentage of the stock is required to establish control, that percentage should be Mexican owned.

Out of deference to the defence of the country the constitution prohibits foreigners from acquiring land (or bodies of water) within 100 kilometres (about 62 miles) of the land borders or 50 kilometres (about 31 miles) of the sea coast. No foreigner is allowed to hold shares in a Mexican company owning land in the prohibited zone.

As far as the acquisition of real property outside the prohibited zone is concerned, foreigners can do so to the extent that such acquisitions are necessary to the operation of their enterprise, and to the extent that they are prepared to abide by certain national requirements, one of these being the Calvo Clause.

As a footnote we should add that since May, 1973 foreign investment policy has been regulated by the 'Law for the Promotion of Mexican Investments, and the Regulation of Foreign Investments.' Essentially the law brings together all previous legislations in force since 1944. 'According to this Law, foreign investors who wish to engage in joint ventures in Mexico are welcome, particularly those who bring labour intensive technologies, who contribute to the geographical decentralisation of the economy, who will have a favourable effect on the balance of payments and who will integrate into their production the largest amount of local raw materials, and finally, who will not reduce the local sources of credit for local firms and who will not impose patterns of consumption judged to be useless.'[32] As was the case previously, certain activities are reserved for the state. Among them are petroleum and hydro-carbons, the exploitation of radio-active minerals and the production of nuclear energy, mines, electricity, railways and telegraphic and radio communications. There are also certain areas which are reserved exclusively for Mexicans or Mexican firms. These include radio and television, urban and inter-urban transport services, aerial and maritime transport exploitation of forests and gas distribution. There are certain activities where foreign investors can participate, but only up to a fixed percentage. These are as follows: exploitation and use of minerals subject to regular concessions up to a maximum of 49 per cent; special concessions for minerals judged to be of national interest, up to 34 per cent; secondary products of the petrochemical industry, up to 40 per cent; manufacture of spare parts for the automotive industry, up to 40 per cent. In all other cases, foreign participation is allowed up to 49%, but not if the effective control of such a joint venture would be in foreign hands.[33]

As indicated earlier, about 80% to 90% of Mexican investment in the post-war period has been financed from domestic resources. Foreign capital, however, has not been unimportant. Direct foreign investment in Mexico increased from $449 million in 1940 to $1.7 billion in 1965, to $2.8 billion in 1970 and to $4.2 billion in 1975. About 75% of this investment has gone into the rapidly expanding manufacturing sector. For example, US direct investment alone in Mexico was estimated to be $7.0 billion at the end of 1981. Of this, 74% was in manufacturing.

It is clear from the above that, despite the increasing policy of Mexicanisation and the national requirements which foreign investors must satisfy, private foreign capital has continued to be attracted by opportunities created by Mexican development. There have been periods when foreign flows have slowed as a result of uncertainty stemming from domestic policies, but over the long term, there has been a sustained flow of private foreign capital into the Mexican manufacturing sector. One such period was the Echeverria years of 1970s which were marked by an upsurge of economic nationalism. In fact an outflow of foreign capital took place in this period as a result of certain new policies on taxation and investment, and one might add the general political climate of the Echeverria administration. For example, foreign companies found the Echeverria regime insufficiently tough on labour.[34] Some observers have used this episode in the context of the post-war experience to make a very telling point. 'Mexico, one of the richest and best-behaved nations in the Third World, had only to stray slightly from the path of sound business practice to end up shifting the impact of TNC capital and profit flows from a positive $179 million in the 1960–69 period to a negative $349 million in the period from 1970 to 1976. Since one can hardly accuse Echeverria of being a radical, it would appear that the band of acceptable policy is exceedingly narrow and that the penalties for straying outside it are strict and swift.'[35]

Despite the differences in approach taken by Mexico and Brazil respectively, the consequences of their policies bear certain similarities. The Mexican economy, as indicated earlier, has been one of the fastest growing among developing countries. Between 1960 and 1975 it experienced the highest and most regular growth rate among Latin American countries. In constant prices per capita income is estimated to have tripled between 1950 and 1970.[36] From available data, however, it would appear that the distribution of this income has become worse over time. For example, between 1950 and 1970 the relative share of total income received by the poorest 40% of the population dropped from 14.3% to 11.6%.[37] Even though Mexico is a net exporter of oil, its current account balance has inreased significantly in recent years, reaching almost $13 billion in 1981. The external public debt, as we saw earlier, has also been increasing, amounting to more than $40 billion at the end of 1981. What is also interesting is that despite 'the official "Mexicanisation" policy, majority control is still in foreign hands in the majority of firms with foreign participation, i.e. joint ventures. At the end of 1975, out of 4,083 joint ventures, 64.2 per cent were under foreign control, 27.3 per cent had a foreign participation between 25 per cent and 49.9 per cent, and in only 8.5 per cent of the firms was foreign control less than 25 per cent of the capital.'[38]

Even though both Brazil and Mexico have made considerable strides in the diversification of their production and exports, their economies remain vulnerable on several fronts. The present dynamic appears to rest heavily on the infusion of foreign capital, both private and public. In this kind of situation foreign investors can easily overturn or cause to be modified nationalistic regulations which they may have been willing to tolerate in different circumstances. The greater the dependence on foreign capital, the more easily can domestic political behaviour be affected. Even large countries like Brazil and Mexico which have made significant progress in the industrial field have not been able to escape the implications of this relationship. In reviewing the experience of these two countries, two writers have made the observation that however successful dependent-developing countries might be 'at emulating or even surpassing the rates of industrial growth that are found in the capitalist core, (they) do not have the same possibility of exploring the welfare side of capitalist development.'[39] The exercises which compare the growth rates of developing countries today with the growth rates of the now industrialised countries at a similar stage of development in an effort to highlight how well the former are doing often completely ignore not only the different historical contexts, but the costs in social, economic and political terms at which some of these growth rates are being achieved. And this may also explain why it is often so difficult for the people who make this kind of comparison to understand why these growth rates cannot be sustained, or if sustained can only be done by a particular type of policy which eventually leads to unrest and instability. There is no necessary connection between growth and the improvement in broad social and economic conditions.

The Andean Common Market

The Andean Subregional Integration Agreement (Acuerdo de Integration Subregional Andina) which brought the Andean Common Market into being was signed by Bolivia, Colombia, Chile, Ecuador and Peru in May 1969. Venezuela (who was due to sign but backed out at the last minute partly as a result of disagreement over certain issues and partly as a result of the intense pressure exerted by domestic and foreign business interests) joined the group in 1973. Chile withdrew in 1976. Together the five remaining countries have a land area of approximately 1,723,219 sq miles and a population of 75 million (1980 estimate). Per capita GNP varies from around $600 for Bolivia to about $4,000 for Venezuela.

The Andean Group, which was formed as a sub-group within the Latin American Free Trade Association (now the Latin American Integration Association) was born out of dissatisfaction with the rate of progress LAFTA was making and out of a need to create an entity to counter the power of the larger countries such as Argentina, Brazil and Mexico. In order to accelerate the process of integration the Andean Group adopted its own timetable for attaining specific objectives and instituted its own procedures and instruments in pursuit of desired developmental goals. Economic integration was seen as an instrument for the 'balanced and harmonious' development of member states. In this connection it was felt that industrialisation should take place within a rational framework designed to maximise use of scarce capital and other resources, and at the same time allow all member states to benefit. To attain these objectives industrial programming was seen to be an important instrument and there was, therefore, need for agreement on a range of issues related to investment policy. One aspect of this policy concerned the treatment of foreign capital. Through Article 27 of the Cartagena Agreement, member states pledged themselves to the adoption of a common system for the treatment of foreign capital and of similar systems for trade marks, patents, licences and royalties, *inter alia*, 'within the six months following approval by the Commission'.

In December 1970 the Standard Regime for the Treatment of Foreign Capital, and for Treatment of Trademarks, Patents, Licences and Royalties was approved by the Cartagena Agreement Commission (Decision 24) and went into effect on June 30, 1971. The Agreement that went into operation contained several modifications to the text approved in 1970. While recognising a role for foreign capital and techniques, the agreement lays down certain conditions under which foreign capital would be accepted and defines the areas where it would be welcomed or discouraged. During the first ten years of the common system (i.e. until 1981) member states were free to authorise the activity of foreign enterprises in the field of basic products provided the contract did not exceed twenty years and deductions were not authorised on depletion for tax purposes. Basic products are defined as those related to 'primary activities for exploration of any type of minerals including liquid and gaseous hydro-carbons, gasducts, pipelines and forestry exploitation.' In the area of exploration and exploitation of liquid hydrocarbon and gas deposits a preference is expressed for foreign participation in the form of contracts with government entities in the particular country. The regime forbids new investments in the field of public services (drinking water, sewage, electric power, illumination, garbage collection, and sanitary, telephone, mail and telecommunication services), insurance, commercial banking and other financial institutions. Foreign banks operating in member states were given a period of three years (from the date the system went into effect) within which to suspend the receipts of local deposits for current accounts, saving accounts, or fixed terms. Foreign banks which wished to continue receiving any type of local deposits were required to sell at least 80% of their capital stock to nationals within the three year period indicated. New direct investment is also forbidden in the field of internal transportation, publicity and radio station, newspaper and magazine enterprises devoted to internal commercialisation of any type of products. In the field of manufacturing, new or established foreign enterprises wishing to enjoy the advantages of the integration exercise were required within a specified period to sell the necessary percentage of their stocks (assets or rights to nationals) or convert these concerns into a national enterprise (a local company with 80% of its capital owned by nationals). In Colombia, Chile and Peru the maximum period was fifteen years, while for Bolivia and Ecuador it was twenty years. In the case of Colombia, Chile and Peru the agreement (with the foreign investor) was required to stipulate that the participation of national investors in the capital of the enterprises should be not less than fifteen per cent at the time of initiating production, not less than thirty per cent upon expiration of one third of the period agreed upon, and not less than forty-five per cent upon expiration of two thirds of the same period. In the case of Bolivia and Ecuador, the progressive participation of national investors in the capital of the enterprise was not less than five per cent after three years of initiating production, not less than ten per cent at the expiration of one third of the period agreed upon, and not less than thirty-five per cent upon expiration of two-thirds of the same period.

According to Article 37 foreign investors could by previous

authorisation, remit abroad (in freely convertible foreign exchange) net proven profits up to 14% of direct investment per year. In special cases the Committee could authorise higher percentages at the request of a member. Under Article 13 foreign enterprises were permitted to re-invest up to 5% of paid capital per year without specific authorisations. Beyond this permission was required from the government concerned. Re-invested profits were considered new investment and were subject to the same norms as the latter. We should point out here that, subsequently, some countries found the remittance of profit rate too restrictive and sought to have it changed. In 1977, for example, Colombia adopted the Andean Pact's Decision 103 which increased the remittance proportion from 14% to 20% of investment and the re-investment ratio from 5% of net proven profits to 7%. That part of the profit which could not be legally remitted the government sought to direct into local developmental agencies through the sale of five year bonds.[40]

The Common System contains norms governing a wide range of transactions. With respect to technology, member states are required to exercise strict control over the importation of techniques, patents and trademarks. Articles 19 and 20 lay down a number of guidelines for the evaluation of imported techniques. For instance, member countries are not permitted to approve contracts on transfer of foreign techniques which include clauses prohibiting the use of competitive techniques, or clauses which commit the purchaser of technology to disclose to the supplier the inventions or improvements accomplished through utilisation of said technology. With respect to internal borrowing foreign enterprises (those with less than 51% national ownership) are restricted to short term credit. Foreign investors are free to re-export their capital invested upon sale of shares, assets or rights to national investors or upon liquidation.

One aim of the common policy is to remove the possibility of foreign investors playing off one country against another, leading each to give greater and greater concessions in order to get the investment. It also seeks, of course, to increase the contribution of foreign capital to national and regional development and to the process of economic independence. It is not surprising, therefore, that the decision to put into operation a common system for the treatment of foreign capital attracted a great deal of hostility from foreign businessmen (particularly American). The system put into operation, it needs to be pointed out, was the product of long and careful study and was not simply an instant piece of rhetoric designed to arouse emotion to serve some short term purpose. The powerful Council of the Americas (a group of American businessmen then headed by David Rockefeller) circulated a document far and wide (including the US Congress) which, among other things, stated:[41]

1 far from providing potential new foreign investors with guarantees

of stability, it would create new and greater elements of instability;
2 certain provisions would discriminate against foreign companies in technology transference operations with both their affiliates and local companies of the Andean Group of countries; and
3 few foreign companies would seriously consider a fixed-term investment for a short period of 15 to 20 years in any country unless they could be sure that such an investment would earn exceptionally high profits during the major part of this period.

In correspondence with the then President of Colombia the Council expressed the view that the common system would not only discourage the inflow of foreign private capital, but it would have a debilitating effect on the entire development process by undermining private local investments. 'Once the stimulus supplied by foreign administration, technology and capital has disappeared, the business opportunities that foreign investment provides to local investors would be restricted and local investors might possibly diminish their activity in the fear that the restrictions applied to foreigners could be extended to include them.'[42] The President of Colombia was informed that, unless he withdrew his support to the Common System, he would be responsible for a violent revolution, not only in Colombia but in 'other countries of the Americas' as well.[43]

This position was taken by the Council of the Americas despite the fact that there was increasing evidence in various parts of the developing world that foreign investors (including American) were being made to alter traditional forms of operations and adapt to the demands of national aspirations and expectations. A basic fear of the American companies was no doubt that the assertiveness of the Andean Group would spread to other parts of the hemisphere, thus leading to a serious curtailment of their activities in the region. The position of the Andean countries was that the Common System by providing certain guarantees would remove a great deal of the uncertainty surrounding the operation of foreign capital in the region, particularly in the light of the nationalisations that took place during the 1960s.[44]

In their application of the Common System, member countries of the Andean Group were free to be more restrictive than the minimum requirements laid down in the code. They were certainly not expected to be less liberal, since this would have betrayed the whole purpose of a common policy on foreign investment. The Agreement, however, did make provisions for the special circumstances of certain member states, who found some standards initially too restrictive, and took advantage of Article 44 to apply regulations different from those in the common code. Peru and Ecuador, for example, initially sought exemption from the application of Articles 40 to 43 which outlined the areas where new investments were to be restricted.

Because of differences in the application of the Common System it is difficult to gauge its true impact on the movement of foreign capital in the region. Table 6.2 gives a picture of the net flow of foreign direct investment into Andean countries in the period between 1969 and 1981. While some capital may have left the region as a result of Decision 24 a high proportion of the outflows seemed to have stemmed from internal economic and political problems (e.g. Chile, between 1971–74 and Bolivia in the late sixties/early seventies) or nationalisations (e.g. the Venezuelan oil industry in the 1970s and Peru's in the 1969–72 period). According to data released by the Common Market technical secretariat foreign investment in the Andean Group between its creation in 1969 and 1979 totalled some $8 billion. This was distributed as follows: Venezuela $3.6 billion, Peru $2.0 billion, Colombia $1.4 billion, Ecuador $800 million and Bolivia $120 million. United States capital is reported to have accounted for 56% of the total.[45]

Table 6.2 *Annual flow of direct investment into Andean Countries, 1969–81*

SDRs millions

Years	*Bolivia*	*Chile*	*Colombia*	*Ecuador*	*Peru*	*Venezuela*
1969	9.1	85	50	39	6	224
70	−75.9	−79	39	89	−70	−23
71	1.9	−66	40	162	−58	210
72	−9.7	−1	16	74	22	−346
73	3.9	−4	19	44	59	−71
74	21.5	−463	29	64	48	−358
75	44.0	41	29	79	260	344
76	−7.0	−1	12	−17	147	−770
77	−1.0	14	37	30	46	−3
78	9.2	141	54	39	20	54
79	13.9	180	81	49	55	68
80	31.9	131	179	54	21	42
81	50.9	319	177	51	226	136

Source: IMF, *Balance of Payments Statistics*, various issues.

The Andean countries, for various reasons, have not been able to attain many of the objectives they aspired to at the beginning of the 1970s. The common system for the treatment of foreign capital is still far from being strictly adhered to or uniformly applied. There are groups both within and outside the Pact countries who are bitterly opposed to the full implementation of the agreement, and even implicitly blame the problems of the region on the sections that have been in effect. The position of some of the member countries themselves has shifted over time. Venezuela, for example, who initially had grave reservations over the impact of the code became one of its strongest supporters in the latter part of 1970s. This was no doubt due to her enhanced position stemming from the increases in oil prices during the 1970s. Her views on strict implementation of the code could once more change, if the need to encourage greater private inflows begins to exert a stronger than usual influence on official policy.

The Caribbean Community (CARICOM)

In a technical sense the Caribbean Community grew out of the Caribbean Free Trade Association agreement signed by Antigua, Barbados and Guyana in 1965, and which later provided the basis for an extended association. The Agreement for the enlarged Caribbean Free Trade Association (CARIFTA) went into effect on May 1st, 1968 with the three countries named above plus Trinidad and Tobago as members. By the end of 1968 Dominica, Grenada, St Kitts-Nevis, St Lucia, St Vincent, Jamaica and Montserrat had also become members. Belize joined in May 1971. While there were questions surrounding CARIFTA as a framework for Caribbean development, it was nevertheless seen as a beginning on which more appropriate arrangements could be built. On the 4th July, 1973 the Treaty of Chaguaramas, establishing the Caribbean Community, including the Caribbean Common Market, was signed at Chaguaramas (Trinidad) by the governments of Barbados, Guyana, Jamaica, and Trinidad and Tobago. The Treaty became effective from 1st August, 1973 with these four countries (referred to as the More Developed Countries or MDCs) as members. The other members of CARIFTA (referred to as the Less Developed Countries LDCs) joined on 1st May, 1974.

The Caribbean Community (CARICOM) does not fit neatly into any of the text-books schemes of integration, since the areas in which it seeks to promote cooperation goes beyond the purely economic. The structure of the organisation is intended to preserve and advance traditional areas of cooperation, while opening up new horizons for regional development. There are three main elements. One is the Common Market which is largely concerned with regional trade and production. It should be pointed out that while the 'Common Market' aims at the establishment of a free trade area and the setting up of a common external tariff, no provision is made for the movement of labour and capital. The second is functional cooperation in certain non-economic areas (e.g. education, health, meterological services, etc). And the third is the recognised need of member states to coordinate their foreign policies. The necessity for this latter stems from the fact that foreign policies are linked with external economic relations and these can by no means be divorced from domestic and regional economic strategies.

As can be seen in Table 6.3 CARICOM members are generally small countries in both physical size and population. Taken together the population in 1979 was estimated to be a little over 5 million people. Per capita GNP varies widely from country to country. In 1979 the limits were less than \$500 for St Vincent and almost \$4,000 for Trinidad and Tobago. The member states also differ widely in natural resource endownment, and one dare say potential, at least as far as industrial development is concerned. Taken individually the resource base of the various countries tends to be very narrow, and this acts as a major constraint to national development. Taken as a group, however, the greater resource diversity offers considerable scope for industrial development within certain limits.

Table 6.3 *Selected data on Caribbean Community countries*

Countries	*Area (sq. miles)*	*Total Population (mid-1979) '000*	*Per Capita GNP[1] 1979 US\$*	*Real Growth Rate of Per Capita GNP 1970–79*
MDCs[2]				
Barbados	166	248	2,680	2.1
Guyana	83,000	790	630	0.0
Jamaica	4,411	2,159	1,110	−3.7
Trinidad & Tobago	1,980	1,150	3,910	4.5
LDCs[3]				
Antigua	170	74	1,150	−2.6
Belize	8,866	142	980	4.1
Dominica	305	82	580	−3.2
Grenada	133	109	650	−1.3
Montserrat	32	11	1,310	3.8
St Kitts-Nevis	101	50	820	1.3
St Lucia	233	122	840	2.8
St Vincent	150	106	480	−1.7

1 GNP at market prices. The estimates for the LDCs are tentative.
2 MDCs – More Developed Countries.
3 LDCs – Less Developed Countries.

Source: World Bank *Atlas* 1981; *West Indies and Caribbean Yearbook*, various issues.

The integration experience in the post-war period (both among the developed and developing countries) has demonstrated in no uncertain terms that if all participating member states are to share in benefits of integration there has to be co-ordination of policies in a number of areas which at first sight might not seem directly related to the integration effort. One of these areas is the question of foreign investment. There are a number of issues involved here. It is obvious that in an integration context there would be certain activities that could be undertaken by locals (be they governments or private entities) that would not be possible within a national framework. These activities would need to be identified and a common approach taken with respect to the kind and extent of foreign involvement that would be tolerated. In addition, there are certain issues that have to be addressed directly. In a grouping which consists of countries at different stages of development and with different levels of infrastructural development, it is obvious that where location is the critical consideration foreign capital would be attracted to the more developed members, thus giving these a further advantage over the less developed members. Where a country does not have a locational advantage, or whose advantage is shared by other member states, it may be tempted to offer greater and greater concessions in order to attract investors. In this kind of competitive situation governments could easily be pitted against each other. Foreign investment offers certain short-term benefits, but could also frustrate the goals of national and regional development, unless it operates within a clearly articulated perspective conforming with long run social and economic objectives.

Out of concern with the questions raised above, and out of a conviction that there is a role for foreign investment in regional development, many of the officials engaged in the integration exercise[47] (and also many West Indian economists[48]) have long advocated the need for a common policy (if not a code) for the region. The recent Report by the group of Caribbean experts set up in March 1980 by the Council of Ministers of the Caribbean Common Market to review the functioning of the Caribbean integration movement and to prepare a strategy for 1980s again reiterated the need to establish a set of principles and guidelines for foreign investment.[49] The purpose for such a regime, the experts argue 'is not to discourage foreign investment and the transfer of technology, but to seek through joint approaches to increase the region's bargaining power in this area in order to maximise the benefits and reduce the costs to the countries of such extra-regional inflows and to maximise the participation of national and regional ownership, entrepreneurship, management and technology in the process of national and regional economic development.'[50]

Despite the cogent arguments in favour of a common policy in foreign investment and the transfer of technology, and despite efforts at the national level to increase localisation of their respective economies, the Governments of CARICOM countries have so far not been able to formulate a regional policy. There might be many reasons for this. Some obviously place greater store on the role of foreign private capital than others, and for these, the adoption of guidelines far from removing uncertainties might serve to frighten off foreign investors. It is also possible that given the differences in political outlook, some would want to be more restrictive than others. In this situation, too liberal an approach would be seen by some as a betrayal of ideology. On the other hand, too restrictive a policy may attract the criticism that it is likely to give the wrong signal on the political position embraced. Countries desperately seeking foreign aid may feel that they have to adopt particular postures with respect to the private sector generally and this factor complicates the situation.

In the following sections we examine the significance of foreign capital in a few of the CARICOM countries for which we have data and outline their respective policies on foreign investment where this is possible. First we provide a general background to the present foreign investment situation in the region.

The earliest interest of foreign investors in Commonwealth Caribbean countries appear to have centred around the plantation and mining sectors of the various economies. Major investment in tourism, the services and manufacturing came later. The growth of the manufacturing sector is largely a post-war development, and though it had taken some root during the war years and the 1950s, it was after political independence was attained in the 1960s that a concerted and deliberate attempt was made to promote industries as a major sector. Foreign capital, following the Puerto Rican lead, was seen as an essential ingredient in the process. The writings of the well known West Indian economist Sir Arthur Lewis in the early 1950s provided inspiration. Lewis argued, as we saw in an earlier chapter, that excess labour in the agricultural sector was such that its marginal product was zero. Labour, therefore, could easily be drawn away from agriculture without any adverse effect on production. The key to economic expansion lay in the availability of capital and the re-investment of profits.[51]

In order to attract foreign capital regional states found themselves competing with each other by offering increasingly generous incentives. These incentives took several forms: exemption from the payment of corporate taxes on profits for a period of time (tax holidays), exemption from import duties on essential equipment and supplies, accelerated depreciation allowances, etc. Some of these devices proved to be self-defeating in that they encouraged the use of capital intensive techniques, and therefore the number of jobs created was not as great as was expected. Governments, of course, also lost revenue. As far as exports are concerned many of the products manufactured have either not been of a price and quality level to enable them to compete abroad, or those that could compete have found themselves facing severe restrictions in foreign markets. This latter feature marks a fundamental difference with the Puerto Rican model, since as part of the US customs area Puerto Rican products enter the US market free from restrictions. Another factor here is that many of the foreign investors who came entered the local markets merely to get behind the protective walls, and have not been particularly keen in developing exports. With respect to re-investment, there has been some of this, but available data for certain countries tend to show annual investment outflows to be in excess of annual inflows.

Trinidad and Tobago

Trinidad and Tobago is one of the wealthiest of the CARICOM countries. On the basis of per capita income it would easily qualify as a middle-income developing country. In 1979 it had a per capita GNP of almost US$4,000 as compared to US$1,110 for Jamaica, US$2,680 for Barbados, US$3,770 for Singapore.

Growth in the post-war period has been somewhat uneven. At current prices GDP (at factor cost) grew at an annual rate of between 11 and 12% during the 1950s, just over 6% in the 1960s and around 27% in the 1970s.[52] The latter figure has a high inflationary content. Real growth rate is estimated to have been in the region of 4 to 5% as compared to about 8% in the 1950s. Generally real income has grown at a faster rate than population in the post-war period, resulting in a positive growth rate for per capita income. In the 1970s real per capita GNP grew at an average rate of 4.5% per annum.[53]

The main economic force in Trinidad and Tobago's economy is the petroleum sector which tends to determine the pace of overall economic activity. The growth rates of the 1970s were heavily influenced by the boom in the petroleum industry resulting from the price increases won by OPEC during the decade. In recent years the oil sector has contributed over 60% (on average) to government's current revenue. Since 1974, it has accounted for between 80 and 90% of export earnings and contributed almost 40% (on average) to GDP (at current factor cost). The comparable percentage contribution to GDP in the 1950s was around 31%.

Value added in manufacturing has grown since the war, but its relative share in total product has tended to decline in recent years in the face of developments experienced in the oil sector. The share of manufacturing (including construction) in GDP (at current factor cost) grew from TT$52 million in 1951 to TT$149 million in 1960, to $151 million (manufacturing excluding construction) in 1970 and to TT$912 million in 1980.[54] Manufacturing (including construction) averaged about 16% of total product during the 1950s as compared to 7.5% (manufacturing alone) during the 1970s. The sector has been promoted as a means of diversifying the economy particularly with respect to job creation and exports. Success in these objectives, however, has been limited. As indicated earlier, the main interest of foreign investors has been to 'capture' the local market by getting behind the high protective 'walls' which government has used to encourage local industry. Penetration has usually been effected through various kinds of commercial arrangements with local business. Once a satisfactory profit level could be obtained on the basis of local sales the incentive to export tends not to be very strong. The fact that the framework used has also tended to create local monopolies free from competition has generally removed the stimulus for quality improvement and the incentive to undertake policies designed to reduce prices. Given this situation and given the fact that the manufacturing sector is heavily dependent on imported raw materials, equipment and end products (which are merely assembled locally), the sector's contribution to net foreign exchange earnings has tended to be very small. The situation described here applies more or less to all the other Commonwealth Caribbean countries.

The role of direct foreign investment Trinidad and Tobago has long been a recipient of direct foreign investment.[55] As a colony of Britain the sugar plantations were developed by British enterprise in the 17th century within the imperial commercial framework in which the colonies supplied food and raw materials to Britain in return for manufactured goods. The growth of the oil industry from the beginning of the 20th century has also been associated with foreign capital. Though a small oil producer, Trinidad and Tobago is reputed to be one of the oldest. The data we have at our disposal on the role of foreign capital in the economy pertain largely to the post-war period, and we shall use these to give some indication of its contribution to development.

Table 6.4 gives some idea of the contribution of the respective sources of savings to capital formation from the early 1950s to the early 1960s. Between 1952 and 1962 private foreign capital accounted for 36% (on average) of gross capital formation. If we take the period between 1956 and 1966 FDI accounted (on average) for 54% of total net domestic capital formation (public and private) and 68% (on average) of net private sector capital formation.[56] The extent of foreign capital inflows in this period should not necessarily be taken as a reflection of inadequate domestic savings. The data presented in the Table indicate that domestic savings financed about 62% (on average) of gross capital formation in the period. (Central government borrowing took place in two years, and this amounted to about 2% (on average) of gross capital formation in the period.) Between 1952 and 1962 gross local (national) savings averaged about 19.4% of GDP (at factor cost) and net local (national) savings (i.e. excluding depreciation allowances) about 10%. A large part of these savings would have flowed out of the country through financial institutions which were largely foreign owned in this period. Another point is worth noting here. A substantial part of DFI is often financed from re-investment of earnings. This latter represents resources generated by local production. We do not have data on the proportion of total foreign investment financed from re-invested profits in the 1950s and 1960s. Data for the 1970s, however, reveal that re-invested earnings accounted for a significant proportion of DFI in this period. According to IMF figures, between 1973 and 1980 total direct investments amounted to 789.5 millions SDRs. Of this, new capital amounted to 31.7 million SDRs and re-invested earnings 824.3 million SDRs. These last two figures were offset by capital outflows of 66.5 million SDRs.[57]

Table 6.4 *Trinidad and Tobago: finance of capital formation, 1952–62*

(Percentage Contribution)

Year	*Provisions for Consumption*	*Savings of Locally-Owned Corporations*	*Savings of Households*[1]	*Savings of Gov't.*	*Private Capital Inflows*	*Other Trans-actions*	*Total*
1952	31.0	3.6	25.0	11.6	36.8	−8.0	100.0
53	44.8	5.9	36.2	8.7	31.8	−27.4	100.0
54	40.7	6.1	37.6	6.2	44.0	−34.6	100.0
55	37.9	3.0	22.2	6.7	30.1	0.1	100.0
56	42.9	7.3	20.3	8.4	38.5	−17.4	100.0
57	28.2	4.8	16.9	15.2	58.3	−23.4	100.0
58	30.7	8.1	15.5	18.4	33.7	−6.4	100.0
59	29.0	5.3	11.5	14.1	43.8	−3.7	100.0
60	32.5	3.6	15.3	13.0	32.0	3.6	100.0
61	38.4	2.6	26.2	4.6	24.9	3.3	100.0
62	37.8	3.1	20.4	5.5	24.9	8.3	100.0

1 include unincorporated enterprises.

Source: CSO, *The National Income of Trinidad and Tobago, 1952–62.*

Savings data have not been published since 1962. The indications are that the national ratio has increased over the years. Government savings alone in the period since 1974 has averaged around 18% of GDP (at current factor cost). Domestic resources have financed an increasing proportion of capital formation. A glance at Table 6.5 shows that whereas net direct investment averaged about 31% of gross domestic capital formation in the 1956–75 period, the proportion for the period 1976–79 was around 14%. The resource situation since 1974 has been such that the Government has allowed regional financial institutions like the Inter-American Development Bank and the Caribbean Development Bank to float bonds on the local market. Government foreign debt outstanding increased from TT$158.2 million at the end of 1970 to an estimated TT$1,049 billion at the end of November 1981, but this was not motivated by any pressing need for foreign savings. In the same period the foreign reserves of the Central Bank increased from TT$96.2 million to TT$7.328 billion. One of the arguments put forward by Government to justify its resort to foreign finance in a period when its reserves were increasing was that this would help establish its credit rating in foreign capital markets,[58] to which at some time it believes it may have to turn on a more significant scale. The external debt outstanding at the end of 1981, it should be pointed out, was still small when measured by certain standards. In relation to GDP it amounted to about 6%, while service payments (interest and amortisation) in the period since 1970 have averaged under 3% of the earnings of goods and services on current account.

In the post-war period a significant proportion of private capital has gone into the oil industry. In the 1950s this averaged about 36% of gross domestic capital formation and about 44% of private sector

Table 6.5 *Trinidad and Tobago: selected direct investment statistics and service payment data, 1956–79*

			Service Payments (TT$mn)		
Years	*Net Direct Investment as a % of Gross Domestic Capital Formation*[1] *(1)*	*Direct Investment Income as a % of Exports*[2] *(2)*	*Management Fees*[3] *(3)*	*Royalties, Patents & Similar Fees*[3] *(4)*	*Professional & Technical Fees*[4] *(5)*
1956	38.2	24.5	1.6	4.3	a
57	58.5	34.1	1.8	5.6	a
58	33.9	21.8	2.0	6.3	a
59	43.7	27.1	3.5	6.6	a
60	26.6	22.5	n.a.	n.a.	n.a.
61	20.5	22.9	n.a.	n.a.	n.a.
62	24.7	22.1	n.a.	n.a.	n.a.
63	36.6	20.5	4.7	10.0	n
64	21.2	17.8	4.8	10.1	a
65	32.8	15.3	4.0	10.0	a
66	14.7	28.9	3.7	1.7	n.a.
67	14.4	27.0	4.0	1.6	n.a.
68	16.8	31.2	6.3	3.7	n.a.
69	46.9	27.2	3.4	2.9	n.a.
70	39.4	26.2	4.1	3.7	0.0
71	32.2	28.1	5.2	3.9	0.0
72	25.8	26.2	2.0	1.2	0.0
73	20.6	24.0	7.6	2.0	13.8
74	28.8	30.2	7.2	2.7	26.3
75	38.2	24.2	7.4	3.7	31.7
76	16.2	26.6	13.9	4.9	51.3
77	16.4	34.5	13.9	9.7	81.7
78p	11.2	31.0	14.8	8.1	134.9
79p	13.7	33.4	11.5	11.7	189.5

1 capital formation data used from 1963 onwards are IMF estimates.
2 exports excluding petroleum falling under Petroleum Agreement.
3 the data for the 1956–65 period include unspecified miscellaneous services and are therefore not strictly comparable with the data for the period 1966–79.
4 including commissions.
a included in (3).
n.a. not available.
p provisional.

Sources: Table 6.6; CSO, *The Balance of Payments of Trinidad & Tobago*, various issues; IMF *Financial Statistics*, various issues; A. McIntyre and B. Watson, *Studies in Foreign Investment in the Commonwealth Caribbean, No. 1, Trinidad and Tobago*. ISER 1970.

capital formation. Table 6.6 shows that oil and related industries continue to be the major attraction for foreign private investors. Between 1973 and 1979, over 80% of foreign direct investment has been in oil and related industries.

Table 6.6 *Trinidad and Tobago: annual net direct investment[1] in private sector enterprises by sectors, 1973–79*

TT$mn.

Sectors	1973	1974	1975	1976	1977	1978	1979	Cumulative 1973–79	
								Total	%
1. Petroleum Industries	108.1	206.4	470.8	254.9	250.5	260.2	353.5	1,904.4	89.3
1.1 Mining, exploration and production, refineries, petrochemicals.	(108.5)	(204.7)	(464.9)	(261.2)	(169.0)	(244.1)	(355.1)	(1,807.5)	(84.8)
1.2 Service contractors, marketing and distribution	(−0.4)	(1.7)	(5.9)	(−6.3)	(81.5)	(16.1)	(−1.6)	(96.9)	(4.5)
2. Food processing and drink including tobacco	13.2	6.3	3.0	4.2	30.4	5.0	19.2	81.3	3.8
3. Chemicals and non-metallic minerals	1.9	18.8	10.3	−39.0	6.9	3.2	12.2	14.3	0.6
4. Assembly type and related industries	4.1	6.0	3.6	4.5	18.6	8.9	0.5	46.2	2.2
5. Distribution	4.0	1.6	0.3	0.9	10.7	11.9	14.7	44.1	2.1
6. All other sectors	−2.9	7.6	−47.9	35.6	19.1	15.5	16.4	43.4	2.0
Total	*128.4*	*246.7*	*440.1*	*261.1*	*336.2*	*304.7*	*416.5*	*2,133.7*	*100.0*

1 Investment minus dis-investment.

Source: CSO, *Balance of Payments of Trinidad and Tobago*, 1979.

Investment in resource industries (where high returns are expected) tends to give rise to significant capital outflows. An examination of Table 6.7 will show that in the period between 1956 and 1972, direct investment capital inflows exceeded direct investment income outflows in only four years. Total direct investment inflows for the period amounted to TT$3,020 million while income outflows relating to direct investment amounted to TT$5,320 million. The figures in column (4) of Table 6.7 largely reflect direct investment income paid abroad and interest on the external debt. 'Net' implies that the figures have been adjusted for foreign investment inflows. In recent years, the interest income from the investment of the country's foreign reserve has been relatively large compared to returns prior to 1975. In the absence of these positive inflows, net investment income outflows would obviously have been higher. For the entire period 1956–83, *total net investment income* outflows amounted to TT$6,115 million while direct investment inflows amounted to TT$5,310 million. For the period 1956–81, direct investment inflows was TT$4,563, as compared to TT$7,243 for *direct investment income outflows*.

Table 6.7 *Trinidad and Tobago: selected balance of payments data, 1956–83*

TT$mn.

		Current Account			*Capital Account (Non-monetary Sector)*		
Year	*(1) Current A/C Bal.*	*(2) Net Direct Investment Income*	*(3) Other Investment Income*	*(4) Net Investment Income (2) + (3)*	*(5) Direct Investment*	*(6) Other Private Capital*	*(7) Public Sector*[1]
1956	−30	−71	2	−69	48	–	–
57	−59	−111	2	−109	101	–	–
58	−53	−80	3	−77	70	–	–
59	−90	−105	3	−102	109	–	–
60	−88	−98	4	−94	76	−8	–
61	−72	−126	6	−120	61	−6	–
62	−97	−123	4	−119	73	−6	12
63	−102	−122	6	−116	105	−5	43
64	−84	−123	2	−121	58	−5	23
65	−118	−108	5	−103	107	−5	17
66	−62	−106	−1	−108	43	–	10
67	−25	−113	−1	−114	43	–	3
68	33	−129	2	−127	51	–	12
69	−38	−137	4	−133	128	–	5
70	−116	−119	−3	−122	166	7	−8
71	−233	−121	−2	−123	206	17	31
72	−283	−129	−4	−133	167	−2	34
73	−51	−157	−14	−171	128	−66	58
74	576	−576	–	−576	247	13	−192
75	716	−222	52	−170	440	−31	−65
76	619	−351	104	−246	261	−21	−383
77	516	−605	164	−441	336	8	332
78	97	−410	246	−164	305	128	233

Table 6.7—*(Cont'd)*

TT$mn.

Year	*Current Account*				*Capital Account (Non-monetary Sector)*		
	(1) Current A/C Bal.	*(2) Net Direct Investment Income*	*(3) Other Investment Income*	*(4) Net Investment Income (2) + (3)*	*(5) Direct Investment*	*(6) Other Private Capital*	*(7) Public Sector*[1]
1979	−87	−840	252	−588	417	444	135
80	945	−1,150	427	−722	329	50	163
81	751	−1,011	555	−456	488	261	−229
82	−1,786	n.a.	n.a.	−186	637	263	231
83[e]	−2,320	n.a.	n.a.	−505	110	142	164

1 excludes SDRs allocations.
n.a. not available.
e estimate.

Source: CSO, *Balance of Payments of Trinidad and Tobago*, various issues; Ministry of Finance, *Review of the Economy 1983*; IMF, *Balance of Payments Statistics Yearbook*, various issues.

Besides profits remittances, direct investment also tends to be associated with other types of payments such as royalties, management fees, etc. As indicated earlier, penetration of the manufacturing sector has been affected through a variety of arrangements with local businessmen who make payments for the use of brand names, formulae, techniques, etc. Table 6.5 gives some indication of the magnitude of these outflows. The data, it should be noted, do not distinguish between payments made by foreign controlled firms and payments made by local enterprises using (or renting) foreign know-how and management skills. The figures have shown a tendency to increase significantly in recent years. Management fees more than doubled between 1974 and 1978, but dropped slightly in 1979. Royalties and patent payments increased from TT$2.7 million in 1974 to TT$11.7 million in 1979. Professional and technical fees grew from TT$13.8 million in 1973 to TT$189.5 million in 1979. These figures were affected by the importation of skilled personnel (such as architects, engineers, etc.) required by the booming construction industry during the 1970s.

Since the McIntyre-Watson study was published in 1970, there have been some significant developments in the ownership pattern of Trinidad and Tobago's economy. The draft Third Five-Year Plan (1969–73) published in 1968 had, as once of its main objectives, a reduction in external economic dependence. In describing the position at the time, the Plan had this to say: 'There has been economic growth and expansion, it is true, but nearly all the decisions bearing on this growth and expansion have been taken by metropolitan Governments and metropolitan producers. This state of affairs has carried the corollary that the process of economic growth has not been internally propelled.'[59] In discussing the strategy for the 1970s, the Plan saw the need for a more diversified economy 'with considerably more economic decision-making being located internally, and with full-employment'.[60] Increasing the proportion of local ownership and participation in the economy was a primary objective. In order to accomplish this, emphasis had to be placed 'on the development and utilisation of local resources of trained manpower, trained management entrepreneurship, raw materials and capital – and on more local scientific and technological research.'[61]

By opting for a policy of localisation and seeking to have greater national involvement in areas representing the 'commanding heights' of the economy, the Trinidad and Tobago Government has not declared itself to be anti-foreign investment. What it has done in the various statements issued since 1970 is to indicate the conditions under which foreign investment would be accepted and the areas where it expects foreign investors to contribute. The policy statement contained in the Third Five-Year Plan, 1969–73 (pp. 54–56) provided the framework for action in the 1970s. There was one section in that statement, however, which remains substantially in abeyance. Paragraph 9 of that statement reads as follows: 'Branches and subsidiaries of foreign companies will be required to re-invest locally a minimum of a certain percentage of their after-tax profits. Where they do not wish to re-invest in their own line of business, they will be required to invest their funds in locally controlled public companies or in the proposed Development Finance Company, in such a manner that they do not acquire controlling or dominant interest in these enterprises.' The 1970 statement is summarised in clearer terms in the 1972 Budget Speech (p. 11) as follows:

1 We acknowledge new foreign investment which brings in expertise, new technology and access to export markets to assist and supplement national efforts in our development.
2 No new 100 per cent foreign owned enterprise will be allowed in key sectors of the economy and national participation in joint ventures involving the new foreign firms must be of meaningful proportion.
3 Alienation of land will not be permitted.
4 Existing foreign owned enterprises must take steps to facilitate national participation, including in particular worker-participation.
5 Certain areas of our economy are reserved exclusively for national effort.
6 All firms, whatever the structure of their ownership, must in their operations give ample opportunity to transfer to nationals the skills, knowledge and expertise required to run the business.
7 Government will take a leading part, including the use of direct participation, to expedite national control and ownership.

'An integral part of our overall policy towards private foreign investment is to diversify the sources of investment funds and, in particular, to seek the participation in our national development of European and Japanese capital and entrepreneurship, in addition to capital from the traditional sources such as the United Kingdom, the United States of America and Canada.'

At the time of the Black Power disturbances in April, 1970 the Government had already taken a number of steps to increase local ownership of the economy, including its own participation in a number of areas. For example, in 1968 the Alien Land-Holding Law was amended and modernised to enable the Government to exercise greater control over purchases of land, securities and physical assets by non-nationals. The international carrier BWIA was purchased as far back as 1961. The 1970 disturbances accelerated the localisation process. In a nationwide radio and television broadcast of 3rd May, 1970 the then Prime Minister boasted that with respect to the enlargement of national decision-making, Trinidad and Tobago had gone further than any other country in the Caribbean except Cuba. He summarised the position then as follows:

100% national ownership in the Hilton Hotel
100% national ownership in the Orange Grove Sugar Company (purchased in 1968). (Later in 1970, Government purchased 51% of Caroni Ltd., the other major Sugar Company, owned by Tate & Lyle of Britain.)
100% national ownership in the new National Commercial Bank which was set up on the basis of assets purchased from the Bank of London and Montreal in 1970. (This was the first nationally-owned commercial bank.)
100% national ownership in the public utilities, electricity, water, sewerage, transport.
100% national ownership in Radio Guardian (one of two radio stations operating in the country).
100% national ownership in Trinidad and Tobago Television (the only-Television Station in the Country).
51% national ownership in Port Landing Company.
51% national ownership in Cable and Wireless (now Textel).
51% national ownership in the new company for the manufacture of particle board from bargasse.
51% national ownership in Trinidad Tesoro which took over (in 1969) the former British Petroleum Properties.
50% national ownership in the Telephone System.

During the 1970s the localisation process was further intensified. In the Third Five-Year Plan published in 1970, government indicated (p. 46) that no new foreign insurance companies or commercial banks or hire purchase institutions would be allowed to be established in the country, except in special circumstances. In 1972 another locally-owned bank (the Workers' Bank) came into operation, with substantial government participation. By the beginning of 1973 the Government had also undertaken investments in a number of manufacturing and other enterprises including a printing and packaging company, a meat processing plant and the Point Lisas Development Company. The list has since been expanded further to include activity in agriculture, fisheries, electronics, etc. The sugar industry which was dominated by foreign firms in the 1960s has now been completely nationalised. In 1967, the Government had indicated to the private foreign-dominated financial sector that it should take steps to localise its operations. In the 1970s branches of the British and Canadian banks operating in the country were converted by their owners into local companies and shares offered to nationals. The eventual objective is for nationals to obtain a controlling interest in these institutions. The two American banks operating in the country refused to comply with government's policy and, in the Budget Speech of 1981, the Prime Minister froze the deposits of these banks and allowed them one year to phase out their deposits. The Chase Manhattan has since sold out to the government-owned National Commercial Bank, while Citibank has since decided to bow to government's policy. In his 1975 Budget Speech, the Minister of Finance revealed that, with one exception, foreign insurance companies were resisting government's localisation policy. In order to force compliance he announced that with effect from 1st January, 1978, only premiums on new policies issued by companies with at least 25% local shareholding would qualify as a tax expense. Since the tax benefit is an important incentive for purchasing life insurance, companies which issued policies that did not qualify for this concession would have been at a disadvantage to other companies. Another measure aimed at increasing localisation was the requirement that with effect from 1st January, 1975 companies should keep 70% of their Statutory Fund in local assets and 80% in local plus CARICOM assets. A few companies found that they could not accept government's policy on the insurance industry and closed their local operations. The slack was taken up by other companies, and there has been no discernible adverse effects on the industry stemming from the measures described. With respect to other financial companies, a number of local entities have emerged in recent years to provide services previously monopolised by foreign concerns. Finance no longer seems to be the estoric business it was some years ago.

Through its National Petroleum Company, Government participates with foreign investors in oil and gas exploration, and has now largely taken over the distribution of refined petroleum products in the domestic market. The government also participates in oil mining and refining through Trinidad and Tobago Oil Company Limited (TRINTOC) (wholly-owned) and Trinidad Tesoro Petroleum Company Limited (majority-owned). The major part of the country's refining capacity, however, is still owned by Texaco whose operations continue to exert a major influence on the level of economic activity in the country. For some time the Government has been under pressure by the powerful Oilfield Workers Trade Union to nationalise the assets of the Texas-based company. The Government, however, has opted to seek participation in the company rather than nationalise it, and negotiations have been going on for some time. In the 1974 Budget Speech, the then Minister of Finance, Mr George Chambers (now Prime Minister), announced that agreement had been reached in principle for Government participation in the company. In August, 1984 the Prime Minister announced that the government had decided to buy Texaco's assets (excluding the marine operations) for US$175 million.

Since 1974 the significant increase in government revenues stemming from the increases in oil prices has encouraged government to get involved in a number of energy-based industries. In seeking participation in new activity there were three routes open to it.[62] One was to make participation a condition of a licence as is being done in new issues of oil exploration licences. This approach has been used in invitations for bids for new acreage. In these invitations a minimum carried participation of 35 per cent has been stipulated and provision is also made for Government to secure a 51 per cent interest eventually at its option. The second route was to agree with a sponsor of a specific project on a particular percentage of Government participation and to negotiate the terms for payment. The negotiations on the liquid ammonia plant and on the liquified natural gas project fall in this category. The third route was for government on its own initiative to develop projects and seek out private or official partners for joint-venture operations. This latter was favoured with respect to projects based on petroleum and related natural resources. There were three reasons given for adopting it:

1 These projects involve large sums of money.
2 They depend on complex and rapidly changing technology.
3 They require an export market.

A list of energy based projects undertaken or proposed was given in the 1980 Budget Speech and is reproduced below.

Projects	*Estimated Cost TT$mn*	*Gov't. Share*	*Status*
Tringen	264	51/49 W.R. Grace	Begun 1975. Completed 1977
ISCOTT (Iron & Steel)	840	100%	Begun October, 1977 Completed 1981
Fertrin (Fertiliser)	600	51/49 with AMOCO	Begun 1978.

Trintoc Refinery (up grading)	850		Decision 1979 Possible completion date-1982
Aluminium Smelter	1,400		Decision 1979 Not yet begun
Methanol	300		Decision in 1981
LNG (including tanker fleet and pipeline	6,000	Partners: Tenneco and People Gas	Decision in 1981

Without fanfare and without resort to ideological posturing the Government has taken over a large part of the operations in the economy that were under foreign control. It has opted to permit substantial foreign participation in the petroleum and energy-based industries, which comprise the most dynamic and vital sectors of the economy. Despite a desire to diversify the sources of foreign investment, the US remains the most significant. At the end of 1981 US direct investment in Trinidad and Tobago amounted to US$932 million. Of this US$808 million (87%) was in petroleum, and US$102 million (11%) in manufacturing. Besides the direct investment undertaken by US based transnational corporations in the petroleum and energy-based sectors, US financial institutions have provided a substantial part of the debt finance in the projects. The US Export Import bank loaned the Government US$200 million with respect of Fertrin, ISCOTT and the new Point Lisas Power Plant. US commercial banks are also involved heavily in the financing of Fertrin, Tringen, ISCOTT and the power plant.[63]

The Government's reasoning for its partnership with foreign transnational corporations in the development of its energy-based industries was outlined earlier. When this policy is viewed against its action in other areas of the economy, it is clearly an attempt to reconcile what it sees as an essential need for markets and technology (which are controlled by transnationals) with nationalist aspirations. To the Government this is practical policy. To nationalists it represents economic re-colonisation. Leaving aside the degree of foreign participation, there has been strong criticism of the strategy which has sought to concentrate so large a part of the nation's resources in a few huge projects whose impact on development is far from certain. The government, for its part, feels that these core industries could form the basis of secondary and tertiary activities and so add a new dimension to the assembly-oriented industrial sector that has grown up in the post-war period. For a small country with limited resources and choices operating in an international environment of highly protective structures, the options tend to be neither simple nor straightforward. Since mistakes stemming from the economic paths chosen can be costly, and can eventually affect the standard of living of the general population, the formulation of strategies needs to be open to the largest possible intellectual inputs and not confined to small groups of handpicked technocrats whose vision may go on further than their particular training.

The government has indicated that it intends to sell some of its shares in various companies to citizens of the country. One of its major concerns expressed from time to time is that ownership should not be concentrated in the hands of traditional commercial and business elites whose behaviour often differs little from that of foreign investors. This has been a basic factor in the ambivalence towards the private sector not only in Trinidad and Tobago but in other Caribbean countries as well. Despite all the efforts to promote small business, and to get the average citizen more involved in commerce and business, economic power still tends to be concentrated in the hands of small groups who are best placed to take advantage of the incentives offered by government. The concept of cooperatives which could strengthen the position of the small man in society is still far from developed.

As a final comment here it should be pointed out that localisation was a natural outgrowth of nationalist aspiration in the post-independence era. But it is not an end in itself. To view it as such could easily lead to stagnation. With localisation there is need for a wide range of supporting policies designed to encourage innovation, entrepreneurship, technological research, etc. in the context of the effort to internalise the growth.

Jamaica

During the 1950s and 1960s Jamaica experienced high rates of growth by international and historical standards. Between 1954 and 1961 the economy grew in real terms by almost 8% as compared to between 5 and 6% in the 1960s. Between 1971 and 1973 the real growth rate (based on 1970 prices) averaged about 5%. This was followed by 7 consecutive years of negative real growth. In 1981 there was a real growth rate of 2% (See Table 6.8). In average terms, per capita GNP (at current prices) increased from about US$300 in 1960 to about US$720 in 1970 and to US$1,110 in 1979. Real GNP per capita is estimated to have grown by about −3.7% between 1970 and 1979.[64]

Table 6.8 *Jamaica: average annual growth rates of GDP at current and constant prices, 1954–81*

Year/Period	*Current Prices %*	*Constant Prices %*
1954–61	11.0	7.8[a]
1962–70	14.1	5.2[b]
1971	9.6	3.1[c]
72	12.2	9.2
73	20.6	2.8

Year/Period	*Current Prices %*	*Constant Prices %*
1974	25.0	−5.4
75	20.5	−0.6
76	3.9	−6.1
77	10.2	−1.7
78	25.7	−0.3
79	14.2	−1.5
80	10.6	−5.4
81	11.6	2.0

a based on 1956 prices.
b based on 1960 prices.
c 1971 onwards based on 1970 prices.

Sources: Five year Independence Plan, 1963–68; Department of Statistics, *National Income and Product*, various issues.

Bauxite production began in Jamaica in 1952 and has now become one of the leading sectors in the Jamaican economy, accounting in 1981 for about 13% of GDP as compared to less than 2% in 1952. (See Table 6.9.) In 1981 bauxite and alumina accounted for almost 80% of total exports as compared to about 6% for sugar and rum, less than 1% for bananas, and just over 1% for citrus, coffee and related products. Previous to the 1950s the manufacturing sector was based mainly on the processing of local agricultural products and the production of a limited range of consumer goods for local consumption and exports, such as sugar, rum, cigars and cigarettes, non-alcoholic beverages, and a range of food products.[65] Since then a range of assembly-type industries has sprung up, producing mainly for the local and CARICOM markets. As can be seen in Table 6.9 the contribution of manufacturing to GDP grew from about 11% in 1950 to around 15% in recent years. There was a concomitant decline in the share of agriculture from 30% in 1950, to 8% in 1981. Over this same period the public sector's share increased from 6% to around 15%.

Table 6.9 *Jamaica: composition of GDP at current factor cost, 1950–81*

(Percentages)

Sectors	*1950*	*1952*	*1955*	*1965*	*1970*[c]	*1975*[c]	*1980*	*1981*
Agriculture, Forestry & Fishing	30.4	25.1	19.2	11.6	6.7	7.7	8.4	7.9
Mining & Quarrying	a	1.7	4.6	9.7	12.7	10.6	14.2	12.7
Manufacture	11.3	12.2	13.4	15.0	15.4	16.1	15.5	14.8
Construction and Installation	7.6	10.8	9.5	10.7	16.3	11.3	5.9	6.8
Distributive Trade	15.1	16.3	16.8	14.4	15.4	15.2	19.6	20.9
Transport, Communication, Storage	7.1	5.9	7.0	7.4	5.4	6.7	5.1	4.7

Table 6.9—*(Cont'd)*

(Percentages)

Sectors	*1950*	*1952*	*1955*	*1965*	*1970*[c]	*1975*[c]	*1980*	*1981*
Financing and Insurance Services	b	b	b	4.4	4.8	5.0	4.2	5.0
Real Estate and Business Services	b	b	b	b	8.4	8.2	8.6	9.5
Producers of Gov't Services	6.0	6.3	6.6	7.5	7.8	13.5	14.7	14.7
Other	22.5	21.7	22.9	19.3	7.1	5.7	3.8	3.0
Total	100.0	100.0	100.0	100.0	100.0	100.0	100.0	100.0

a included in Agriculture, Forestry and Fishing.
b included in 'Other'.
c at market values.

Sources: Five Year Independence Plan, 1963–68. Department of Statistics, *National Income and Product*, various issues.

Despite this growth performance, and the structural changes which have taken place in the economy since the Second World War, the country faces serious social and economic problems. The unemployment ratio has increased from about 18% in the late fifties to over 20% in recent years. The figure in April, 1982 was 27%. Of the 757,000 persons employed in April, 1982, 35% were in agriculture, forestry and fishing, 1.1% in mining, quarrying and refining, 11.6% in manufacture 4.3% in construction and installation, 13.8% in public administration and the rest in other services. In the context of the structure of the economy we discribed earlier, this in itself should give some indication of the distribution of income. Large differences exist in the earnings from different types of activity, particularly between agriculture and the other sectors.[66] Recent data on the distribution of total income among the population is not available. A study[67] done in the late fifties indicated that the top 5% of households accounted for 30% of total income (before tax) while the 60% at the lower end of the scale received 19% of total income. There is no evidence to indicate that the situation has improved significantly since.

Growth during the 1950s and 1960s was significantly influenced by foreign investment in the bauxite industry and public sector investment. Girvan has indicated that out of an estimated total capital inflow of J$290.4 million in the period 1950–66, the bauxite sector accounted for 58%, the public sector for 16% and the banking sector for 4%.[68] Between 1956 and 1971 the mining sector accounted for about 18% of total domestic capital formation on average, as compared to 12% for manufacturing and 13% for the public sector (excluding the utilities). The share of financial intermediaries in the period 1961–71 averaged about 1.6%. Some idea of the contribution of other sectors to total fixed capital formation (for selected years) in the period between 1956 and 1970 can be got from Table 6.10.

Table 6.10 *Jamaica: fixed capital formation by sectors, 1956–71*

(Percentages)

Sectors	*1956*	*1961*	*1966*	*1969*	*1970*
Agriculture, Forestry & Fishing	9.0	11.3	8.9	4.4	4.4
Mining, Quarrying & Refining	29.9	2.7	14.4	35.5	35.9
Manufacturing	10.6	18.3	11.9	9.8	9.8
Construction & Installation	a	4.5	7.0	4.4	4.4
Electricity, Gas & Water	1.5	4.6	2.3	6.2	6.2
Transportation, Storage & Communication	a	12.0	11.9	7.5	7.5
Distribution	a	14.6	7.2	3.5	3.6
Financial Intermediaries	a	1.7	1.6	1.7	1.6
Ownership of Dwellings	10.3	15.2	13.9	7.4	7.4
Public Administration	7.2	11.2	15.9	16.4	16.1
Other	31.5	3.9	5.0	3.1	3.1
Total	100.0	100.0	100.0	100.0	100.0

a included in 'Other'.

Source: Department of Statistics, *National Income and Product*, 1970; Five Year Independence Plan, 1963–68.

Available data indicate that since 1956 gross capital formation as a proportion of GDP has generally been over 20%. In more recent years the proportion has tended to fluctuate greatly. (See Table 6.11.) Between 1956 and 1975 the ratio averaged 26.5%. In the period between 1976 and 1981, however, the figure fell to 18.3%. A significant part of capital formation over the years has been financed from domestic savings. As can be seen in Column (2) of Table 6.11, gross national savings as a proportion of GDP averaged 19.4% between 1956 and 1975. In the 1976–81 period the figure fell to 7.6%. Net capital inflows (including undistributed profits of resident foreign corporations) averaged about 7.1% of GDP between 1956 and 1981. In terms of the respective contributions made by domestic resources and foreign resources, the published data, while not being sufficiently detailed, does permit us to draw certain conclusions. The figures on 'Gross National Savings' used in Table 6.11 include only the savings of local households, local unincorporated businesses, locally-owned corporations and government. The re-invested profits of resident foreign-owned businesses derived from domestic production is treated as a capital inflow. McIntyre and Watson[69] have made the point that in terms of gauging the capacity of the economy to generate its own savings for development, 'Gross Domestic Savings' is a better concept than either 'Gross National Savings' (which excludes the re-invested profits of foreign-owned corporations) or 'Total Savings', (which is equal to 'Gross Domestic Savings' plus new inflows from abroad). An examination of Table 6.12 will show that on average 'Gross National Savings' financed over 70% of gross capital formation between 1956 and 1981. Net capital inflows averaged about 30%. If we take net capital inflows as a percentage of net capital formation, the average would be nearer 50%. In recent years foreign inflows have tended to account for an increasing proportion of net capital formation. (See Table 6.11.) There is a point (to which we have already alluded) worth noting here, however. To the extent that capital inflows include undistributed profits of resident foreign corporations, the figures will tend to exaggerate the contributions of foreign savings to domestic capital formation. We do not have data on the re-investment of profits by resident foreign corporations for the period prior to 1973. Figures published by the IMF[70] indicate that of the J$2,200 million of capital inflows in the period 1973–81, re-investment accounted for about 20%. Since this was a period in which a certain amount of disinvestment was taking place this proportion may not be a true reflection of the position in the 1950s and 1960s, when re-investment may have accounted for a higher proportion of inflows.

In Table 6.12 we show the contribution of the various sources of savings to gross domestic investment. Private savings (which include both personal and corporate savings) contributed about 28% (on average) to gross capital accumulation in the period between 1956 and 1981. We do not have data on the breakdown of private savings between personal savings and corporate savings for the entire period. The figures available for the period 1956 to 1969 indicate that corporate savings tended to account for over 60% of the total. It is clear from Table 6.12 that depreciation accounts for a significant proportion of total capital accumulation. Between 1956 and 1981 this contribution averaged about 38%. Government savings between 1956 and 1975 financed about 12% (on average) of total investment. Since 1976 government saving has been negative, reflecting the different rates of growth between revenue and expenditure.

Table 6.11 *Jamaica: selected investment and savings statistics, 1956–1981*

Year	*Gross Capital Formation as a % of GDP*[1] *(1)*	*Gross National Saving as a % of GDP*[1] *(2)*	*Net Capital Inflow as a % of GDP*[1] *(3)*	*Direct Investment as a % of Gross Cap. Formation (4)*	*Net Capital Inflow as a % of Net Cap. Formation (5)*
1956	26.2	15.6	10.7	n.a.	54.3
57	29.8	21.3	8.5	n.a.	38.0
58	25.6	18.1	7.5	n.a.	41.5
59	24.1	16.3	7.8	n.a.	47.0
60	23.3	16.1	7.2	n.a.	45.7

Year	Gross Capital Formation as a % of GDP[1] (1)	Gross National Saving as a % of GDP[1] (2)	Net Capital Inflow as a % of GDP[1] (3)	Direct Investment as a % of Gross Cap. Formation (4)	Net Capital Inflow as a % of Net Cap. Formation (5)
1961	22.2	20.7	1.5	n.a.	10.1
62	20.8	19.6	1.2	n.a.	1.6
63	19.3	20.6	−1.3	n.a.	−11.7
64	22.1	16.7	5.6	n.a.	38.6
65	21.9	18.2	3.7	n.a.	25.9
66	22.5	18.0	4.5	n.a.	29.7
67	24.6	18.0	6.5	n.a.	37.7
68	29.6	20.2	9.4	43.5	42.5
69	30.0	19.4	10.5	32.6	47.3
70	34.4	27.2	7.2	36.6	30.7
71	35.2	22.9	12.3	23.8	49.7
72	29.9	21.0	8.9	5.3	46.9
73	34.1	23.9	10.2	3.7	43.8
74	26.4	19.4	7.0	4.0	43.6
75	28.2	15.6	9.7	−0.3	52.5
76	19.9	7.6	12.3	−0.2	124.4
77	13.1	8.7	4.5	−1.8	153.5
78	16.3	12.5	3.8	−7.3	58.2
79	20.6	15.5	5.1	−5.6	47.7
80	16.8	10.3	6.6	6.8	88.8
81	23.3	10.0	13.3	−1.8	97.6

1 at factor cost.
n.a. not available.

Source: Dept. of Statistics, *National Income and Product*, various issues; *Balance of Payments of Jamaica*, various issues.

Table 6.12 *Jamaica: financing of gross domestic investment, 1956–1981*

(Percentages)

Year	Gov't Savings (1)	Private Savings[1] (2)	Depreciation (3)	Net Foreign Borrowing[2] (4)	Total (5)
1956	11.5	22.6	25.2	40.7	100.0
57	15.2	31.6	24.6	28.6	100.0
58	14.3	26.9	29.5	29.3	100.0
59	13.7	23.1	30.8	32.4	100.0
60	12.3	24.4	32.4	30.9	100.0
61	10.4	48.8	34.2	6.6	100.0
62	9.1	48.7	36.1	6.1	100.0
63	5.7	59.0	42.1	−6.8	100.0
64	10.2	30.0	34.7	25.1	100.0
65	12.7	35.4	35.0	16.9	100.0
66	16.1	31.3	32.6	20.0	100.0
67	12.4	31.6	29.5	26.5	100.0

Table 6.12—*(Cont'd)*

(Percentages)

Year	*Gov't Savings (1)*	*Private Savings*[1] *(2)*	*Depreciation (3)*	*Net Foreign Borrowing*[2] *(4)*	*Total (5)*
1968	11.2	31.8	25.4	31.6	100.0
69	16.9	22.3	25.6	35.2	100.0
70	13.7	33.6	31.7	21.0	100.0
71	15.8	19.6	29.7	34.9	100.0
72	10.9	22.8	36.6	29.7	100.0
73	3.2	35.1	31.9	29.8	100.0
74	23.4	10.9	39.0	26.7	100.0
75	10.4	20.7	34.5	34.4	100.0
76	−4.9	−7.2	50.2	61.9	100.0
77	−25.2	13.3	77.8	34.1	100.0
78	−18.1	34.7	60.3	23.1	100.0
79	−5.2	32.2	48.2	24.8	100.0
80	−17.7	22.6	56.0	39.1	100.0
81	−13.1	14.5	41.6	57.0	100.0

1 personal savings plus corporate savings.
2 as measured by current account deficit.

Source: Dept. of Statistics, *National Income and Product*, various issues, *Balance of Payments of Jamaica*, various issues.

With respect to foreign capital inflows there are two elements worth exploring in further detail: one is government external borrowing, and the other is direct foreign investment.

Government's total (net)[71] debt outstanding increased from J$239.2 million at the end of 1970 to J$5,065.0 million at the end of 1981. Over the same period the external component grew from J$80.3 million to J$1,959.2 million or by more than 24 times. Besides the size of the figures, the debt position at the end of 1981 differs in several ways from that at the end of 1970. For one thing, the government has grown increasingly more reliant on dollar sources for funds. Of the total debt outstanding at the end of 1981, 28.8% (13.4% in 1970) was repayable in US dollars. Sterling's share dropped from 21.3% to 2.9% over the same period, while the Jamaican dollar's share also fell slightly from 62.5% to 61.4%, and the Canadian dollar share from 2.8% to 1.7%. While detailed information on the maturity structure of the external debt outstanding in 1970 is not readily available, the evidence points to a shortening in the maturity structure of loans. Forty-four (44%) per cent of the external debt outstanding at the end of 1981 was repayable within five years while over 60% was repayable within 10 years. Increasing resort to borrowing has meant increasing debt service payments. While external debt charges in 1970 amounted to less than 3% of gross exports of goods and services, the proportion in 1980 was 18.5% and in 1981

29.3%. External debt charges (J$186.6 million in interest and J$251.2 million in amortization) amounted to 32.9% of cash inflows from exports of goods and services in 1980 and 56.7% in 1981.

This significant increase in the public debt has been brought about by several factors. One has been the rapid expansion of public expenditure in the context of a stagnating or declining economy reeling from the effects of a mixture of both domestic policies and developments in the international economy. One of the factors that had a severe effect on the government finances was the increases in oil prices won by OPEC during the 1970s, which affected all oil-importing countries. The oil bill (including related products) of Jamaica increased from J$66.3 million (10.8% of total imports in 1973) to J$817.7 million (39.9% of total imports) in 1980.

Exact data on the flow of foreign direct investment into Jamaica or the sectors where it went in the post-war period are not readily available. Between 1956 and 1981 total gross capital formation is estimated to have been in the region of J$8,894 million. Net capital formation amounted to roughly J$5,180 million. Over the same period net capital inflows (including government borrowing) totalled J$3,027 million. What part of the latter constituted direct investment we are unable to say. The figures available since 1968 indicate that total direct investment between 1968 and 1974 amounted to J$481 million. Between 1975 and 1980 disinvestment totalled J$46 million. For the period 1968 to 1980, therefore, total direct investment amounted to J$435 million. Over the same period investment income amounted to J$996 million. (See Table 6.13.)

Table 6.13 *Jamaica: selected balance of payments data, 1960–81*

J$mn

		Current Account			*Current Account (Non-monetary sectors)*			
		Net Investment Income						
Year	*Current A/c Balance (1)*	*Direct Investment (2)*	*Other (3)*	*Total (2)+(3)*	*Direct Investment (5)*	*Other Private Long-Term (6)*	*Other Private Short-Term[1] (7)*	*Official Account (8)*
1960	−20	n.a.	n.a.	−26	a	a	11	7
61	−9	n.a.	n.a.	−30	a	a	10	−4
62	−7	n.a.	n.a.	−30	a	a	14	2
63	−8	n.a.	n.a.	−32	a	a	23	5
64	−31	−30	1	−29	a	a	3	8
65	−22	−32	1	−31	a	a	10	6
66	−30	−67	2	−65	a	a	46	5
67	−51	−70	3	−67	a	a	80	3
68	−86	−65	4	−61	101	–	5	12
69	−103	−76	3	−73	85	–	3	10
70	−127	−87	5	−82	135	3	−2	−1
71	−97	−40	2	−38	98	8	2	4

Table 6.13—*(Cont'd)*

J$mn

		Current Account			*Current Account (Non-monetary sectors)*			
		Net Investment Income						
Year	*Current A/c Balance (1)*	*Direct Investment (2)*	*Other (3)*	*Total (2)+(3)*	*Direct Investment (5)*	*Other Private Long-Term (6)*	*Other Private Short-Term*[1] *(7)*	*Official Account (8)*
1972	−100	−42	−1	−43	21	11	9	19
73	−164	−46	−7	−53	20	69	2	33
74	−152	−42	−20	−62	21	102	16	82
75	−257	−54	−40	−94	−2	73	6	112
76	−275	−39	−54	−93	−1	9	−35	65
77	−32	−26	−91	−117	−6	4	59	5
78	−125	−132	−125	−257	−42	254	50	257
79	−253	−147	−212	−359	−46	−95	−2	125
80[4]	−264	−200	−273	−417	50	−82	82	369

Note: The figures from 1976 onwards have been converted from US dollars at the average annual rates of exchange published in IMF, *Financial Statistics*.

1 The figures for the period 1960–67 are presented in the official statistics as 'Identified Foreign Inflows'.
a Included in column (7).
n.a. not available.

Source: Dept of Statistics, *Balance of Payments of Jamaica*, various issues; National Planning Agency, *Economic Survey*, various issues; IMF *Balance of Payments Yearbook*, various issues.

The main areas which have attracted foreign private capital in the post-war period are the bauxite-alumina industry, tourism and the manufacturing sector. As indicated earlier, however, a significant part of the capital inflows into Jamaica in the 1950s and 1960s went into the bauxite-alumina sector. Jefferson has estimated that out of the roughly J$430 million foreign capital that flowed into Jamaica between 1950 and 1968, some J$300 million or 70% went into bauxite and alumina operations.[72] As far as the sources of private capital are concerned investment in the 'modern' sectors has originated largely in North America. US direct investment in Jamaica at the end of 1977 amounted to US$556 million. A substantial part of this would have been in the mining sector. Manufacturing accounted for US$221 million or 40%.

Foreign investment policy As indicated earlier, the incentive legislations enacted in the 1950s and 1960s were aimed primarily at attracting foreign investors. Foreign capital, whether attracted by the incentives offered or by the country's natural resources and assets, played a significant part in the structural changes and the high growth rates experienced by the Jamaican economy in the 1950s and 1960s.[73] In the period following independence (in 1962) some attempt was made to link concessions with local participation in ownership within a framework which continued to place heavy reliance on foreign capital as a critical factor in the process of economic development. In order to increase local savings and to gain a greater measure of national control over the financial sector, banks and insurance companies particularly, which had traditionally used the branch form of operation, were urged to form local companies with the eventual aim of placing majority ownership in local hands. The establishment of institutions like the National Commercial bank and the Workers Savings and Loans Bank was a reflection of a policy which saw the need for greater Jamaican participation in certain sectors of the economy.

By the time the People's National Party (PNP) government under Michael Manley's leadership assumed office in 1972, the need for greater local involvement in economic activities was already recognised and some further steps taken in this direction. The democratic socialism philosophy of the PNP had as one of its basic tenets greater control over the country's natural resources and general economic life of Jamaicans. This did not, however, mean the complete repudiation of a role for foreign investors, though the early rhetoric gave precisely that impression. 'We are interested in foreign capital that begins with a commitment to accept standards of good corporate citizenship. We believe that the guest investor proceeds most harmoniously and therefore, most successfully when he is in partnership with his Host. And, last but not least, we recognise absolutely both the need for and the legitimacy of just and adequate profits.'[74]

There was no doubt, however, that the policy of the Michael Manley administration in the context of the 'politics of participation' was less open than that of previous governments. First of all, it expressed a clear interest that foreign investors should undertake their investments in the form of joint ventures with local interests, whether in the public or private sector or both.[75] It also specified certain areas where government ownership would be essential, whether in partial or full form. These included the utilities, communications and certain basic and strategic industries like mining and cement. There were certain areas which were reserved for residents on the grounds of 'adequate capability' within Jamaica. These included, *inter alia*, internal distribution (except in cases of highly sophisticated equipment which requires continuous and highly technical development and servicing), restaurants and catering, internal transport, services such as hair-dressing and dry cleaning, auditing and accounting, entertainment, real estate development, the mass communication media, advertising and public relations, quarrying, automobile and other repair services, production for the domestic market in the areas of agriculture, garments, handicrafts, printing and publishing, architecture, structural, mechanical, electrical and civil engineering and contracting (in special cases where foreign expertise is required in any of these areas it shall be obtained by way of consortium with an appropriate local firm or group of local firms). With respect to the 'open' areas the Government expressed particular interest in investment which could 'increase domestic income, employment, foreign exchange earnings or savings and transfer technology to the local society'. Investments supplying exclusively overseas markets were particularly welcome. Where the operation was based on the processing or assembly of foreign raw material and components (which were processed and paid for outside the country), the Government indicated its willingness to approve 100% non-resident ownership. Where the operation was based mainly on local mineral or agricultural raw materials, some degree of local participation would have had to be considered. Non-resident controlled enterprises were required to obtain all their funding from non-resident sources. Local banks were permitted to make loans to non-resident enterprises up to 25% of their paid-up capital and revenue reserves.

Despite the policies of the Michael Manley administration, a study[76] published by the National Savings Committee in 1980 showed that while local participation in the economy had increased over the years there was still substantial foreign ownership in major sectors of the economy. The critical bauxite sector, for example, was still largely in the hands of some five or six transnationals based in North America. The traditional impact of governmental policy has been mainly 'to secure greater royalty and tax payments and to increase aluminum processing capacity'.[77] Manley seemed content for the time being to continue this policy, but convinced that the industry had long been undertaxed as a result of the transfer price system used by the companies and the weakness of government stemming from lack of knowledge of the industry, he instituted measures designed to bring about a substantial increase in government's revenue from the industry. While staying away from the issue of ownership, this move was widely interpreted as anti-foreign investment particularly in the context of other social and economic policies that were being put into effect. As we saw earlier, in the few years that followed a certain amount of disinvestment took place, and this further added to the foreign exchange problem faced by the country in these years. Also there was very little new investment taking place. Despite state policy, in practice the problem was compounded by the left-wing rhetoric which projected Jamaica as an unsafe place for private foreign capital and injected a deep sense of uncertainty into the investment climate.

The PNP Government of Michael Manley was ousted by the Jamaica Labour Party (JLP) under Edward Seaga in the elections of 1980. Since then an intensive campaign has been in operation aimed at attracting foreign investors who are viewed as one of the key elements in the regeneration of the economy. A reduced role is envisaged for the public sector in the production process. This policy is founded on a particular type of perception arising from the experience of the 1950s and 1960s when the high growth rates were fuelled by large injections of foreign capital into the mining sectors and to a lesser extent in other industries. 'In Caribbean economies, for the most part the dynamic sector that produces most of the real growth is the private, not the public sector. In contrast to the limited resources of public investment channels, the real sources of major financing are private investment inflows that, aside from magnitude reach the sector that generates most of the productive growth.'[78] The results of this approach remain to be seen.

Guyana

Though Guyana is classified as a 'More Developed Country' in CARICOM, its estimated per capita GNP of US$630 in 1979 was in fact lass than most of the so-called 'Less Developed Countries' (See Table 6.3). At current prices GDP (at factor cost) grew by about 6% during the 1960s and by between 11% and 12% during the 1970s. For most of the years in the latter decade the annual growth rate was in fact lower than the average which was significantly affected by the high prices received for sugar in 1974 and 1975. In current dollars per capita GNP increased from about US$270 in 1960 to US$340 in 1970 and to around US$700 in 1980. During the 1970s the real growth rate of per capita GNP was close to zero.[79]

Though the country has a land area of 83,000 square miles the bulk of the population (about 790,000 in 1980) is concentrated in a coastal strip comprising about 3% of the total land space. At present less than 2% of the land area is under cultivation. To say that the hinterland remains largely undeveloped is to say that the country has remained undeveloped. While the full resource potential of Guyana is still unknown, the known resources have either eluded development, or have not been exploited in a manner to make any significant impact on the standard of living of the average Guyanese. The agricultural and farming potential remains largely untapped while there is dependence on foreign sources for a wide range of essential food items. Though well endowed with the natural resources to produce hydro-electric power the country has been exporting bauxite in raw form since the start of exploitation in 1917. In addition to bauxite, other minerals that are known to exist include sand (suitable for the manufacture of glass), shell resources (which can be used in cement production), gold, diamonds, copper and radio-active minerals including uranium, iron and nickel. Manganese was also mined at one time.[80]

As can be seen in Table 6.14 the Guyanese economy is essentially agriculture-based with sugar and rice as two of its main products. In 1980 agriculture accounted for about 25% of GDP as compared to about 27% in 1960. Mining and quarrying contributed 17% (11% in 1960), while manufacturing's share was only 8% (5% in 1960). One of the noticeable features of Table 6.14 is the significant increase of government's contribution between 1960 and 1980, the percentage share moving from 10% to 19%. With respect to exports these are concentrated in a few products. The 1980 data show that out of a total domestic exports figures of G$977.6 million in that year, sugar accounted for 31%, rum and molasses for 4%, rice for 9% and bauxite and alumina for 49%.

Table 6.14 *Guyana: composition of GDP (at factor cost), 1960 and 1980*

	1960		*1980*ᵖ	
Sectors	*G$mn*	*%*	*G$mn*	*%*
Sugar	46.3	17.6	198.0	14.8
Rice	13.9	5.3	51.0	3.8
Other agriculture[1]	12.2	4.6	89.5	6.7
Fishing & forestry	11.8	4.5	32.5	2.4
Mining & quarrying	29.1	11.5	221.0	16.5
Manufacturing	13.9	5.3	108.0	8.1
Distribution	37.2	14.1	115.0	8.6
Transport & communications	19.8	7.5	75.0	5.6
Engineering & construction	25.0	9.5	90.0	6.7
Financial services	8.5	3.2	54.0	4.0
Government	25.6	9.7	250.0	18.7
Other	20.2	7.7	52.0	4.0
All Sectors	*263.5*	*100.0*	*1,336.0*	*100.0*

p provisional.
1 including livestock.

Source: Bank of Guyana, *Annual Report*, various issues.

The role of direct foreign investment An examination of Table 6.15 will show that between 1960 and 1970 there was a net flow of direct investment of G$186 million[81] into Guyana. Between 1978 and 1980 the flow was G$43 million. Because of the unavailability of data on direct investment income we are unable to gauge the net movement of direct investment funds. The figures in column (2) of Table 6.15 include interest payments on the government external debt. A salient feature of Table 6.15 is the fact that since 1970 official capital receipts has been the main autonomous factor in the financing of the current account deficit.

In terms of the relative importance of DFI in domestic capital formation some indication can be got from Table 6.16. Between 1960 and 1970, it is clear that private investment was a more important source of capital formation than public investment. The former averaged 17.1% of GDP while the latter averaged only 7.1%. In the period between 1971 and 1980, however, the average for public investment rose to 20%, while that for private investment fell to 6.6%. Columns (3) and (4) of Table 6.16 show the relationship of foreign direct investment to total

Table 6.15 *Guyana: selected balance of payments data, 1960–1981*

G$mn

Year	*Current Account*		*Capital Account (non-monetary sector)*			
	Current A/c Bal. (1)	*Net Investment Income*[1] (2)	*Net Direct Investment* (3)	*Other Private Long-Term* (4)	*Private Short-Term* (5)	*Official Capital Receipts* (6)
1960	−45	−24	30	4	–	5
61	−20	−23	10	1	−1	8
62	9	−37	−3	2	−2	12
63	26	−29	7	2	1	3
64	−10	−30	10	1	2	1
65	−25	−27	16	−2	−2	−1
66	−41	−33	27	−3	−4	3
67	−41	−33	38	–	3	17
68	−22	−30	16	−9	3	14
69	−21	−42	17	−2	8	12
70	−46	−43	18	−1	−4	22
71	−13	−36	−4	15	−5	32
72	−23	−22	5	5	1	24
73	−123	−27	18	10	2	33
74	−17	−38	18	2	15	58
75	−35	−40	4	8	−5	102
76	−351	−59	−4	−20	−5	177
77	−251	−60	3	−15	−5	85
78	−72	−44	−2	−11	2	103
79	−208	−73	4	−7	11	74
80[e]	−300	−83	1	–	7	72

1 includes interest on the public debt which is not available separately.
e estimate.

Source: Bank of Guyana, *Annual Report*, various issues; IMF, *Balance of Payments Statistics Yearbook*, various issues.

investment and private investment respectively. Here again the decline of FDI in the Guyanese economy since 1971 is apparent. As a proportion of total capital formation, FDI averaged 18.7% in the period 1960–70 as compared to 2.3% in the period 1971–80. As a proportion of private investment FDI averaged 26.8% in the period 1960–70 as compared to 8% between 1971–80. With the decline of private sector activities, the Government's position in the economy has assumed greater and greater importance as investor and provider of jobs. To carry out its functions the Government has had to resort increasingly to borrowing, both internally and externally. The internal debt increased from G$18.2 million at the end of 1960, to an estimated G$1,889 million at the end of 1981. The external debt on the other hand, increased from G$78.9 million to G$1,210.5 million over the same period. As a per-

Table 6.16 *Guyana: selected investment, and foreign debt statistics, 1960–80*

Year	*As a % of GDP*[1]		*FDI*[2] *as a % of Gross Capital Formation*		*External Public Debt*[3] *G$mn*		*Net Investment Income as a % of Exports*[4]
	Public Investment (1)	*Private Investment (2)*	*Total Investment (3)*	*Private Investment (4)*	*(5)*	*(5) as a % of GDP*[1] *(6)*	*(7)*
1960	6.3	25.0	36.8	46.1	78.9	29.9	19.2
61	8.0	18.3	12.6	18.1	86.2	29.7	15.7
62	6.5	11.6	−5.4	−8.5	96.7	31.5	23.0
63	4.5	14.0	14.3	20.0	102.1	37.0	16.8
64	3.3	14.4	17.7	21.7	104.6	31.9	18.0
65	5.0	19.6	20.1	24.4	106.4	32.7	16.3
66	7.6	19.1	29.0	45.8	113.7	33.3	18.1
67	7.2	21.8	34.5	46.9	124.1	33.1	15.8
68	7.9	15.7	15.4	25.6	125.3	30.9	13.5
69	9.7	14.2	16.6	27.9	141.1	32.2	17.2
70	12.0	14.3	14.5	26.7	160.0	34.3	16.6
71	13.4	7.9	+3.4	−9.2	291.6	58.9	12.9
72	13.9	8.9	4.3	11.0	310.2	58.6	7.5
73	19.8	7.6	11.1	39.3	348.6	60.5	9.6
74	17.9	7.5	8.2	27.7	403.6	46.7	6.4
75	22.8	6.4	1.2	5.7	533.4	48.7	4.8
75	34.6	6.8	−0.9	−5.6	662.5	64.6	8.5
77	22.6	5.9	1.0	5.0	689.8	67.7	9.2
78	17.2	4.1	0.4	2.1	744.0	65.5	5.9
79	22.3	5.6	0.5	2.3	811.7	69.7	9.9
80p	25.0	5.2	0.3	1.7	911.3	68.2	8.5
81p	n.a.	n.a.	n.a.	n.a.	1,210.5	76.0	n.a.

n.a. not available.
1 at factor cost.
2 Foreign Direct Investment (Net).
3 outstanding at the end of each year.
4 domestic exports.
p provisional.

Source: Bank of Guyana *Annual Reports*, various issues; IMF, *Financial Statistics*, various issues.

centage of GDP the external debt outstanding increased from 30% in 1960 to around 75% in 1981. We do not have separate data on the servicing of the internal and external debt components. It has been estimated, however, that in 1981 the service of the foreign debt as a proportion of exports of goods and services amounted to 18% as compared to 3.2% in 1970–1. With respect to interest paid on the external debt this, as indicated earlier, is included with income accruing to private capital in the investment income figures published in the balance of payments. As can be seen in column (7) of Table 6.16, investment income as a percentage of domestic exports fluctuates from year to year. In recent years, it has tended to be less than 10%. The payments of interest on the total public debt (internal and external) increased from G$7.6 million (9.1% of revenue) in 1965 to G$189.6 million (40.6% of revenue in

1980). Over the same period debt funding and repayment increased from G$4.5 million (5.4% of revenue) to G$143.1 million (30.7% of total revenue). In other words total scheduled debt servicing in 1980 amounted to over 70% of revenue. As far as the structure of the external debt is concerned, almost all of it is long term. Of the G$1,211 million outstanding at the end of 1981, 13.8% was owed to the United Kingdom, 12.9% to the US Government, 5.9% to the Canadian Government, 13.7% to the IBRD and IDA and 53.8%, to 'others'. The latter included government debt for nationalised assets.

Policy towards foreign direct investment In recent years the government has sought to promote what it calls a tri-sectoral economy, i.e. an economy comprised of:

(a) a public sector;
(b) a co-operative sector; and
(c) a private sector.

When Guyana was declared a Co-operative Republic in 1970 one of the avowed aims of the Government was to increase national ownership of basic and strategic resources. This policy did not rule out foreign participation in domestic economic activity. In addressing the 12th Congress of the People's National Congress in 1969, the President, Mr Forbes Burnham, stated:

> In cases when for one reason or another, we do not have internally the means to be immediately responsible for the development of a particular resource, we shall have to rely upon external assistance, public or private. In the latter case, particularly, we shall have to make the particular project attractive, profit-wise. There is no room for quibbling over this; philanthropy is dead, if it ever lived. What has to be ensured is that Guyana shares substantially in the profits and advantages and is not raped, exploited and given the jackal's pickings. There will be occasion when rather than sell our birthright we shall have to refuse offers of assistance.

These sentiments were repeated in Mr Burnham's speech to the 13th Annual Conference of the People's National Congress on 5th April, 1970, when he said, *inter alia*: '. . . the Hinterland, as we all know, contains the greatest part of our natural resources especially in forests and minerals. In the exploitation of these, especially of the latter, we are prepared to enter in consortia with foreign investors, but only on certain conditions, and one such condition henceforth will be that government alone or government cooperatives hold in each case no less than 51 per cent of the equity.'

Until 1970, the Government had pursued what might be called a very accommodating policy towards foreign capital. Political independence was gained from Britain in 1966, but economic decision-making affecting almost all the major sectors of the economy was in foreign hands.

Until the government established the National Cooperative Bank in 1970, commercial banking was controlled by the branches of five expatriate banks. Since then, Government's policy has been aimed at 'miniaturising' the operations of the foreign banks by excluding the latter from the local deposit business which is being diverted towards the National Cooperative Bank. Until 1975 when the Government decided to nationalise sugar, the industry was effectively controlled by Booker McConnell Limited of the United Kingdom through local subsidiaries and agencies. The latter were also engaged in fields such as shrimping, dairying, stockfeed manufacture, shipping, printing, cattle ranching, general engineering, etc.[82] In 1975, sugar was not only the largest employer of labour in the country, but contributed 30% to GDP in that year. Some of the reasons given for nationalisation were: wasting the country's resources, inefficient operations, unsatisfactory agricultural practice, primitive industrial relations and appalling workers' housing conditions.[83] The key bauxite industry, too, remained in foreign hands until 1971, when the largest of the two companies (the Demerara Bauxite Company or Demba) mining Guyanese bauxite was nationalised. Since the complete take-over of Demba by the Guyanese Government tended to give the impression that the Government had taken an anti-foreign investment position it would be interesting to examine the context in which this was done.

In 1970 there were two companies engaged in Guyanese's bauxite industry: The Demerara Bauxite Company, or Demba (which was a subsidiary of the Canadian based Alcan Alumina, Limited)[84] and Reynold Metals Company of the United States. The former accounted for over 80% of the bauxite production in Guyana. Demba's assets in Guyana represented about 15 to 20% of Canada's private direct investment in the Caribbean which was estimated in 1970 to be around C$435 million.[85] Alcan's total assets in 1969 was estimated to be about G$5 billion, while its income of over G$2.6 billion was over 5 times the GDP of Guyana.[86] In 1970 bauxite mining contributed about 20% to GDP, while bauxite and alumina accounted for a little more than half of total domestic exports. The industry also made some contribution to government revenue, but this was insignificant in relation to the level of profits that was being generated. 'Even such value as was created by the production and minor processing of bauxite within the country was distributed iniquitously. For 1917–69 of the industry's total exports, which were worth over G$1,200 million, the government's revenue from royalties and export duties amounted to G$21.1 million, or 1.6 per cent, even adding income tax, the government's total revenue from the company in the 1963–68 period amounted to only 3.4 per cent of the value of exports. The take of the country as a whole – that is with taxes, labour incomes and other local payments added to taxes – normally amounted to just over one-third of the value of the company's exports. The company's small tax payments bear eloquent testimony to Alcan's power and manoeuvrability as a large, oligopolistic, vertically integrated transnational enterprise. The "prices" for Demba's "sales" to its parent Alcan were fixed by the latter so as to minimise the corporation's overall tax burden, and as a direct result, Guyana experienced some of the lowest prices and taxes per ton recorded in the Caribbean. Moreover, when the company decided to build its small alumina plant in Guyana (opened in 1961), it secured so-called pioneer industry tax concession from the colonial administration – although it had by then been operating in the country for some forty years. The result was that for the first ten years of the plant's operation it paid virtually no taxes at all.'[87]

When the Guyana government first approached Alcan in November 1970 with respect to participation in Demba it was only interested in majority ownership and 'the control which inheres in such majority holding'. The exact size of the majority holding was negotiable. It offered to pay for its share of the assets out of future profits of the joint undertaking after tax. The value of the company's assets was to be no greater than that given by the company as the written down book value for income tax purposes on 31st December, 1969.[88] These terms were not acceptable to Alcan and a counter proposal was made by the company. It suggested that the 'Government of Guyana should raise a loan from the World Bank for expanding the production of calcined ore and put it into the new entity as equity. Alcan would then put all of Demba's assets into that entity, part of these assets to represent Alcan's equity, the rest to be an interest-bearing loan to be repaid in instalments – presumably annual. These instalments were to be chargeable against cash generation and before tax. Alcan desired freedom from exchange control and from withholding tax and proposed that she should appoint the Chief Executive Officer of the new Company.'[89] The Government rejected these proposals for three reasons: first, it premised the Government's having to pay in advance for participation; second, repayment for assets was to be before tax; and third, Alcan's right to appoint the Chief Executive Officer meant that she should in fact control the operation of the new entity. Alcan responded with a new set of proposals which the government found even more objectionable. These were as follows:[90]

1 A new company would be formed after the Government had agreed in advance to commit the new entity to Alcan's scheme for the expansion of calcined bauxite and after the Government had undertaken to provide the G$50 million needed for the scheme.
2 The new company would be capitalised at G$100 million in $1 shares, 50 to Government and 50 to Alcan. (The company later conceded 51 to Government and 49 to Alcan.)
3 The existing assets of Demba (approximately G$100 million) would be put in as a fully interest bearing loan at current commercial rates.
4 The new entity and its shareholders would not be subject to any

Income Tax, Corporation Tax, Property Tax, Withholding Tax, Import Duty, Export Duty, Royalty or any Guyana Tax or Import, nor any Exchange Control restriction with respect to any interest, dividends or fee for its shareholders.

5 If the Government should sign with any other bauxite producer an agreement containing any single term more favourable than the corresponding term reached with Alcan, the agreement with Alcan would be changed to include the more favourable term.

The government saw these proposals as reflecting 'a kind of arrogance and lack of concern with the realities in Guyana'. As worded, it meant that before any agreement could take place the Government first had to find G$50 million to help 'finance an expansion scheme over which it would have no control'. Alcan, it felt, was trying to eat its cake and have it too. The contribution of Demba's assets of G$100 million (estimated book value) would not only have to be repaid with interest (at commercial rates), but during the period of repayment the company would continue to hold 49% of the equity and share in the profits. When the loan had been repaid, Alcan would still have retained its share of 49% in the enterprise. The government also felt that the proposals would have restricted its sovereignty since they sought to remove from its fiscal power an important part of the authority in dealing with other bauxite producers. Finally, it felt the repayment out of cash generation (rather than out of future profits) would have placed responsibility for expansion on the government and its ability to borrow.[91]

On the 23rd February, 1972, (on the occasion of Republic Day) the Prime Minister announced the nationalisation of Demba. The Government eventually agreed to pay a total of G$107 million (US $53 million) in instalments over twenty years with interest effectively at 4.5%. The total sum was higher than the book value of Demba's assets. Payments were not linked to the profits of the new enterprise. Reynolds was nationalised in 1975. By the end of 1970s the state owned and controlled more than two-thirds of the economy.

Prior to 1970 sugar and bauxite accounted for the major part of private capital formation in Guyana. During the 1970s, foreign direct investment inflows were reduced to a trickle. In order to reduce some of the uncertainties surrounding government's policies towards private domestic and foreign capital, the government found it necessary to produce what it calls 'The Guyana Investment Code' in 1979. In this document it is stated that the state recognises and welcomes both local private investment and foreign private investment. The state also welcomes and will promote in certain circumstances joint ventures between the state and foreign states or between the state and foreign state corporations. (The largest hotel in Guyana, the Pegasus, is a joint venture between the Guyana Government and Trust House Forte.) With respect to the patterns of ownership, the foreign investor can enter into business alone, or with local individuals, companies or cooperatives or with the State. Where the foreign investor is a foreign government or the official arm of a foreign government, the only permissible ownership arrangement is one which includes the state.

In cases where the state is not a participant in an enterprise involving a foreign investor, the enterprise is subject to a licence approved by the state for joint ventures. Such licence shall be issued upon consideration of:

1 The proportion of equity held by the foreign investor and the private investor or cooperative.
2 The terms of transfer of technology.
3 The condition of financing.
4 The conditions governing:
   (a) Management
   (b) Marketing
   (c) Disbursement of Dividends.

The object of such licencing is to ensure that the interest of the local investor is protected and that the policy of the state as regards development is adhered to.

Private and cooperative sector activity is encouraged in the area of manufacturing and agriculture. The government takes the position (which is by no means uncommon in developing countries) that the state has the responsibility 'for control of the economy and the nature of the economic development which occurs'. In order to do this the state must exercise strict control over the ownership and use of the country's natural resources. 'Strategic Activities' (i.e. activities or areas which are of strategic importance to the health and the course of the economy) are to remain under the strict control of the Public Sector and Cooperative Sector. The government recognises that majority ownership is not synonymous with control and pledges that the state 'will seek to maintain that control by examining in each case the nature of the investment proposed and work out a formula consistent with Government's overall policy.'

The Code (which itself is far from clear on many issues) has had no noticeable effect on the investment climate in Guyana. The economy continues to stagnate or decline, and this in itself is a disincentive to investment. The stagnation, however, appears to have far deeper causes related to socio-political factors than simply lack of investment. Recently, the IMF has been putting pressure on the Burnham government to return some of the nationalised industries to private hands in the hope that they could once more lead the economy. This is being resisted both by the Government and Opposition parties who view it as a step towards re-colonisation.

Other Caricom Countries[92]

Unlike Guyana, Jamaica and Trinidad and Tobago, Barbados does not have a mining sector on any significant scale. Early foreign investment was mainly in the sugar industry which is now in local hands. In recent years direct investment has flowed largely into the manufacturing and tourism sectors. An examination of Table 6.17 will show that between 1964 and 1981 total direct investment flows into Barbados amounted to some B$272 million. Over the same period direct investment income totalled B$151 million or 56% of investment inflows.

Table 6.17 *Barbados: selected balance of payments data, 1964–81*

B$mn

	Current Account				*CAPITAL ACCOUNT (Non-Monetary Sector)*		
Years	*Current A/C Bal.*	*Direct Investment Income*	*Other Investment Income*	*Net Investment*	*Direct Investment*	*Port-folio Investment*	*Public Sector*
1964	−23	−1	1	–	7	–	1
65	−25	−2	1	−1	3	–	7
66	−32	−2	1	−1	13	4	–
67	−30	−2	1	−1	12	2	−4
68	−40	−5	1	−4	16	−1	–
69	−68	−6	1	−5	14	3	1
70	−84	−8	2	−6	17	7	1
71	−69	−8	−1	−9	29	3	–
72	−83	−12	−1	−13	33	–	5
73	−102	−12	−2	−14	5	1	41
74	−98	−11	−5	−16	12	16	−7
75	−84	−16	−4	−20	45	7	−1
76	−128	−8	−1	−9	12	27	6
77	−103	−9	−8	−17	9	19	11
78	−63	−10	−1	−11	19	−7	32
79	−69	−11	−12	−23	10	28	9
80	−54	−11	−6	−17	2	12	54
81	−250	−17	−18	−35	14	42	99

Source: Barbados Central Statistical Service, *Balance of Payments of Barbados*, various issues; Central Bank of Barbados, *Balance of Payments of Barbados*, various issues; IMF, *Financial Statistics*, various issues.

We do not have detailed or reliable balance of payments data for the Less Developed Countries (LDCs) of CARICOM, but the indications are that these countries have not been able to attract private foreign capital on the scale that their more developed partners have been able to do. The reasons for this might be several: lack of mineral resources, small local markets, inadequate infrastructural facilities, etc. Out of recognition of these handicaps the CARICOM scheme for the Harmonisation of Fiscal Incentives permits the LDCs to grant more generous incentives than the MDCs can give, and also allows them to do so in a wider range of activities than the MDCs are permitted to do.

The inability to adopt a common approach to foreign private capital by CARICOM countries is related to several factors of both a historical and contemporary nature. Some of the member states who have been gradually nationalising or localising sectors of their economies which have for long been under foreign control are reluctant to adopt policies which may have the effect of reversing this process. There are others who see private foreign capital as the passport out of underdevelopment and want an environment accommodating to foreign investors. The posturings differ from country to country, reflecting perceptions based on what seems to be pragmatism in some cases and ideology in others. It is important to note that, while none of the CARICOM countries is completely opposed to private foreign investment, utterances, sometimes deliberate, sometimes in unguarded moments, do give the impression of a hostile attitude towards all private foreign capital which tends to be associated with imperialism.

As indicated earlier, CARICOM countries have been unable to properly conceptualise the role of the private sector *vis-à-vis* the role of the government sector in the process of economic development. And this may not be unrelated to the ambivalence towards private foreign capital and the consequent uncertainty that prevails in some cases. The absence of a common policy on private foreign capital has in effect meant the lack of a CARICOM policy on intra-CARICOM investments which tend to be treated in a very *ad hoc* manner. In the context of the effort being made to initiate a policy of industrial programming, this would seem to be an essential prerequisite.

It has often been stated that the region must recognise the trend towards ideological pluralism and that there can be different paths towards the satisfaction of the material needs of the Caribbean people. In the context of the integration movement the real test of compatibility would be the ability to take a common position in the interest of advancing the integration process and strengthening its fabric. Since it appears that the pooling of financial and other resources within the region could reduce the dependence on private foreign capital and thus introduce a greater element of rationality in existing national policies, this may be one area where member states can demonstrate the commitment. There is clearly a need for legislation which could facilitate intra-CARICOM capital movements of a productive nature. To the extent that foreign investments are needed, the setting up of an institution to appraise such investments and evaluate their potential contribution to regional development may be necessary. This may be a useful approach even where there may be differences in perceptions with respect to the role of private foreign investment.

Notes

1 See the UN, *Foreign Capital in Latin America* op. cit., quoted in Bernstein op. cit. p. 31.
2 For a good review of Brazilian economic growth in the 20th century, see Werner Baer, *Industrialisation and Economic Development in Brazil* (Homewood, Illinois: Richard D. Irwin, 1965).
3 Because of methodological differences in compilation, the figures in this year are not strictly comparable with those of 1920. See Baer, op. cit., p. 28.
4 Baer, op. cit., p. 4.
5 Ibid., p. 17.
6 Ibid., p. 28.
7 See D.E. Syvrud, *Foundations of Brazilian Economic Growth*, (Washington, DC: American Enterprise Institute for Public Policy Research, 1974), p. 28.
8 See H.J.O. Struckmeyer and T.M. Reichmann, 'Brazil Seeks to Strengthen External Position and Re-evaluate Strategy for Resumed Growth', in IMF *Survey*, March 21, 1983.
9 Ibid.
10 Ibid.
11 Ibid.
12 L.C. Marinho, 'TNCs and Latin America's Present Growth', in CEPAL *Review*, August 1981, p. 13.
13 See P.T. Knight, 'Brazil's Socio-economic Development: Issues for the Eighties', in *World Development*, Nov/Dec., 1981.
14 S.H. Roboch, *Brazil: A Study in Development and Progress* (Lexington: Lexington Books, 1975), p. 61.
15 Ibid.
16 P.T. Knight, op. cit.
17 Ibid.
18 Latin America, *Weekly Report*, 4 March, 1983.
19 Latin America, *Weekly Report*.
20 Joseph S. La Cascia, *Capital Formation and Economic Development in Mexico* (New York: Praeger Publishers, 1969), p. 2.
21 Ibid.
22 See E.W. Baklanoff, *Expropriation of US Investment in Cuba, Mexico, and Chile* (New York, Praeger Publishers, 1975), p. 56.
23 Ibid., p. 45.
24 Harry K. Wright, *Foreign Enterprise in Mexico: Laws and Policies* (University of North Carolina Press, 1971), p. 94.
25 Baklanoff, op. cit., p. 48.
26 For an excellent discussion on Mexican laws and policies before 1970 see Harry K. Wright, op. cit. This section draws heavily on this study.
27 Ibid., p. 97.
28 Ibid., p. 127.
29 Ibid., p. 132.
30 Ibid., p. 137.
31 Ibid., p. 147.
32 Remy Montavon *et al.*, *The Role of Multinational Companies in Latin*

America (New York: Praeger Publishers, 1980), p. 14.
33 See ibid.
34 See Peter Evans and Gary Gereffi, op. cit.
35 Ibid., p. 151.
36 See Remy Montavon, op. cit., p. 3.
37 See L.C. Marinho, op. cit., p. 13.
38 Remy Montavon, op. cit., p. 13.
39 Peter Evans and Gary Gereff, op. cit.
40 See *Latin American Economic Report* of March, 16, 1979.
41 Quoted by Miguel S. Vionczek in 'US Reaction to the Andean Group System for Treatment of Foreign Capital', *Commercio Exterior de Mexico*, June, 1971.
42 Ibid.
43 Ibid.
44 See Alicia Puyana de Palacios, *Economic Integration among Unequal Partners: The Case of the Andean Group* (New York: Pergamon Press, 1982), p. 182.
45 See *Latin America Economic Report* of May 25, 1979.
46 See Comercio *Exterior de Mexico*, of October, 1981, pp. 447–48.
47 For a useful discussion on the nature of direct foreign investment and its consequences for development, see Commonwealth Caribbean Regional Secretariat, *From Carifta to Caribbean Community*, Georgetown, 1972. pp. 65–68.
48 See, for example, A. McIntyre and B. Watson, *Studies in Foreign Investment in the Commonwealth Caribbean, No. 1, Trinidad and Tobago* (Jamaica: ISER, USI, 1970), pp. 54–63.
49 *The Caribbean Community in the 1980s* (Georgetown: CARICOM Secretariat, 1981), p. 74.
50 Ibid.
51 See W.A. Lewis, 'Economic Development with Unlimited Supplies of Labour', *The Manchester School*, May 1954. See also W.A. Lewis,' The Industrialisation of the British West Indies. *Caribbean Economic Review*, Vol. 11, No. 1, May 1950.
52 See Frank Rampersad, *Growth and Structural Change in the Economy of Trinidad and Tobago, 1951–61* (Mona, ISER undated); CSO, *The National Income of Trinidad and Tobago, 1952–62*; Central Bank, *Annual Reports*, and IMF, *Financial Statistics*, Various Issues.
53 World Bank estimate.
54 Since 1976 the TT dollar has been worth about US$0.42. In November 1984, it is still so.
55 For an excellent discussion on the foreign investment situation in Trinidad and Tobago until the late 1960s, see McIntyre and Watson, op. cit.
56 Ibid., p. 19.
57 IMF *Balance of Payments Statistics Yearbook*, Vols. 32 and 33.
58 See 1978 *Annual Report* of the Central Bank, p. 23.
59 Draft Third Five Year Plan, p. 7.
60 Ibid., p. 16.
61 Ibid.
62 1977 Budget Speech, pp. 32–33.
63 1979 Budget Speech, p. 8.

64 World Bank estimate.
65 See Five Year Independence Plan, 1963–68, p. 14.
66 For instance in 1980 the average weekly earnings in the mining sector was in the region of J$250 as compared to about J$110 in manufacturing and J$113 in construction. See Dept. of Statistics, *Statistical Abstract*, 1980.
67 E. Ahiram, 'Income Distribution in Jamaica 1958', *Social and Economic Studies*, September, 1964.
68 N. Girvan, *Foreign Capital and Economic Under-development in Jamaica* (Mona: ISER 1971), pp. 12–13.
69 A. McIntyre and B. Watson, op. cit., 67.
70 IMF, *Balance of Payments Yearbook*, Vols. 32 and 33.
71 i.e. excluding Sinking Fund provisions.
72 See Owen Jefferson, *The Post-War Economic Development of Jamaica* (Mona: ISER, 1971), p. 220.
73 See Girvan, op. cit., p. 260.
74 Speech by Michael Manley at the Waldorf Astoria Hotel, New York, in October, 1977.
75 For details, see *Foreign Investment – A Statement of Policy*, published by the then Government of Jamaica, (undated.)
76 National Savings Committee, *Ownership Within the Jamaica Economy*, Kingston, 1980.
77 See G.M. Meier, *Problems of Cooperation for Development* (London: Oxford University Press, 1974), p. 182.
78 Address by Mr Edward Seaga to the CARICOM Foreign Ministers meeting in 1981.
79 See World Bank *Atlas*, 1981.
80 See the *Guyana Investment Code*, published by the Ministry of Information, Nov., 1979, p. 7.
81 The average value of a Guyanese dollar in 1981 was around 35 US cents.
82 See Eusi Kwayana, 'Economic Relations in Pre-Republican Guyana', in *Co-op Republic*, Government of Guyana, Georgetown, June, 1970.
83 The Prime Minister's address to the nation on the occasion of the celebration of the fifth anniversary of the Co-operative Republic held at the National Park on Feb., 23, 1975.
84 Alcan was incorporated in Canada in 1928 by the US based Aluminum Company of America (ALCOA) to take over its Canadian and foreign properties including Demba which was incorporated in Guyana in 1916. See Norman Girvan, *Corporate Imperialism: Conflict and Expropriation* (New York: M.E. Sharpe, Inc., 1976), Chap. 4.
85 See I.A. Litrak and C.J. Maule, 'Nationalisation in the Caribbean Bauxite Industry', *International Affairs*, Jan. 1975.
86 'Control of Our National Resources', Prime Minister's address to the nation on the occasion of Republic Day, Feb, 23, 1971.
87 N. Girvan, op. cit., pp. 164–5.
88 For details on the proposals and counter proposals of the two parties, see the President's Speech 'Control of Out National Resources', op. cit., See also Girvan, op. cit., for a detailed account of the negotiations.
89 'Control of Our Natural Resources', op. cit.
90 Ibid.
91 Ibid.

92 For a useful discussion of the foreign investment situation in some of the CARICOM countries during the 1960s, see B. Watson, *Supplementary Notes on Foreign Investment in the Commonwealth Caribbean*, Mona, ISER Working Paper No. 1, 1974.

7

US Direct Investment in the Broader Context of US–Latin American/Caribbean Relations

Because of its geographical location, the US takes a special interest in developments in the Latin American and Caribbean Region. For a long number of years this interest was largely of a political/security nature. The concern with European interventions in the hemisphere until the turn of the century has given way in the post-war period to a concern over the encroachment of communism in the region and the threat this poses to American security. Increasingly this has become more of an obsession than a concern, and has tended to have a great influence on American relations with the rest of the hemisphere and on the conduct of United States foreign policy. One of the main features that has come to characterise the latter is the support given to regimes sympathetic to US interests (be these political, military or economic), regardless of their behaviour or performance on the domestic front. Scant attention has tended to be paid (particularly previous to 1960), to local social or economic conditions. As a result of this, the US has often found itself associated with (or supportive of) regimes that can claim to be neither popular nor democratic. In fact, some of them have been downright repressive.

A wave of rebellions in the 1950s and the overthrow of a number of military dictators (including the Cuban strongman Fulgencio Batista in 1959 by Fidel Castro) 'whom the US State Department had previously hailed as champions of anti-communist stability in Latin America'[1] instigated some change in the American attitude in the final years of the Eisenhower administration. The latter put up $350 million as the initial capital of the new Inter-American Development Bank and Congress authorised a $500 million fund for social investments in Latin America.[2] Previous to this, the prevalent view was that private capital was a sufficiently powerful force in itself capable of dealing with the problems of poverty and under-development. The Eisenhower gesture was followed in 1961 by the launching of the Alliance for Progress by President John F. Kennedy who described it as 'a vast cooperative effort, unparalleled in magnitude and nobility of purpose, to satisfy the basic need of the American people for homes, work and land, health and schools.[3] The Charter of Punta del Este which established the Alliance had as one of its main objectives an acceleration of the economic and social development of Latin America in order to bring about a narrowing in the gap between the Latin American countries and the industrialised nations. The ten-year programme of action envisaged an average rate of growth in per capita income of no less than 2.5% per annum in the decade of the 1960s. While no reference was made to the growth of population a growth rate of 2.5% in this variable would have required a 5% growth in total income. Other objectives covered a wide area in the economic and social field. These related to a more equitable distribution of income, diversification of the national economy, an increase in agricultural productivity and production through comprehensive agricultural agrarian reform, better credit and technical facilities and improved marketing arrangements. It was also hoped 'to increase resources from the external sector of the economies by maintaining stable prices for basic export products, undertaking programmes to avoid excessive fluctuations in the foreign exchange receipts from exports and strengthening economic integration agreements, with a view to achieving a Latin American common market; and to adopt a broad social welfare programme in the fields of education, health and housing.'

The Alliance was in a large part a reaction to Cuba's growing ties with the Communist World, and as such it sought to offer an alternative path to the countries of the region. It was cast in a particular ideological framework which is readily apparent in the following statements: 'This Alliance is established on the basic principle that free men working through the institution of representative democracy can best satisfy man's aspirations including those for work, home and land, health and schools. No system can guarantee true progress unless it affirms the dignity of the individual which is the foundation of our civilization.' Again, one of the goals of the Alliance was seen to be the improvement and strengthening of 'democratic institutions through application of the principle of self-determination by the people.' Another was the stimulation of 'private enterprise in order to encourage the development of Latin American countries at a rate which will help them to provide jobs for their growing populations, to eliminate unemployment, and to take their place among the modern industrialized nations of the world.'

One of the main assumptions of the Alliance was that partnership with the US (or more specifically United States aid) would act as a catalyst in bringing about change in Latin America's economic and social structure. It was indeed idealistic to assume that ruling cliques would easily give up their positions of wealth and power in the interest of a commitment to democracy and democratic political institutions. In the decade following the launching of the Alliance many of the objectives were only partially fulfilled, while others were not. Total product for the region as a whole grew by about 5.4% annually, while there was a 2.4% annual growth rate in per capita product.[4] At the individual level seven countries (Panama, Nicaragua, Mexico, Bolivia, Brazil, Costa Rica and El Salvador) registered per capita growth rates above the level set for the decade.[5] Despite this performance the problem of unemployment and underemployment continues to afflict every country in the region. The distribution of income, as we saw earlier, in most cases has tended to get worse. The ownership of land which is one of the most intractable problems in Latin America remains highly concentrated. Action in agrarian reform has been mainly in the legal area, rather than in effective implementation of programmes. Political power is still exercised by ruling cliques who resist any attempt to dilute their power or deprive them of their privileges. Social conditions with respect to housing, literacy and health care though improving remain far from satisfactory. The industrial sector may have improved its position in domestic product and even made an impact on the export trade and market diversification in some cases, but a state of self sustaining growth still appears to be a long way off for most countries. Many years later economic integration continues to be a slow and painful exercise. With respect to the external sector, the region as a whole paid out in the 1961–70 period a total of $20.2 billion for financial services whose growth rate was higher than that of exports. Given a surplus of $60 billion in the balance of non-financial goods and services, the accumulated deficit for the period was around $14 billion, of which net direct investment financed $5.1 billion (35%) and net official financing most of the rest.[6]

If nothing else the initiation of the Alliance programme did appear to recognise the fact that stability in the region was linked to social and economic conditions, and the traditional reliance on force was not the way of the future. In subsequent years with the unfolding of the Vietnam War and the persistance and intensification of the Cold-War atmosphere, the concern with security took control, and the US seemed unwilling to pressure regimes (perceived to be sympathetic to US interests) into undertaking social and economic reforms of the kind envisaged in the Charter of Punta del Este. Dwindling US economic assistance, coupled with a feeling that the Alliance was not having the desired impact led to a surge of anti-US feeling in several countries in the hemisphere. This took the form of nationalisation, increased taxation of US companies engaged in the mining sector, local participation in foreign-owned enterprises, new regulations regarding profit remittance and re-investments, greater local processing of raw materials, etc. As indicated earlier, such measures have not been confined to leftist regimes but have grown out of the nationalist fervour reacting to what is perceived to be years of exploitation and the need to secure control over vital sectors of the economy, such as mineral industries, fishing etc.

The take-over of US enterprises by Latin American governments or the expansion of their territorial waters has not necessarily meant the adoption of an anti-foreign investment policy, or even an anti-US posture. The economic ties between the US and Latin America have remained strong despite periodic and sometimes bitter differences over particular issues. An examination of Table 7.1 will show that in recent years the US has supplied about 35% of the region's requirements as compared to about 40% in the early 1960s. In recent years about 34% of the region's exports has gone to the United States as compared to 37% in the early 1960s. (See Table 7.2.) These exports include a wide range of minerals and raw materials. Of course, the proportion of trade taking place varies from country to country. It is worth pointing out that, although the proportions of overall trade with the US have declined in recent years, one should not under-estimate the value of this trade in terms of the significance for individual countries and the strategic nature of the goods traded. As we saw earlier, trade and investment are closely linked. Investment in Latin America is often designed to facilitate exports from the US. According to some of the modern theories of international trade the flow of factors of production to other regions may often have the effect of changing the pattern of comparative advantage. But even when this is accomplished in practice, trade barriers in the factor exporting countries tend to discourage the trade effects of such shifts. Trade policies in the developed countries are so structured that they discourage the export of goods from the developing countries in processed form, and this is to some extent explains the heavy reliance on primary exports by developing countries. While a significant proportion of the region's exports enter the US market duty-free or at low rates of duty, the products involved are largely confined to raw materials (including mineral products) and food items. So dependent is the region on certain exports (sugar, beef, bananas, coffee, bauxite, etc.) that a small change in the prices of these commodities could result in the loss of import capacity several times the amount of aid received.

The Caribbean Basin Initiative

Traditionally the US has tended to treat Latin America and the Caribbean as one area. With Canada at one extreme and Mexico (and the rest of Central and South America at the other) the Caribbean has come to be regarded as the United States third border. 'The Caribbean region is a vital strategic and commercial artery for the United States. Nearly half of the US trade, two-thirds of our imported oil, and over

Table 7.1 *Origin of Latin American/Caribbean imports, 1961–63[a] and 1978–80[a]*

Sources	*US*		*EEC*[1]		*Japan*		*Canada*		*Middle East*		*Latin Am.*		*Other Countries*	
Importers	*1961–63*	*1978–80*	*1961–63*	*1978–80*	*1961–63*	*1978–80*	*1961–63*	*1978–80*	*1961–63*	*1978–80*	*1961–63*	*1978–80*	*1961–63*	*1978–80*
Argentina	26.8	20.9	39.5	27.6	3.9	7.2	2.6	1.7	—	2.3	12.7	22.2	14.5	18.1
Bahamas	56.4	39.5	22.1	26.4	0.2	1.6	6.1	2.2	—	15.6	9.0	6.3	—	8.4
Barbados	14.7	32.3	44.5	23.6	1.8	3.8	10.5	7.4	—	0.1	10.4	22.3	18.1	10.5
Bolivia	43.6	22.7	27.6	18.2	7.3	11.0	0.3	0.7	—	0.1	15.1	36.3	6.1	11.0
Brazil	32.3	19.4	24.5	17.3	4.6	6.5	1.7	2.9	4.8	30.3	15.0	11.7	17.1	11.9
Chile	37.9	26.0	30.1	16.6	2.8	8.6	0.1	1.9	1.1	5.1	19.3	27.8	8.7	14.0
Colombia	51.8	38.2	26.2	18.6	3.2	9.5	2.0	2.6	—	0.1	5.6	18.3	11.2	12.7
Costa Rica	47.3	33.2	26.4	12.3	7.0	12.9	3.3	1.9	0.1	0.1	9.5	29.0	6.9	10.6
Dominican Rep.	47.4	45.3	28.0	9.5	6.8	7.6	6.0	2.4	0.1	—	2.7	24.4	9.0	10.8
Ecuador	43.8	36.4	33.5	21.2	3.5	13.8	3.5	2.0	0.1	—	7.4	13.0	8.2	13.6
El Salvador	36.5	31.4	29.9	13.0	6.9	8.0	2.1	1.4	—	—	21.4	41.8	3.2	4.4
Guatemala	47.8	32.5	24.9	14.5	5.2	9.0	2.0	1.6	0.1	0.1	11.2	31.0	8.8	11.3
Guyana	21.2	27.3	45.9	29.7	2.2	3.0	7.6	4.2	—	—	13.0	30.7	10.1	5.1
Haiti	57.9	57.4	23.2	13.1	0.2	6.4	2.6	6.5	—	0.1	2.5	6.4	13.6	10.1
Honduras	50.1	43.7	15.2	11.0	7.7	8.9	1.3	1.9	—	—	14.8	30.8	10.9	5.6
Jamaica	27.7	35.8	43.0	14.1	3.4	2.5	10.6	5.3	—	—	7.4	24.8	7.9	17.5
Mexico	69.1	62.9	18.1	16.1	1.8	6.6	3.2	1.7	—	—	1.3	4.6	6.5	8.1
Nicaragua	49.4	29.8	21.2	9.3	5.9	4.5	2.3	1.4	—	—	13.2	49.6	8.0	5.4
Panama	47.7	35.8	14.8	8.4	3.2	5.5	1.3	1.3	0.2	10.0	12.4	28.8	20.4	10.2
Paraguay	25.2	10.9	24.5	18.6	8.3	8.2	—	0.1	—	0.1	22.4	45.6	19.6	16.5
Peru	4.3	38.6	30.9	27.3	5.3	8.3	2.3	2.2	0.1	0.4	13.4	12.0	7.7	11.2
Suriname	n.a.	31.9	n.a.	26.2	n.a.	6.4	n.a.	1.0	n.a.	—	n.a.	29.2	n.a.	5.3
Trinidad & Tobago	13.3	24.7	27.0	17.0	1.1	7.3	4.8	4.8	20.4	24.8	26.6	6.5	6.8	14.9
Uruguay	19.0	9.4	37.8	18.9	1.5	2.9	1.5	1.0	5.3	14.2	21.6	38.0	13.3	15.6
Venezuela	53.5	45.4	28.1	22.2	4.1	8.7	4.4	4.1	0.1	—	2.6	9.0	7.2	10.6
All Countries	*41.8*	*34.9*	*28.1*	*18.8*	*3.7*	*7.5*	*3.0*	*2.6*	*1.8*	*9.5*	*10.7*	*15.1*	*10.9*	*11.6*

a average for period
n.a. not available

1 Belgium, Denmark, France, W. Germany, Ireland, Italy, Luxembourg, Netherlands and the UK.

Source: IDB, *Annual Report*, 1982.

half of our imported strategic minerals pass through the Panama Canal or the Gulf of Mexico.'[7] Increasing economic difficulties and growing political and military conflicts in Central America and the Caribbean during the 1970s and early 1980s convinced the Reagan Administration that there was need for an approach which paid special attention to the problems of this area. In a speech to the Organisation of American States on February 24, 1982 he outlined a programme of assistance to the region, comprising a mixture of aid, trade and investment. The Caribbean Basin Initiative (CBI), as the programme is popularly known, has its origins in a conference held at Ditchley in February 1981 to discuss the problems faced by the Caribbean economies and the suggestion of a mini-Marshall plan for the region.[8] Among those present were United States officials and Dr Nicolas Ardito-Barletta, the Vice President of the World Bank Group and Chairman of the Caribbean Group for Cooperation and Economic Development. The initial idea was apparently for a common effort by the US, Canada, Mexico, Venezuela and by certain developed countries from outside the region. However, unable to agree on the scope and conditions of a joint programme the US announced its own proposals in early 1982. The CBI[9] consists of six main elements:

1 The creation of a one-way free trade arrangement under which exports (with certain exceptions) from Caribbean Basin countries will receive duty-free treatment in the US for 12 years.
2 The provision of tax incentives to encourage US private investment in Basin Countries.
3 Increased financial assistance in 1982 amounting to US$350 million.
4 The provision of technical assistance and training to assist the private sector to benefit from the opportunities of the programme. The areas proposed include investment promotion, export marketing and technology transfer efforts, 'as well as programmes to facilitate adjustments to greater competition and production in agriculture and industry.'
5 A commitment to work closely with Mexico, Canada and Venezuela 'to encourage stronger international efforts to coordinate our own development measures with their vital contributions and with those of other potential donors like Colombia. We will also encourage our European, Japanese and other Asian allies, as well as multilateral development institutions, to increase their assistance to the region.'
6 The provision of special measures to ensure that Puerto Rico and the US Virgin Islands also benefit from the programme.

Since the programme was unveiled, there has been a number of significant changes to the original proposals. Of the $350 million in supplemental aid proposed for fiscal year 1982, the division was as follows: El Salvador, $128 million (36.6%); Jamaica, $50 million (14.3%); The Eastern Caribbean $10 million (2.8%); Belize $10 million

Table 7.2 *Destination of Latin American/Caribbean exports, 1961–63[a] and 1978–80[a]* (Percentages)

Destinations	*US*		*EEC*[1]		*Japan*		*Canada*		*Mid. East*		*Latin Amer.*		*Other Countries*	
Exporters	*1961–63*	*1978–80*	*1961–63*	*1978–80*	*1961–63*	*1978–80*	*1961–63*	*1978–80*	*1961–63*	*1978–80*	*1961–63*	*1978–80*	*1961–63*	*1978–80*
Argentina	9.1	8.4	60.1	31.2	3.5	4.6	0.4	0.7	0.4	3.1	13.1	24.9	13.4	27.1
Bahamas	91.7	64.6	5.5	29.1	—	1.1	1.8	0.9	—	—	1.0	2.3	—	2.0
Barbados	6.7	33.7	53.5	17.6	—	0.1	13.8	4.5	—	—	1.2	18.3	24.8	25.8
Bolivia	31.7	27.7	58.9	25.6	2.4	3.0	—	1.1	—	0.2	5.4	34.2	1.6	8.2
Brazil	39.3	19.8	31.0	28.5	2.6	5.7	1.6	1.2	0.7	3.7	6.4	16.3	18.4	24.8
Chile	35.7	2.4	42.1	36.9	6.3	11.2	0.1	1.0	0.1	1.6	8.9	25.4	6.8	11.5
Colombia	56.7	28.8	24.8	33.1	0.8	3.0	1.7	1.2	—	0.2	6.5	15.9	9.5	17.8
Costa Rica	57.4	34.6	32.1	25.6	0.6	0.9	0.6	0.5	—	0.4	5.4	29.0	3.9	9.0
Dominican Rep	74.1	55.1	14.5	9.9	1.9	1.9	0.8	0.5	0.3	—	1.4	8.6	7.0	24.0
Ecuador	61.0	36.8	24.2	10.4	4.8	4.9	0.6	1.2	—	—	6.8	24.4	2.6	22.3
El Salvador	30.7	31.1	31.5	32.1	20.0	5.4	0.5	5.5	—	—	15.4	24.7	1.9	5.5
Guatemala	49.6	29.3	27.8	24.5	9.4	5.9	0.5	0.3	0.1	2.7	7.5	28.9	5.1	8.4
Guyana	18.7	24.9	27.5	37.1	0.5	4.6	28.8	8.0	—	0.2	13.6	18.2	10.9	7.0
Haiti	52.4	68.2	36.8	26.0	4.8	0.2	0.2	1.7	—	0.1	1.8	1.5	4.0	2.3
Honduras	60.7	56.3	13.1	23.0	0.8	3.7	2.9	0.2	—	0.2	19.2	12.8	3.3	3.8
Jamaica	36.0	40.1	29.7	21.7	0.2	0.5	21.3	6.2	—	0.3	1.7	9.7	11.1	21.5
Mexico	60.6	67.0	6.6	6.0	6.9	3.3	0.8	1.0	0.1	3.0	4.3	7.3	20.7	12.4
Nicaragua	42.6	35.4	25.1	26.7	20.3	5.9	3.3	2.5	—	—	5.3	18.6	3.4	10.9
Panama	75.1	49.7	6.0	16.6	0.5	0.3	5.1	1.3	—	1.0	5.0	18.4	8.3	12.7
Paraguay	22.5	9.8	26.0	35.2	0.1	7.1	—	0.3	—	—	30.3	35.2	21.1	12.4
Peru	35.4	38.1	40.1	18.0	7.3	13.4	0.5	1.7	0.3	0.3	9.3	14.0	7.1	14.5
Suriname	n.a.	29.2	n.a.	38.8	n.a.	6.7	n.a.	1.2	n.a.	0.1	n.a.	5.3	n.a.	18.7
Trinidad & Tobago	25.7	63.4	38.1	10.8	0.1	0.1	4.8	0.7	0.1	—	5.1	13.2	26.1	11.8
Uruguay	13.9	12.1	56.3	31.6	2.0	1.2	0.6	0.8	0.4	4.8	6.1	35.5	20.7	14.0
Venezuela	35.7	35.0	16.4	10.1	0.6	1.7	7.1	10.0	—	—	10.1	11.2	30.1	32.0
All Countries	*37.2*	*33.7*	*29.4*	*21.0*	*3.3*	*4.3*	*3.2*	*2.8*	*0.2*	*1.8*	*8.4*	*15.6*	*18.3*	*20.5*

a average for period
n.a. not available

1 Belgium, Denmark, France, W. Germany, Ireland, Italy, Luxembourg, Netherlands and UK.

Source: IDB, *Annual Report*, 1982.

(2.8%); Dominican Republic $40 million (11.4%); Costa Rica $70 million (20.2%); Honduras $35 million (10.0%); Haiti $5 million (1.4%); and the American Institute for Labour Development US$2 million (0.6%). The financial package was eventually approved by the US Congress, but not before a provision limiting each beneficiary to $75 million was included. This necessitated some adjustments in the division of the $350 million, the most significant of which was the scaling down of El Salvador's allocation to the stipulated limit. The trade proposals (which tend to be viewed as the most important element in the programme) ran into even more serious difficulties. The arrangements eventually passed into law in August 1983 were a watered-down form of the earlier idea. In the original proposals the only exceptions from the free trade arrangements were textile and apparel products because of the fact that these products were 'governed by other international agreements'. Fearing increased competition many business groups in the US have successfully lobbied for the insertion of provisions which would either put restrictions on a wider range of goods (e.g. frozen orange juice, sugar, beef) or exempt them (e.g. oil products) from the duty free arrangements. Reagan had suggested a ten cent tax credit for new investments in the region, but this was rejected in favour of write-off for business conventions held there. Prospective beneficiaries would also have to satisfy certain conditions with respect to freedom to join unions and work-place conditions of workers. These amendments were strongly supported or instigated by the American Labour Movement which felt that the CBI would result in the loss of jobs for American workers. The American Federation of Labour–Congress of Industrial Organisations (ALF–CIO) working in collaboration with certain American companies has been engaged in an intensive campaign designed to restrict imports of certain items from so called 'low-wage' areas, which it believes pose a threat to American industry. One of the items which has recently received attention (and which is currently under investigation) is steel products from Trinidad and Tobago, which AFL–CIO and US steel companies argue are subsidised by the Trinidad and Tobago government.

The criticisms of the CBI tend to be directed at two levels: firstly, the technical proposals and the benefits it seeks to convey, and secondly, the framework in which it is cast. Let us address ourselves to the first, and later the second.

In putting forward his proposals for the establishment of a free trade area, President Reagan conceded that 87% of Caribbean Basin exports already entered the US market duty free under the Generalised System of Preferences. His rationale for the new trading arrangements was that the GSP excluded a wide variety of products which Basin countries are capable of producing, if only they had a guaranteed market. The offer of the latter would also stimulate new investment. We indicated earlier that textile and apparel products (which Basin countries are capable of producing competitively) were excluded from the original proposals which have since been further whittled down by the protectionist lobby in the US. Given the reaction of steel producers in the US to the small volume of steel exports from Trinidad and Tobago, it is clear that exporters in Basin countries would find it extremely difficult to sell to the US products in which they have a comparative advantage, if these products pose the slightest threat to US production. The free trade idea seems to be more symbolic than anything. As we indicated earlier, the labour movement in the US has succeeded in preventing any significant tax incentives (for US companies to invest abroad) from being incorporated into the programme. Even if Basin countries decided to enter into bilateral Investment Treaties with the US in order to attract US private capital, it is unlikely that this device by itself could have any significant effect in this direction. The supplementary aid proposed is not only miniscule compared to the needs of the region, but its distribution seems to bear little relationship to real needs. The fact that this aid will be directed largely towards private sector development implies that, in situations where infrastructural developments are needed before production can take place, the effect may be negligible.

The more fundamental criticism of the CBI has been directed towards the framework in which it is cast and the assumptions inherent in this framework. President Reagan's stress on the 'magic of the market place' and the assignment of a key role to the private sector reveals the ideological basis of the programme. One critic has stated that the CBI 'not only fails to come to grips with deep structural features that engender conflict, but its assumptions concerning the relationship between politics and development, the state and market are fundamentally flawed.'[10] While the Reagan administration sees the present conflicts and instability in the region in terms of an East–West confrontation and attributes a large part of the current economic difficulties to the steep rise in oil prices during the 1970s, many critics blame domestic, social and economic policies aided and abetted by the short-sightedness of successive US administrations. In this respect it is widely felt that the CBI as an aid programme does not even measure up to the Alliance for Progress which at least recognised the range of policies that would be required to foster growth and development in the region. In attacking Reagan's market economics, Petras has this to say: 'It was precisely this free market growth (protected by dictatorial regimes) that engendered the social and regional inequalities and mass landlessness, that provoked social polarisation and led to political warfare; and it is precisely these consequences that undermine any efforts to induce free marketeers to invest in the region, no matter how lucrative the tax incentives. Paradoxically, unmitigated market-induced growth has created political conditions that undermine long term, large scale private investment provoking the economic crisis that has led to increased US public sending. Reagan has fallen into the very policy that he has accused the liberals of pursuing: throwing state money at problems. Unless the underlying structural problems are dealt with – the re-structuring of ownership of land, commerce, credit – the new funds will be dissipated into inefficient bureaucratic machinery, when they are not siphoned off into foreign bank accounts.'[11]

While conceding that there are certain positive features in the CBI, other observers see serious flaws in the approach adopted which has a clear underlying political motive. 'An East–West focus distorts every aspect of the CBI. The allocations for assistance suggest that obtaining aid from the United States will depend more on a country's attitude towards Cuba, US foreign policies, and US private investment than on the country's economic need or development prospects.'[12] The clear hint that countries like Cuba, Nicaragua and Grenada would be excluded from the programme reflects the dominant concern with security. 'The CBI reflects the administration's interest in military security, political loyalty, and advantages for US firms, rather than US concern for the region's long term development.'[13]

Another issue which has caused concern in certain quarters is the lumping of the insular Caribbean with countries in Central America. 'Despite divergent colonial traditions, the insular territories of the Caribbean share social, ethnic, economic, and cultural patterns. They also share historical relationships with the United States and other Western Powers that differ sharply from those in Central America. Most Caribbean countries are handling social and economic pressures within a framework of established, functioning political institutions, while Central America is wracked by civil war.'[14] This situation, it is felt, calls for approaches which recognise these differences and use social and economic factors as criteria for aid rather than the level of insurgent activities.[15]

While there are aspects of the CBI which have aroused interest among the business community in Basin countries, other aspects have given rise to concern. The Cold-War atmosphere in which it is cast leads to suspicions about its real motives. While the US concern with security is understandable, its assessment of the causes of instability and armed conflict in the region is questionable. Unless the root social and economic causes are addressed, the CBI may have little impact on the prevailing conditions. This would not have meant that the CBI has failed, but simply that it was the wrong cure. The resulting increase in social and political instability could then become, according to Petra's scenerio, a pretext for greater military intervention, and the perpetuation of client-state relationships with little hope of independent development.

A final point is worth making, and this is with respect to the various integration movements in the region. Clearly the focus on bilateral relations could affect the construction of an integration framework if individual members cannot take common positions on question which have a critical bearing on the fabric of their respective movements. In this connection bilateral treaties and the role of private foreign capital are issues which cannot be dealt with individually, if the integrity of the various movements is to be maintained.

Notes

1 J. Levinson and J. De Onis, *The Alliance that Lost Its Way* (Chicago: Quadrangle Books, 1970) p. 6.
2 Ibid.
3 Quoted in Inter-American Institute of International Legal Studies, *The Inter-American Systems, Its Development and Strengthening* (New York, Oceana Publications, Inc., 1966) p. 214.
4 OAS, *Latin America's Development and the Alliance for Progress* (Washington, DC, 1973), p. 38.
5 Ibid.
6 Ibid., p. 15.
7 President Reagan's Speech to the OAS in February, 1982.
8 See *The Economist* of 12–18 Feb, 1983 Special Survey, p. 14.
9 For purposes of the programme the Caribbean Basin comprises an arbitrary group of some 28 countries in the Caribbean and Central America, with a population of around 40 million.
10 See James Petras, 'A Military Policy in Search of an Economic Rationale: Reagan's Caribbean Basin Aid Program', *Comercio Exterior de Mexico*, Nov., 1982.
11 Ibid.
12 A.F. Lowenthal, 'The Caribbean Basin Initiative', *Foreign Policy*, Summer, 1982.
13 Ibid.
14 Ibid.
15 Ibid.
16 Ibid.

8
Concluding Observations

Economic development is a very complex process for the reason that it involves a broad range of political, social and economic factors whose behaviour is often difficult to control or predict. In such a situation models and theories often have to be constructed at such a high level of abstraction that they are of little use to policy-makers. Any variable can be given a critical role in a model or theory, depending on the kind of assumptions that are made with respect to objectives, performance or the environment. For this reason, the best formulated theory or model may be the least useful from a policy point of view. The choice of variables and the role assigned to them would, of course, be influenced by the perspectives and biases of the model-makers and theoreticians, and this can further add to the confusion of policy-makers.

The emphasis in the early post-war literature was on factors that could be easily quantified or cast in mathematical terms. The framework used drew heavily on the history of the developed countries and largely failed to grasp the significance of the internal structural relations bequeathed by colonialism or the nature and implications of the changing political context. The world was assumed to be one big happy community with the strong yearning to help the weak and the rich, the poor. All the forces (internal and external) were assumed to be on their best behaviour. Thus, the mere transfer of financial resources to developing countries could be seen to exert a sufficiently powerful impact to overcome the legacy of years of economic and social ravages, both natural and man-made. Little attention was paid to the most crucial variables bearing on the transformation process.

In the intervening years the transfer of resources, both from public and private sources, proved to be highly inadequate in terms of the requirements of developing countries. In addition, not all resources went into investment. The savings effort may also have been relaxed in some cases. A glance at Table 8.1 will show that in the case of Latin America the countries of the region generally tended to finance a substantial proportion of their investment from national savings. The need to increase the level of investment, however, coupled with the inadequate flow of resources from governments and multilateral agencies, resulted in policies designed to attract increasing amounts of private capital. The association of technology, marketing connections and managerial skills with the latter gave it a special significance. Private capital may have helped in alleviating some short term economic problems, and may also have made some minimal contribution to national development. Generally, however, there has been no real commitment to national goals and objectives. Directly and indirectly it has helped in the creation of new forms of dependency. Rather than assist in the reduction of external dependency or the integration of the economy at the national level, it has helped in intensifying external dependency and perpetuating dualism in basic forms. Private foreign capital has imparted little to the development of an internal dynamic. Whether intended or not, it has created a need for itself, which can affect the whole spectrum of economic and social policies. The experience of recent years calls for a departure from the traditional framework to new forms of cooperation between foreign capital and the local economy.

Table 8.1 *Latin America and the Caribbean: national savings as a percentage of investment, 1960–78*

	Average						
Country	*1960–64*	*1965–69*	*1970–74*	*1975*	*1976*	*1977*	*1978*
Argentine	92.2	101.1	97.2	76.0	103.8	102.1	n.a.
Bahamas	n.a.	n.a.	73.3	131.1	132.3	142.4	141.1
Barbados	31.4	13.8	2.8	34.5	3.9	30.3	n.a.
Bolivia	45.1	61.8	89.7	71.5	80.9	76.5	54.3
Brazil	95.0	98.2	88.8	81.8	85.4	88.9	86.0
Chile	75.3	89.8	83.1	118.4	121.4	58.7	n.a.
Colombia	87.2	86.5	83.1	91.8	99.1	106.6	101.3
Costa Rica	69.0	54.6	52.7	46.4	62.3	67.5	55.6
Dominican Rep.	96.9	53.2	63.8	87.0	67.4	68.6	56.7
Ecuador	95.1	83.1	88.0	82.5	100.8	90.4	n.a.
El Salvador	82.4	73.4	80.6	69.3	91.9	98.8	59.5
Guatemala	70.2	73.1	82.2	76.8	63.8	87.6	75.4
Guyana	78.5	62.4	64.9	91.5	20.1	20.7	78.1
Haiti	57.0	24.2	54.4	40.8	39.5	45.5	45.0
Honduras	85.4	77.9	65.2	32.8	47.5	51.8	60.3
Jamaica	84.1	75.3	65.8	60.1	35.5	43.6	80.5
Mexico	89.2	90.6	88.0	82.8	89.0	95.2	n.a.
Nicaragua	82.3	61.2	60.1	41.0	85.0	64.0	93.0
Panama	69.9	82.6	72.3	73.6	69.6	71.0	69.6
Paraguay	73.8	70.2	82.1	77.4	73.1	72.5	64.9
Peru	94.2	87.0	90.5	48.7	54.1	50.3	85.0
Trinidad & Tobago	31.0	29.9	50.7	124.6	106.7	n.a.	n.a.
Uruguay	85.4	117.9	85.0	51.1	83.6	82.6	83.9
Venezuela	133.2	105.0	123.3	129.7	111.7	81.0	70.2

Note: The figures for several of the countries have been computed indirectly and are to be regarded as estimates.

n.a. not available.

Source: IDB, *Economic and Social Progress in Latin America*, 1979.

The failure of national policies to satisfy social goals lies at the root of whatever instability there may be in the region. In his situation incentives and guarantees to private capital can play only a limited role. The key issues revolve around the kind of policies needed to redress social imbalances in the system. Here politics is as important as economics. Given the history of the region, economic strategems by themselves can do very little. When these strategems assume an institutional framework that does not exist the result may be to worsen already existing inequities. Each situation has peculiarities that may call for particular solutions.

The desire by various administrations in the United States to impose an American economic model on these countries completely ignores prevailing political and social realities. In the context of the increasing nationalism in the region, stemming in part from the experience with transnational corporations and a dissatisfaction with the results of past policies, and in part from what is viewed as an increasingly unhelpful international environment, there is a tendency to interpret American efforts in the region as an attempt to perpetuate or strengthen its hegemony. There are doubts as to whether the economic policies embraced by the Americans are intended to accelerate the pace of economic development and thus remove 'the conditions which breed Communists', or are simply part of a larger effort to establish systems compatible with that of the US as 'show pieces of democracy', regardless of their developmental efficacy. The perceived connection between ideology and security lead Americans to favour systems based on free enterprise, a reduced role for the state and an open policy towards foreign private capital, but they are often willing to recognise regimes which diverge from these ideals, but which pose no threat to US security. The apparent contradiction which arises out of this position not only challenges US credibility, but ultimately affect the establishment of relationships which could serve the interest of both the US and the Latin American/Caribbean countries. The first step in this direction would be to recognise the welfare of the people of the region as paramount over all other considerations.

Index